‘The First National Museum’

This book is dedicated to
the memory of Dr Alexander Carte,
director of the Natural History
Museum from 1851 to 1881.

'The First National Museum'

Dublin's Natural History Museum in the mid-nineteenth century

SHERRA MURPHY

CORK UNIVERSITY PRESS

First published in 2021 by
Cork University Press
Boole Library
University College Cork
Cork T12 ND89
Ireland

Library of Congress Control Number: 2021932639

Distribution in the USA Longleaf Services, Chapel Hill, NC, USA.

British Library Cataloguing in Publication Data

A CIP catalogue record for this book is available the British Library.

ISBN: 9781782054559

Printed in Poland by BZ Graf

Design and typesetting by Alison Burns at Studio 10 Design, Cork

Cover image: First floor of the Natural History Museum, courtesy of the National Museum of Ireland

www.corkuniversitypress.com

Contents

Acknowledgements

THIS WORK WOULD not have been possible without the support of the people and institutions that aided my research. I owe sincere thanks to the National Museum of Ireland for access to the archives and collections at the Natural History Museum. I am especially grateful for the support and kindness of keeper Dr Nigel Monaghan, who is unfailingly generous in his encouragement to researchers. I would also like to thank Dr Matthew Parkes, Dr Leona Leonard and Dr Rebecca O'Neill for their kind assistance, and for ensuring that I didn't disappear into the depths of Beggars Bush barracks. Dr O'Neill also provided valuable advice at the drafting stages, for which I am in her debt. Many thanks to Clare McNamara of the National Museum of Ireland for her help with some of the images for this volume. I also owe sincere thanks to the Royal Dublin Society for access to its library and archives, and to the staff there, who were always welcoming and generous in sharing their resources. Particular gratitude is extended to archivist Natasha Serne, who has been liberal with her time, attention and knowledge. The staff at the National Library of Ireland never waver from their mission as keepers of the texts and materials which allow us to look back and understand ourselves more fully, and this work is indebted to that collection. These three institutions hold primary archives illuminating the history of museums and collections in nineteenth-century Ireland that were once contiguous, but were separated as a result of the Dublin Science and Art Museum Act of 1877. Piecing some of them back together has been one of the primary pleasures of this work.

My sincere gratitude to Professor Mary E. Daly, who shaped and guided the research that made this volume possible, to Dr Catherine Cox and Dr Eamonn O'Flaherty for offering shrewd and sensible observations at a crucial point in the development of my doctoral project, and to K. Theodore Hoppen for his enthusiastic endorsement of its value. I would also like to thank Dr Elaine Sisson for her constant support and intellectual rigour throughout the long journey of this research. To my friends and colleagues too numerous to list, but who now know more than they ever expected to about nineteenth-century natural history in Ireland, thanks and apologies in equal measure.

My thanks, for varying reasons, to Catherine Levy, Petra Coffey, Juliana Adelman, Karl Grimes, Martyn Linnie and Patrick Wyse-Jackson. I would also like to thank the scholars cited in this volume who pioneered the research on the significance of science in Ireland, as they built the platforms upon which this research rests. Anonymous peer reviewers and copy-editors are often in the thankless position of their contributions going unnoticed in the final text; I would like to acknowledge them here for their rigorous and cogent readings at various stages of the publication process. They have made this book better, and I have silently thanked them many times while writing and editing.

I would like to express my appreciation to my students, as they have surprised and delighted me with their interest in this work, and with their sympathetic encouragement. It always brightened my day when one of them asked how the book was going. They'll never know how much they have bolstered me with their cheerful support.

Many thanks to the staff at Cork University Press, and in particular to Maria O'Donovan, for expertly guiding this project to completion.

I have no words to express the depth of my gratitude to Ronan Murphy, my dearest friend and steadfast companion. His willingness to read all the drafts has been a source of amazement.

Author's Note

It is no secret that Victorian intellectual culture, especially in the realm of science, was decidedly male-dominated. Though women engaged in scientific pursuits as a form of leisure, records of their appearances as researchers in scientific establishments are infrequent, brief, and often tantalisingly incomplete, though there are, of course, notable exceptions. In Ireland, women made a more stable and forceful appearance in the professional realms of natural science from the 1880s onwards. Despite its awkwardness to the sensibilities of the twenty-first century, I have chosen to use the term 'men of science' to refer to the largely male practitioners of natural history in this text. The reasons for this are elucidated by Ruth Barton in her excellent article 'Men of Science: Language, identity and professionalization in the mid-Victorian scientific community'.[1] To summarise, the term 'scientist' was coined in 1833 but was not universally accepted, and did not come into general use until much later in the nineteenth century. Analysing texts and speeches from the mid-century, Barton shows that 'man of science' was the term preferred by the scientific community, as it avoided drawing distinctions between paid professionals and devoted amateurs. In Ireland, the range of people who participated in natural history crossed boundaries of class, education and profession, so that 'man of science' links them in the context of their scientific contributions without the need to resort to more convoluted designations. Though it might rankle contemporary sensibilities, it is faithful to the realities of the Victorian period and its scientific culture.

INTRODUCTION

The Natural History Museum

Dublin's Natural History Museum, an intact nineteenth-century scientific collection, is one of Ireland's most popular cultural sites. On any given day, it is alive with families, tourists, students and locals enjoying its offbeat charms. Affectionately nicknamed the 'Dead Zoo', it is one of four pillars in Ireland's National Museum complex. Often referred to as a 'museum of a museum', it is a mid-Victorian neo-classical edifice filled with mounted animals and natural specimens, arrayed in polished wooden cases and old-fashioned glass jars. Offering visitors a glimpse into the early years of natural history as an organised science, the Natural History Museum preserves the Victorian obsession with collecting and classifying as means of attempting to grasp the ceaseless proliferation of nature. It enjoys a firmly held affection in the hearts of Dubliners, and among those who seek to sense an authentic Victorian past, as the building and collections preserve the priorities of the late 1800s. Unseen by the casual visitor, scientists also regularly conduct research in the vast storage collections at the museum, an important storehouse of historical natural materials. Despite its enduring popularity and the scientific value of its holdings, the museum's historical significance has been largely overlooked. Much more than a 'dead zoo', a repository, or a museum of a museum, it is a gateway to the development of intellectual and scientific culture in nineteenth-century Ireland. Its current patina of nostalgia and genteel stasis conceals the fact that, at its peak, it was a modern and outward-looking scientific establishment that was also Ireland's first and most important public museum.

The heyday of Ireland's Natural History Museum coincided with the golden age of natural history as a scientific pursuit. In the mid-nineteenth century, scholars undertaking the study of nature emphasised direct observation and comparison, working to create universally agreed methods for naming and ordering an explosion of new information about the natural world. Their fundamental goal was to fashion a system for producing and sharing global scientific knowledge, as scholars and collectors corresponded with one another to create a working model for the structure of life on earth. In the form of geology and fossils, they also sought to discover the composition and chronology of the earth itself. As natural history grew, it matured into discrete fields of study such as zoology, botany and palaeontology. Natural history also contributed to the reinvigoration of the Industrial Revolution, as it identified the animal, vegetable and mineral resources that provided raw material for manufacturing and transportation. The discovery of coal fields, the fertility of land, and the growth of cotton and silkworms all relied on information provided by the study of natural science. Natural history was likewise embedded into the ethos of colonial expansion that characterised the century. As the European powers intensified the global drive to amass land and resources, specimens were routinely gathered during missions of exploration and conquest, returning to Europe a dizzying array of new species that found their way into museums and study collections. Men of science compared them against the already known taxonomies of European species, and conducted experiments to test their potential uses. Natural history museums were embedded into these undertakings, storehouses for the collection of specimens, but also for the information that could be gained from analysing them. They developed in tandem with the growth of natural science, and sprang up in Europe at a tremendous rate throughout the nineteenth century.

Originally a long-term project of the Royal Dublin Society (RDS), Dublin's Natural History Museum was established to house then-modern collections that were linked to the development of science and museums throughout the rest of Europe. The society set up displays of raw materials and new inventions in the basement of the Irish Parliament in 1733, informing lawmakers and its own members about discoveries with potential for increasing the productivity of their land and holdings.[1] These collections quickly grew to include books, specimens and scientific instruments, supplemented by experiments and lectures. The RDS gradually established a suite of educational and scientific collections that became a museum, located from 1815 in the society's headquarters in Leinster House, and from 1857 in a purpose-built structure on Merrion Square. In its early days it was the only establishment of its kind in Ireland, and was therefore soon transformed into a civic amenity, an improving institution that would generate and distribute scientific information and techniques for the betterment of Ireland and its people. Over time, it became bound within a complex series of interrelationships as government bodies, influential private societies, men of science and the public each had expectations for how it should address the needs of science and society. The Natural History Museum had a distinct public presence, and the matter of access to its collections was a regular feature of parliamentary inquiries and press accounts. As it grew, the museum became an integral element of scientific and intellectual culture in nineteenth-century Ireland.

The complex circumstances of the museum's governance at its scientific peak are among those that obscure its historical significance. The Royal Dublin Society was a private members' organisation, attracting the well-heeled and powerful, who paid costly membership fees that encouraged a somewhat jealous guarding of the society's aims and reputation. Even so, these funds were not enough to support the scope of the society's ambition for civic improvement. Because its membership was influential, and its intent was to aid Ireland's development, the RDS was also generously funded by the exchequer of the British parliament for its library, museum, art collections, agricultural programmes and educational lectures. Government funding was supervised through the Board of Trade, the Dublin Castle administration and, after 1854, by the Science and Art Department. The relationship between the private society and central government was sometimes difficult and contentious, with the society's amenities caught in a battle of wills between Dublin's most influential private members' body and a central government seeking to exert its influence over Irish civic culture. The tension between the society's private ownership of important civic resources and its support through exchequer funds shaped the Natural History Museum throughout its early history.

The importance of the museum's history is also obscured by the distribution of the records conveying its history. The tension between the public and private aspects of museums in Ireland generally was debated in parliament a number of times in the mid-century, culminating in the Dublin Science and Art Museum Act, 1877, which placed important collections into state control, but was specifically written in relation to the RDS. Significant collections from the Royal Dublin Society and Royal Irish Academy became the basis for state collections in Ireland, and the newly established National Library and Museum of Science and Art opened to the public in 1890.

As these changes unfolded after 1877, the documents that held the history of the Natural History Museum were separated into various places. The new Museum of Science and Art retained collections lists, correspondence and donation records, as they related directly to the objects in the museum. The RDS kept the meeting notes of the Natural History Committee that recorded the museum's role within the society, holding detailed information on how it developed over time. Other RDS publications such as the society's annually published *Proceedings* and the *Journal of the Royal Dublin Society (JRDS)* also convey the museum's role in the development of natural science in Ireland. The relationship between the museum and central government is documented through parliamentary reports, and in the annual reports of the Science and Art Department, showing how the government came to rely on the museum as an important public and educational service. Due to its popularity with the general public, newspapers covered it as a matter of interest, taking especial note when friction between the RDS and central government threatened the museum's future. The Natural History Museum also appeared in a variety of publications such as scientific journals, travel guides and popular magazines, and information on the people involved with the museum can be found in biographies and obituaries.

The picture that emerges from gathering the disparate information belies the moniker 'Dead Zoo', showing that the static display of natural materials was only one of the museum's functions. Reconstructing its past reveals that it was home to vigorous discourse around scientific ideas and developments. In the mid-nineteenth century, the Natural History Museum was not only a locus for collections, but an aggregation of people, objects, publications and practices that were connected to the wider nineteenth-century project of discerning the shape and potential of the natural world. It was also central to the growth of education in Ireland, and was embedded into a series of initiatives that established a formal system for scientific education. It served as a central hub for a network of men of science who used its collections to further both the cause of natural history and the professional scientific environment in Ireland. Most of all, it was as popular with the public in the nineteenth century as it is now, helping to establish fully public museums in Ireland. These numerous and sometimes competing factors mean that the museum was shaped by circumstances particular to its time and place, and looking at them briefly illuminates the wider environment that prompted the emergence of this Dublin landmark. Addressing the history of the Natural

History Museum from its establishment to its transfer into direct control by the state in 1877 shows us the origins of museums in Ireland, and provides a glimpse into the intersections between science and culture; more than that, it shows us how science was understood as a form of culture in the ways that people engaged with it and began to feel its direct effects in their daily lives.

Natural history in the nineteenth century

Science was deeply embedded into Victorian culture. Previously a means of understanding the divine through observing the laws of nature, by the early nineteenth century science had begun to call into question the classical and biblical certainties that had previously formed the foundations for thinking about nature. Developments in the sciences fundamentally altered the conception of humanity's place in the cosmos, and simultaneously changed the quality and texture of daily life. From Darwin's publication of *On the Origin of Species* to the ever-increasing range of uses for electricity and chemistry, the century's social and intellectual discourses were characterised by a constant stream of new scientific information. Historian Barbara T. Gates asserts that this 'shook Victorian culture to its core', and that the 'insights of science forced constant reassessments of self, society and nature, both by scientists and by members of a science-hungry and science-fearful public'.[2]

Natural history, an area of scientific study which built a systematic knowledge of the structure of the earth, and the organisation and relations of living things past and present, was among the sciences most easily grasped by the general public. It enjoyed a popularity that other sciences did not, as it was accessible to the amateur or generalist, but also offered professionals an opportunity to specialise within a broad and emergent field of knowledge. Collecting specimens required little in the way of equipment, and reasonably priced publications conveying information and instruction were plentiful. Anyone could choose an area to study, start a collection, educate themselves, and begin to trade specimens and information with others interested in the same subject. As their knowledge and expertise grew, devotees of natural history could attend lectures or museums, read field guides or periodicals, and take part in meetings of societies devoted to their interests. In comparison to more complex sciences such as chemistry or astronomy, clear introductory knowledge was readily available, and subject matter was, literally, everywhere.

As a consequence, natural history was undertaken by 'numberless amateurs, women and men avidly collecting butterflies, marine animals, ferns, and rocks, filing their discoveries away in Wardian cases, or aquaria, or collecting drawers, or notebooks'.[3] The figure of the amateur naturalist was ubiquitous enough to be pilloried in the satirical magazine *Punch*, and their numbers gave rise to a brisk trade in paraphernalia such as rock hammers and insect nets. The nineteenth century was the zenith of natural history collecting, and the evidence is in museums around the world. Museum historian Samuel Alberti avers that '[h]alf of the 200 million objects in UK museums are in natural history collections; around a third of them are in the Natural History Museum in London alone. There are as many natural history objects as *all other kinds of objects put together*'.[4] Irish collections grew in a fashion similar to those in Great Britain, and the National Museum of Ireland's website puts the number of natural history objects in its collection in the range of two million.[5]

Another dimension of collecting and donation in Victorian natural history may be discerned from reading labels on the objects in the Natural History Museum. The locations listed on specimens from around the globe – Australia, Madagascar, Jamaica, South Africa, Canada, India – read as a compendium of British colonial outposts, revealing the participation of Irish military men and civil servants in natural history collecting while serving within the empire's global colonial apparatus. Throughout the century, natural history and colonial ambition were entwined, and most nations attached men of science to military missions. European natural history collections are rich in materials collected during colonial expeditions, and Ireland is no exception. Historian David Fitzpatrick observes that among 'the attractions of the Empire were the associated opportunities for employment. Colonial services provided a significant outlet for educated Irishmen, Catholic as well as Protestant'.[6] For men of science, this outlet became crucial. As the number of opportunities for paid scientific employment in civilian life were limited, science could be undertaken as an aspect of a career in the military or civil services. This was especially true for surgeons and others with medical training, who were frequent donors to the Natural History Museum from their postings on ships or with battalions. The same held true for the increasing number of men employed by government initiatives such as geological surveys and mapping expeditions, where scientific collection was embedded into their work. A career in the services could provide men of science with opportunities for the collection and identification of new or exotic species, allowing them to pursue their interests while also earning a living. The collections at the RDS Natural History Museum benefited heavily from the contributions of Irish men serving with the crown in colonial outposts.

The abundance of material flowing into museums throughout the century was analysed and ordered by a modest number of men of science who worked in a paid professional capacity, usually in museums, universities and learned societies. They also collected and donated materials themselves, most often in a defined area of interest. The majority of them are treated lightly or entirely overlooked in the literature of Irish science and Irish history, as their contributions were not individually significant, but when combined formed a body of information assembled slowly and carefully by people with common interests who shared their studies and specimens. In aiding one another over time, they formed a network that was built on interlocking relationships and social ties. The RDS Natural History Museum, especially through the work of Alexander Carte, its director from 1851–81, was at the centre of this network of intellectual and scientific exchange that began to shape the understanding of nature in Ireland, and of Ireland's place in the global biosphere.

The popularity of nineteenth-century natural history offers fresh ways of looking at the history of science in Ireland, which has tended to focus on well-known figures and headline events. The building of the massive telescope in 1845 by astronomer William Parsons, Lord Rosse, at Birr Castle in County Offaly remains one of the most celebrated events in Irish science. Mathematician William Rowan Hamilton's flash of insight on quaternions in 1843 opened a new way of thinking about space and geometry, and from 1859 John Tyndall's work on radiant heat opened a new field of study; both retain implications for twenty-first-century technology, and are frequently cited as key figures in the history of science in Ireland. The history of science in general has often been conducted on this 'great deeds' model, with individual achievements signifying advancement in scientific fields. The archives for the Natural History Museum provide another model, detailing the ways that largely unknown people worked together over a long period of time to build a significant body of scientific information. The records suggest that natural history in Ireland was a popular scientific and leisure pursuit, undertaken by a wide variety of people who collected and donated specimens. They possessed varying levels of scientific knowledge, and pursued their interests through differing means, from solitary collecting on farms, to membership of scientific clubs in Dublin. Many of them were in contact with professional men of science who answered their questions, exhibited their donations, and facilitated networks of information and communication. Some established their reputations to the extent that they published papers in scientific journals. Much of this activity was facilitated through learned societies in Dublin and further afield, aided by the complex array of interlocking relationships between them.

Learned societies

Natural history was promoted by learned societies, where, outside the elite ranks of Trinity College, the lion's share of scientific activity in Ireland took place prior to the establishment of the Queen's Colleges in 1845. Historian Juliana Adelman examines the influence of the learned, or voluntary, societies, which directed their efforts towards reforming activities that spanned a wide range of social, educational and political concerns.[7] The Royal Dublin Society and the Royal Irish Academy led these initiatives, establishing access to science, the arts, literature, libraries, exhibitions and lectures for both specialist audiences and a wider public. Others focused their efforts, such as the Royal Society of Antiquaries, which sought to preserve the material relating to Ireland's ancient past, or the Dublin Natural History Society, dedicated to collecting and interpreting the natural history of Ireland. Irish organisations were often closely allied to their counterparts in Great Britain, such as the Royal Society, the Linnaean Society, and the Royal Geological Society. Societies that specifically championed science were dedicated to the emergence of new knowledge, and were central to the cultural atmosphere within which the Victorian vogue for natural science flourished. Membership requirements varied, ranging from the elite Royal Society in London, which extended invitations on the basis of accomplishment and social status, to the more democratic Dublin Natural History Society, which purposely kept its membership fees low and its requirements minimal to encourage participation.

Learned societies had been part of the Irish intellectual landscape since the early eighteenth century. Though Dublin was a focal point, the rest of the island was also home to learned societies, social clubs and mechanics' institutes, especially cities such as Cork, Belfast and Waterford, or larger towns such as Carlow and Wexford. The collection and dissemination of scientific knowledge by these organisations was often undertaken as a means of strengthening Ireland's prosperity through the identification and development of natural resources. Learned societies often functioned as de facto educational outlets, as there was no universal system for science education outside universities in Ireland until the second half of the century. The assumption that an increasingly educated population would utilise Ireland's natural advantages to the full was central to the ambition of reducing Ireland's dependence on outside resources. These ideas were championed by chemist Robert Kane in his book *The Industrial Resources of Ireland* (1844), a collection of his popular lectures delivered at the RDS, in which he declaimed that education, 'more than all else, wanted to give happiness, tranquillity, and wealth to Ireland'.[8] Many of the learned societies took on this project in their own ways. Advances in natural science were considered essential to the project of increasing Ireland's agricultural and industrial output, and divisions were drawn between the theoretical sciences such as astronomy and mathematics favoured by the Royal Irish Academy, and the sciences with practical applications pursued by the Royal Dublin Society. The Board of Trade, the Science and Art Department and Dublin Castle encouraged the aims of education and practicality both notionally and materially, promoting and subsidising the work of learned societies and providing significant funding to the programmes at the RDS.

Irish learned societies also looked to their counterparts in Great Britain and on the continent for the broader context in which their efforts took place. Irish men of science held membership of British scientific and learned societies, ensuring the exchange of ideas and taking advantage of a larger stage to enhance their reputations. One of the most visible and influential, the British Association for the Advancement of Science, was founded in 1831 to bring new ideas in science to a wider audience. Irish men of science were enthusiastic members, routinely presenting papers at its annual meetings, held in a different city each year. Ireland hosted several of them, and the 1857 inauguration of the newly built Natural History Museum was timed to take advantage of a British Association meeting in Dublin. Other organisations such as the Linnaean Society, the Zoological Society of London and the Royal Society all counted Irish men of science as members, and as contributors to their publications. The connections were so close that it is possible to assert that Irish natural science in the nineteenth century was also international science, as the networks of correspondence and intellectual exchange often ignored national boundaries in favour of building an accurate understanding of the natural world.

Museums and intellectual culture

Natural history museums emerged from historical connections between collections and the development of scientific thought. They had their origins in the Renaissance, when cabinets of curiosity assembled by wealthy collectors were seen as an expression of classical humanist learning. Collecting became an essential intellectual activity in sixteenth-century Europe, when apothecaries, gardeners and university men also began to amass collections of natural materials for study. Divisions between *naturalia*, objects produced by nature, and *artificialia*, objects produced by man, settled into a dichotomy between nature and art. In the eighteenth century, collections of natural materials played a role in the rationalising ideals of the Enlightenment, when a focus on experimental methods and objective proofs began to shift thinking about nature into the organised approaches of modern natural science. These Enlightenment ideals were behind the then-Dublin Society's bid to exhibit models of manufacturing and agricultural equipment in the basement of the Irish Parliament building in 1733.[9] The society began to focus on natural history collection per se in 1792 with the purchase of the Leskean cabinet of minerals, a prestigious collection of European geology that also contained zoological and botanical specimens. When the society purchased Leinster House in 1815, six interconnected rooms on the first floor were converted into a natural history museum to house a rapidly growing collection.

By the early nineteenth century, museums had achieved status as an expression of national character. They were increasingly seen as having benefits for the development of a morally sensitive, progressive and educated population, and the availability of public museums was firmly linked with creating social stability. The growth of museums in the Victorian era took place during a period of intense social change and economic reordering, especially in the increasing power of the middle classes, which resulted in 'the emerging social and political force of an ever-more powerful mass public'.[10] Museum historian Jonah Siegel notes that the 'resulting desire to educate it into a grouping of responsible and productive political subjects free from the dangerous passions of the mob are central influences on nineteenth-century social institutions'.[11] In this atmosphere the Royal Dublin Society developed its efforts into an organised strategy, dividing its areas of interest into committees of agriculture, natural history, natural philosophy, chemistry, botany, manufactures and fine art, as well as a standing committee for its expanding library. These groups managed the society's collections and public activities; agricultural shows, botanic gardens, art schools, public lectures, and exhibitions of art objects and manufactured goods operated alongside the natural history museum. The committees commissioned surveys, reports, registers of animal husbandry, scientific publications and practical manuals, all in support of their efforts in the growth and dissemination of practical knowledge in Ireland.

While museums in Great Britain generally evolved as fully public entities, most in Ireland developed as a result of efforts by the learned societies. Aside from the Royal Dublin Society, the Royal Irish Academy held important collections of antiquities and scientific objects, providing another of the premier museums in the city. Many of the smaller societies also held collections, and some had dedicated museums. The Dublin Natural History Society launched its museum on Great Brunswick Street in 1838, intended to rival the RDS in its collections of Irish flora and fauna.[12] In 1831 the Belfast Natural History and Philosophical Society inaugurated its museum, housed in its headquarters on College Square.[13] The Museum of Economic Geology, founded in 1845, became the Museum of Irish Industry in 1854.[14] The Geological Society of Dublin, the Dublin University Zoological and Botanical Association and the Kilkenny Archaeological Society all had collections which they exhibited.[15] These organisations held regular meetings, where members presented new information and the results of research, the resulting papers intermittently published in collected volumes or journals. It was common for members to belong to more than one society, so that collections and publications frequently benefited from close interactions among societies through shared information and resources.

Natural science, culture and Irish history

The endeavours of the learned societies and their efforts in the building of museums, scientific collections and intellectual culture have been elided or downplayed in the historical record of nineteenth-century Ireland. Historian Oliver MacDonagh characterised the period 1845–70 as 'among the most barren culturally in modern Irish history', primarily defining culture in Ireland as the production of literary fiction.[16] That the field of Irish history largely defines culture as the creation of literature is underscored by historian

James H. Murphy. In discussing Prince Albert's influence on Dublin's 1853 Irish Industrial Exhibition and the use of symbols as political expression, he observes that:

> The view of nineteenth-century Ireland that sees a brief literary renaissance in the 1830s and 1840s followed by a period of cultural desuetude until the Anglo-Irish literary revival of the 1890s needs to be modified at least to the extent of recognizing the explicitly cultural texture, albeit of a non-literary variety, of Irish political life. The promotion of science and the arts through exhibitions was a novel form of cultural activity; these became occasions for struggles of political ideology.[17]

Murphy identifies perhaps one of the most glaring oversights in nineteenth-century Irish history, and in the history of Irish intellectual culture generally. Within the corpus of Irish history, the assumption that literature is equivalent to culture, and that a fallow period for literary fiction meant that mid-nineteenth-century Ireland was therefore bereft of cultural activity, is a trope that is ripe for challenge. The general absence of scientific activity, and of this museum in particular, from the historiography of nineteenth-century Ireland echoes the 'two cultures' argument formulated by C.P. Snow in 1959. Snow asserted that science and the humanities, though populated by scholars of equal intelligence and merit, had become largely separate from one another by the middle of the twentieth century, to the extent that scientists were unfamiliar with the key elements of the humanities, and humanities scholars woefully ignorant of basic scientific principles.[18] The widespread proliferation of complex ideas through popular formats in new media and digital communication has corrected this to some extent, but in Irish history there seems to be a lingering reluctance to treat the history of science as history per se, or to acknowledge that science is a deeply embedded aspect of the broader culture that it inhabits, and that its history is therefore of value to scholars of the humanities. This reluctance has obscured an upwelling of intellectual activity in the nineteenth century that produced all manner of knowledge and writing, though not of the literary variety. The growth of science was inextricably bound to wider developments in the period, and nineteenth-century Ireland was abuzz with the discovery of antiquities, with the emergence of photography, with advances in the speed of travel, with lectures and publications on every new invention and discovery – in short, alive with a wealth of new learning and information, all concerned with the seismic shifts in public culture and daily life that defined the Victorian period. The divisions between science and the humanities that became common in the twentieth century were nascent in the nineteenth, so that there was communication between the arts and the sciences, between culture and industry.

The Victorian period was the heyday of science and museums in Ireland and Great Britain, and they were embedded into the social fabric of the period. Influential figures such as Daniel O'Connell, Thomas Davis, Thomas Larcom and William Wilde were all members of learned societies, and championed their potential for creating meaningful social change through education and access to the enriching experiences provided by museums and lectures. Culture in this period was transferred, at least in part, to the exhibition hall, the scientific lecture, the learned paper. When Murphy identified exhibitions of science and art as opportunities for the performance of political positions, he did so in the context of Ireland's reception of Queen Victoria during her visits to the island. However, his postulation about exhibitions of science and the arts as occasions for political expression can be extended; exhibitions of science and art were not simply opportunities to articulate political ideologies, they were expressions of a healthy and vital intellectual culture. That is why unearthing the history of the Natural History Museum is important: it shows that culture in mid-Victorian Ireland was far from 'barren', but was active in the emergent bodies of knowledge that characterised the period overall, and that, outside the field of Irish history, are widely accepted as expressions of culture.

'Blind spots'

Historian R.V. Comerford has argued for the distinctive character of mid-Victorian Ireland, making incisive observations about the impact of social, political and technological shifts in the post-Famine years. He emphasises that 'this era has had its distinctiveness ignored or distorted by the preoccupation of popular historiography with the mythic march of the nation'.[19] Historian John Wilson Foster has proposed that 'there are blind spots in our rear-view vision of Irish culture, episodes that have been overlooked in the creation of a coherent narrative of national history.[20] The importance of Dublin's Natural History Museum as a feature of Irish intellectual and scientific life has become one of those blind spots. Situating the RDS Natural History Museum within the context of Dublin in the mid-nineteenth century reveals that its character and activities were far from the mythology of stasis through which it is viewed today, and uncovers its contribution to the emergence of scientific knowledge within increasingly specific and professionalised fields of inquiry. The following chapters reconstruct the history of the museum into the 1870s, showing how it was woven into the wider concerns of science, museums and intellectual culture in Victorian Ireland. They also examine the people involved with the museum, from donors of single items to the men of science who created new knowledge from the collections, and how they contributed to the growth of natural science, both in Ireland and internationally. Their work often had resonance beyond its particular subject matter, and considering it within the larger Victorian context allows us a glimpse of how the debates of the period unfolded on a local and sometimes personal level. This rear-view look at Dublin's Natural History Museum aims to restore a national treasure to its rightful place in the intellectual history of nineteenth-century Ireland.

PART I

Establishing the Natural History Museum

THE EARLY HISTORY OF Dublin's Natural History Museum also traces the development of natural science in Ireland. It was embedded into wider patterns of European thought, and the people associated with it drew from international influences as they established a natural history of Ireland. Natural science changed radically and rapidly during the same period that the Royal Dublin Society sought to build its museum into a useful and modern civic resource.

The first half of the nineteenth century was also a period of seismic change in the practices of museum collection and exhibition, and those conditions were as influential in Dublin as they were in the rest of the world. The museum's development was shaped by the ambitions of the RDS, but also by the demands of parliament, the growing scientific community and the general public. The curators responded to the conflicting claims on the museum in ways that reflect key concerns in the development of museums and science from the early to the mid-century. These three chapters trace the institutional history of the museum, demonstrating how it was affected by the debates and events surrounding natural history museums at large during a phase of rapid growth and competing demands.

CHAPTER I

Enlightenment Roots, International Contexts

Founding principles

The Royal Dublin Society's Natural History Museum owed its foundation to the rise of learned societies across Europe in the eighteenth century. The wide-ranging shifts in philosophy and the social order explored by Enlightenment thinkers cultivated a broad focus on improving the lot of humankind through the advancement of objective knowledge. Francis Bacon's exhortation that 'we must prepare an adequate and sound natural and experimental history, this being the basis for everything, for we are not to imagine or suppose but to discover what nature makes or does' proposed that natural phenomena be examined directly rather than through received wisdom.[1] Bacon's statement countered educational traditions, in which universities had largely focused on classical texts and lecture-based teaching, with the spirit of direct inquiry and experimentation taken up by newly founded academies and scientific or learned societies. By the late eighteenth century, these newcomers had strengthened intellectual culture in Europe, bolstering a shift away from the conventional certainties of biblical, classical and traditional forms of knowledge towards a type of knowing that derived from observation, practice, and direct experience. Academies and learned societies became centres for the creation and dissemination of new ideas resulting from observation, practising direct engagement with matter and circumstances in the world, developing an ethos of human improvement through the practical application of empirical knowledge.

Experiments, demonstrations and collections were increasingly integral to this process. They were the observational methods through which knowledge was obtained, but were also the means of demonstrating it to those who wished to learn, as demonstrations with scientific instruments and the arrangement of collections became means of conveying new knowledge in natural philosophy and natural history. Collections in particular held a number of attractions. Up to the seventeenth century they had been the purview of the wealthy and scholarly, and found eager audiences when they became more available to a wider public. The eighteenth century was a transitional period as private cabinets of curiosity, where scientific objects mixed with monstrosities, curiosities and rarities, began to develop into more focused resources for studying nature. They were increasingly made available for viewing by the public, though often still limited to an elite audience. Developments in scientific thought changed the way that collections were organised by classifying objects for easy understanding and access. In 1735 Swiss botanist Carl Linnaeus published *Systema naturae*, describing his simplified system for classifying natural specimens using Latin double names for identifying and arranging organisms. His binomial nomenclature created a universally understood system that was consistent and reasonably easy to learn, retaining the use of Latin as the common language of scholars.[2] His system was adopted by men of science in the arrangement of collections, and sometimes also influenced the ways that collections of non-natural materials were classified and displayed.[3] Using a common vocabulary to describe specimens meant that collections could be universally understood across countries and languages, playing a role in an interlocking set of techniques for conveying information, both for specialists and a wider public. Collections, demonstrations and lectures, as well as increasingly available printed material, worked together to spread new scientific knowledge as the eighteenth century rolled into the nineteenth, when these elements became common features of public intellectual life. Learned societies became a locus of these activities, with many societies maintaining lecture halls, libraries and collections of scientific instruments and natural history objects.

The Dublin Society was, from its outset, a product of this environment, one of the many learned bodies spurred into existence by the spirit of the age. Its founders, a group of fourteen well-connected Anglo-Irish gentlemen, fashioned a set of rules and principles that balanced communicating new observation-based knowledge with offering practical advice, and an eye towards communicating with their counterparts in similar societies.[4] The ethos of improvement through learning featured in the society's founding charter of 1731, which declared:

> That every member of this Society, at his admission, be desired to choose some particular subject, either in Natural History, or in Husbandry, Agriculture or Gardening, or some species of Manufacture, or other branch of improvement, and make it his business, by reading what had been printed on that subject, by conversing with them who made it their profession, or by making his own experiments, to make himself master thereof, and to report in writing, the best account they can get by experiment or enquiry relating thereunto.[5]

From its origins, the society encouraged members to educate themselves and others, promoting the Enlightenment principles that were encouraging the growth of science and museums in Europe. Initially, its members chose to focus on subjects with practical implications for Ireland's economic stability. They looked for ways of improving agriculture and animal husbandry, and to reduce the country's reliance on imported goods that could be manufactured domestically. The society initiated competitions in agriculture, husbandry and manufacturing, offering prizes and medals to encourage participation in its improving initiatives. In 1736 it commenced a series of short publications in the form of 'letters', that conveyed information and instruction on topics such as growing flax, soil quality, brewing, tillage and other subjects connected to Ireland's economic potential.[6] In 1750, the society was incorporated by royal charter, in recognition of its efforts. Monarch George II expressed the hope that 'much greater effects might arise there from tending farther to civilise the natives of our said kingdom, and render them well affected to us, and to our royal family' as well as acknowledging the society's efforts in experiments that would increase economic stability.[7] Its initiatives were also generously funded by the Irish Parliament after 1761.[8] Historian Michael Brown points out that with this acknowledgement 'the Society was rhetorically, as well as legally, incorporated into the state' and that any advantages it accrued were purchased at the cost of 'submission to political fortune and a loss of institutional flexibility'.[9] The support of central government would continue to be both boon and burden to the society in its future endeavours.

In establishing a museum in the basement of the Irish Parliament in 1733, the Dublin Society began displaying objects as part of its overall goals of 'improving Husbandry, Manufactures and other Useful Arts', with an accompanying programme of education and information. At the start, this was resolutely practical, consisting of models and examples of the latest manufacturing and agricultural equipment purchased by the society, often too rare or costly for individuals to buy. Interested parties could inspect them, be tutored in how to use them, and arrange to attend hands-on instruction sessions at various locations around the country.[10] These exhibitions were intended to familiarise the landowning classes (and the workers they employed) with advances in technology that could make their holdings, and therefore Ireland, more productive. The displays later moved to the society's premises on Grafton Street, and were transferred to a new premises on Hawkins Street in 1786, heralded in the widely read *Gentleman's Magazine,* which announced that 'above the meeting room is a library and a repository for mechanical models, save those relative to husbandry, which are deposited in another place belonging to the Society'.[11] The exhibitions had by then expanded to include collections of mineral and fossil specimens, and the library housed the society's collection of books on husbandry, natural history and mechanics.[12] The Hawkins Street premises remained the society's headquarters until its eventual move to Leinster House on Merrion Square in 1815.

Mineralogy and the Leskean collection

The society's focus on natural history began in 1792 with the purchase of the Leskean cabinet, a collection of minerals and natural specimens. A branch of geology focused on the physical makeup of rocks and minerals, mineralogy was among the society's primary interests, and by 1786 it had hired a mineralogist named Donald Stewart to collect samples of Irish minerals.[13] The study of geology and mineral specimens was encouraged among the membership as a way of familiarising landowners with potentially valuable natural resources that might be found on their holdings. When the Leskean cabinet of minerals was offered for sale in Germany, chemist and influential Dublin Society member Richard Kirwan was eager to purchase it for the society, as it was celebrated in scientific circles as one of the most comprehensive collections of European minerals.[14] Kirwan secured the support of the Irish Parliament, which provided the £1,350 purchase price, a substantial sum at the time.[15]

He arranged the transfer of the prestigious collection to Ireland, where it was installed in a museum occupying two rooms of the society's Hawkins Street premises.[16] In 1795, the Dublin Society introduced rules allowing access to the Leskean collection for scholars who did not hold membership, signalling the beginning of the society's first public museum. After the installation of the collection, an increased focus on geology naturally followed suit, with the society commissioning a number of geological surveys of Ireland in the late eighteenth and early nineteenth centuries, preludes to the later work of the government's Ordnance and Geological Surveys.[17] In keeping with the society's earlier efforts, these investigations were driven by fundamentally practical aims. Geologist Frank Mitchell notes that 'the founders of the Society were essentially landed proprietors who were imbued with the aim of raising the standard of Ireland's prosperity, an aim which, if successful, would be of benefit to them personally and to the nation as a whole'.[18]

In addition to its practical value, Kirwan's desire to have the Leskean collection in Dublin was motivated by the role it had played in debates about the nature of the earth's surface. Assembled by Nathaniel Gottfried Leske, a professor of natural history at the University of Leipzig, the organisation and contents of the Leskean collection represented the theories of German geologist Abraham Gottlob Werner. Germany was a leading centre of chemical and geological sciences in the eighteenth century, and Werner's theories about the formation of the Earth's surface were among the most influential of his day. Popularly called Neptunian, his theory proposed that the Earth's surface was formed when a body of water that had formerly covered the planet subsided, and that the matter suspended within it behaved in different ways as it settled out to form the strata of land masses.[19] This was contradicted by English geologist James Hutton, who asserted that the formation of the Earth's surface could be attributed to the action of heat underneath it, a process referred to as Plutonian. The advocates of each theory carried on a spirited international debate throughout the late eighteenth and early nineteenth centuries. Kirwan was deeply interested in developments in the fields of geology and mineralogy, and had published the first work in English on the latter, *Elements of Mineralogy*, in 1784. A devotee of Werner and a fierce critic of Hutton, he was a co-founder of the Wernerian Natural History Society in Edinburgh, along with Professor Robert Jameson of the University of Edinburgh, joined by a number of other influential naturalists. Jameson visited Kirwan in Dublin, where they discussed Hutton's theories and found ways to dispute them, and both published robust counter-arguments to his ideas.[20]

Kirwan's acquisition of the Leskean collection put the Dublin Society and its nascent geology collections on the side of the 'watermen' in their ongoing conflict with the 'firemen', one of the most hard-fought scientific debates of its day.[21] It also strengthened Ireland's ties to the experimental sciences in Germany and their preference for practical, hands-on means of discerning new information, strengthening the sense of observation and experiment in the society's scientific activity. Werner had studied widely in mining, metallurgy and mineralogy, proceeding into teaching, and securing the chair of mining and mineralogy at the University of Freiberg in 1775.[22] His system for classifying minerals was loosely based around Linnaeus' principles in the *Systema naturae,* adapting its focus on the sexual characteristics of organisms into a way of identifying and classifying minerals based on application of the human senses to specimens. Werner used physical characteristics such as colour, lustre, streak, taste, and texture, among others, to class minerals into groupings. His 1774 publication *On the External Characters of Minerals* explained his system and made his reputation.[23] Nathaniel Leske, a follower and former student, had assembled his collection according to Werner's classifications, and it had been catalogued by another former student, Dietrich Ludwig Gustav Karsten. An influential mineralogist in his own right, Karsten's 600-page catalogue, *Leske's Mineral Collection Systematically Arranged and Described,* was the first published explanation of Werner's system, further increasing the collection's scientific value.

Museum scholar Susan Pearce suggests that from the Renaissance forward, the thought processes signalling the modern era were bent towards defining and expressing the objective realities shared by all humans. This search for overarching narratives 'gave rise to the discourse of scientific knowledge and understanding arrived at by the operation of human reason upon the observed phenomena of the natural world, for which museums and their collections were perceived as the principal repositories of primary evidence'.[24] The Leskean cabinet exemplifies that collections are not only assemblages of valuable or representative objects, but also serve as propositions about how the world is organised. It represented a modern method of inquiry based on direct observation, its organisation according to Werner's principles behaving as a physical demonstration of a set of new scientific ideas. Its underlying premise was that hands-on interaction with the collection and its catalogue would convey Werner's theories about the shape of the world, and that it could teach his classification system to the alert scholar. The impact of the Leskean cabinet was deeper than simply a source of practical knowledge for landowners about mineral resources. It also represented an intellectual proposition about the origins of the Earth, and placed Dublin scholars into an international debate. The dual configuration of practical use combined with the overall development of scientific thought would remain a feature of the society's natural history collections well into the future. The Leskean collection's value to the Dublin Society and to scholars lay not only in its comprehensiveness, but also in the way that it summarised a system of classification, and physically demonstrated an influential theory of the Earth's formation. Kirwan's ambition in ensuring that it came to Dublin shows that the society's focus on practical information for local improvement was inextricable from the ways that men of science engaged in larger debates in international networks.

International connections

By the time the Dublin Society relocated to its new headquarters at Leinster House in 1815, it had become an ambitious private society with plans for improving Ireland's circumstances through a range of civic initiatives. The Act of Union in 1801 had changed the society's relationship with central government, when the enthusiastic support of the Irish Parliament was replaced by oversight from Westminster. The society adopted the 'Royal' prefix when George IV became its patron during his visit to Ireland in 1821, and from that point 'increasingly became the object of public scrutiny and Government attention'.[25] It continued to receive funding, albeit somewhat reduced, for its provision of civic enhancements that saved parliament the trouble of establishing them itself. In addition to the natural history collections, the society maintained a library, a fine art collection, and agricultural, botanical and veterinary collections. It ran drawing schools, and held scientific lectures. The society also held a series of agricultural shows, encouraging farmers and landowners to continually improve their methods through awarding prizes for the best produce and animal stocks. In the early nineteenth century, it began a series of exhibitions of manufactures, first held in 1835 and then every three years from 1838, showcasing advances in design, manufacturing and raw materials. The stately domestic architecture of Leinster House, the duke

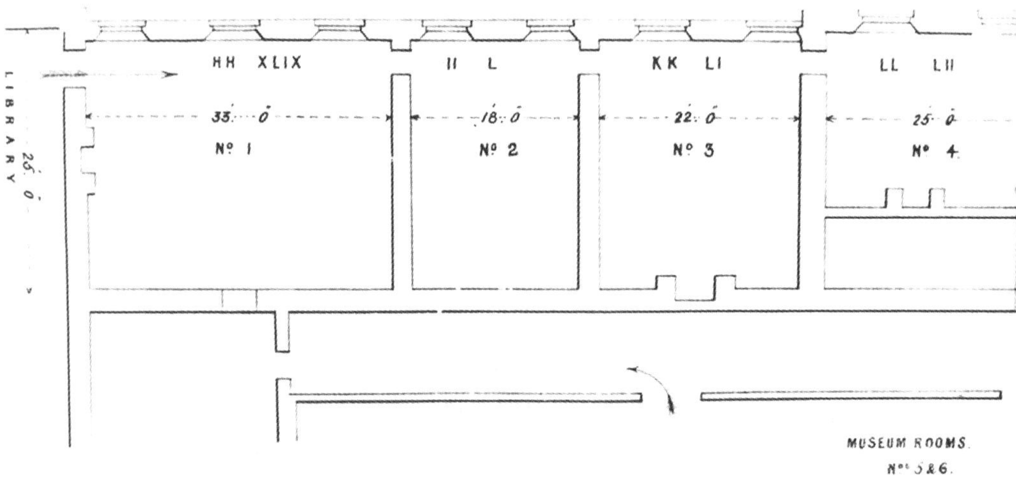

Fig. 1.1 Floor plan of the Natural History Museum on the first floor of Leinster House, showing the layout and modest size of rooms housing the collections. From the Royal Dublin Society's *Catalogue of Exhibition of Manufacture, Produce and Invention, held on 8th July 1850 and Following Days.*
COURTESY OF THE RDS LIBRARY AND ARCHIVES

of Leinster's former residence, was pressed into service as museum rooms, a library, meeting rooms and a lecture theatre (Fig. 1.1). Grand houses were frequently used as museums or repositories; the British Museum began its career in Montagu House, and substantial private collections were often housed in domestic settings, such as the earl of Enniskillen's museum at his home, Florence Court, in Fermanagh. Even so, the restrictions of displaying collections in domestic rooms soon became problematic for the RDS museum, which expanded rapidly from 1815 to 1830. RDS historian Kevin Bright points out that the 'resumption of world trade after 1815, the growth of commerce and of the British Empire, expanded the scope of the RDS museum to global proportions in natural history, geology, antiquities and ethnology'.[26] As the society grew and became more ambitious, its collecting activities were influenced by other institutions in Europe where members had studied or had personal contacts, or that pursued innovative methods of inquiry. The British Museum and the Jardin des Plantes, especially its Muséum d'Histoire Naturelle in Paris, were especially important guides for the development of the museum, and for natural science in Dublin.

The Jardin des Plantes was a French centre of research in natural science, supported by the state for the length of its existence. Founded as a private possession of King Louis XIII, the Jardin du Roi, it was opened to the public in 1640. In 1790, during the French Revolution, naturalist Jean-Baptiste Lamarck proposed to preserve and modify it as a state centre of science education, changing its name to distance it from royal associations. His plan was adopted and expanded upon by the new revolutionary government, which added a new Muséum d'Histoire Naturelle to the site in 1793.[27] The work at the Jardin des Plantes took a comprehensive approach that made it the research institute of note in eighteenth- and nineteenth-century natural science. The Comte de Buffon, Lamarck and Georges Cuvier, key thinkers in the development of natural science, all formulated their influential theories about nature, evolution and the organisation of species during their work in its gardens and museums. Each of them produced multi-volume works on natural history, and were members of the elite learned society the Académie des Sciences. Historian Carla Yanni notes that English men of science looked to Paris as the acme of the natural sciences in the early nineteenth century because of its established tradition of government-supported research and the fact that it was staffed by professors, neither of which was true in Great Britain.[28] The programmes at the muséum were directed at increasing knowledge of nature through research and writing, and attracted scholars from across the globe who came to study the ideas and techniques being developed there.

Ireland's scientific connections to Paris were established primarily through the work of zoologist and palaeontologist Georges Cuvier. Cuvier's influence on nineteenth-century science was considerable: he proposed a system of classification modifying Linnaean taxonomy, created new categories dividing the natural world into living and non-living entities and used comparative anatomy to structure his classifications. One of Cuvier's most important contributions was the principle of extinction: he proposed that localised geological 'revolutions', or catastrophic events, were responsible for the disappearance of certain species.[29] The giant Irish deer was among a group of fossil mammals, such as mammoths and cave bears, that Cuvier had determined were no longer extant as living species. Though a number of the species he examined retained connections to living species, the giant Irish deer, *Cervus megaceros,* was unique, allowing Cuvier to state that extinction was a scientific fact.[30] His influence on natural science in Ireland was significant. References to Cuvier's ideas were scattered throughout the publications and lectures of the Royal Dublin Society, the Geological Society, the Natural History Society and other learned bodies. Cork was home to the Cork Cuvierian Society, founded in 1834. Though its membership was small, it sought to establish itself as a reputable body focused on scholarship, research and the creation of knowledge.[31]

One of the most visible connections between Cuvier and Irish natural science lies in the work of John Hart, surgeon, comparative anatomist and instructor at the Royal College of Surgeons in Ireland (RCSI), and a long-term member of the RDS, serving as chair of its Natural History Committee throughout the 1840s. Hart had studied with Cuvier in Paris in the early 1800s, and his contributions to Irish natural history owed much to his former professor. In 1824–5 Hart was selected by the RDS to reconstruct a skeleton of the giant Irish deer from a collection of fossil bones found in Limerick, donated to the society by Archdeacon William Maunsell. With the support of the society, Hart published a pamphlet on the re-assembled skeleton, acknowledged at the time as one of the finest and most complete examples of the species.[32] In the text, he referenced Cuvier's theories, and placed the skeleton firmly within the scope of his former mentor's assertions about mammal extinctions across the European continent. Hart's pamphlet proved popular: it was reprinted numerous times, prompting the society to publish a separate illustration of the complete skeleton (Fig. 1.2). Hart's work and publications again demonstrate that the Royal Dublin Society's collections were situated within the development of natural science in a pan-European context, in addition to their local significance. Due to its impressive size, this specimen became one of the centrepieces of the collections, and still stands at the museum's entrance today.

Though Paris provided an aspirational touchstone for research, in practical terms the society's natural history museum was allied to the British Museum. They both relied on the state for support and funding, and their collections developed simultaneously throughout the nineteenth century. The British Museum was formed from the private collection of Sir Hans Sloane, wealthy baronet and physician to royalty and gentry, a keen traveller and diligent collector who accumulated a wide range of objects, from books and coins to natural history and curiosities. Rather than entrust them to a learned society, Sloane bequeathed his collections to the state as the foundation for a new national museum. His largesse was accepted in 1753, when it was determined that the collections would be kept intact, opened to the public and installed at a suitable location.[33] Montagu House, a stately home, was chosen, and plans

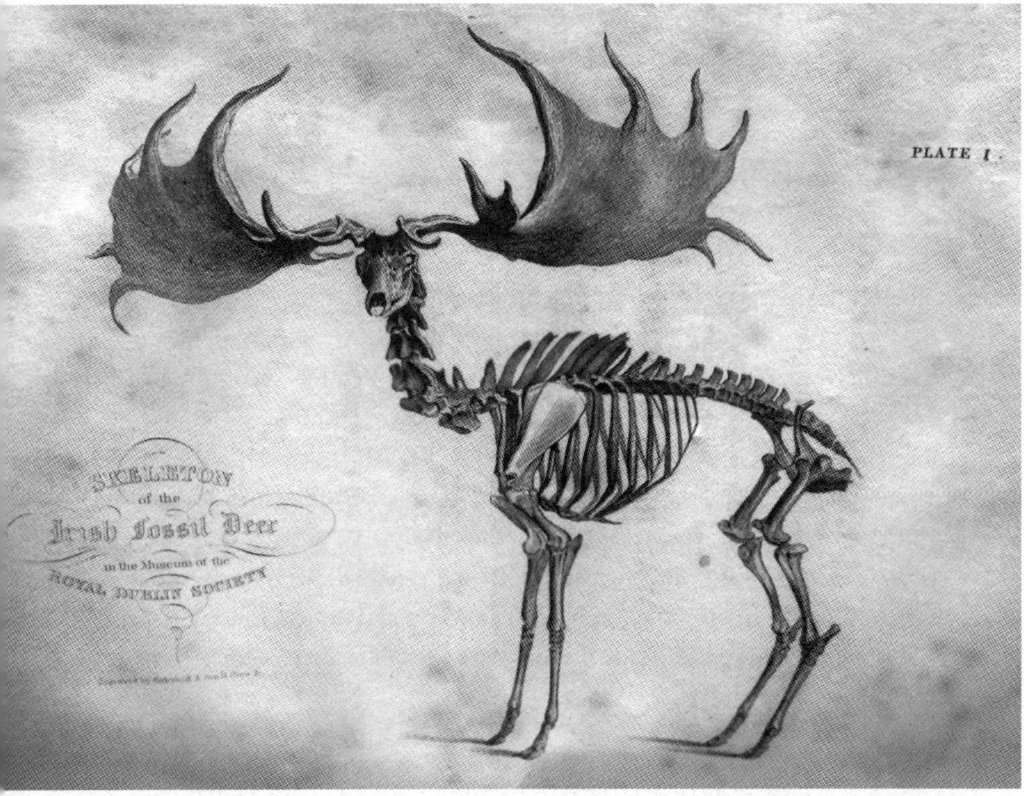

Fig. 1.2 Giant Irish deer fossil skeleton donated to the Royal Dublin Society by Archdeacon Maunsell and assembled by John Hart, from the second edition of Hart's pamphlet on the species.
COURTESY THE NATIONAL MUSEUM OF IRELAND, NATURAL HISTORY

to move the collections were in place by 1755. It was opened to the public in 1759, but the difficulties in arranging and managing a large public collection soon became apparent. The museum staff were at odds with one another over issues of space and status, as funding and facilities were limited. Even though it was conceived as a museum for the benefit of the public, the regime for securing permission to see the collections was famously restrictive. Tickets were procured by application, had to be countersigned by a 'known person', and visitors were sometimes rushed through their tours by overstretched staff. The domestic architecture of the house created difficulties of arrangement and overcrowding, and the preservation of specimens and objects suffered from dark accommodation and exposure to damp and dust. Solving these issues was complicated by the fact that, though parliamentary committees continually asserted the importance of public museums, the British Museum was consistently underfunded, in sharp contrast to its Parisian counterparts.[34]

The Irish learned societies and their memberships looked to both the continent and the Great Britain for guidance in developing their museums. The scholarship and active approaches taken by the Jardin des Plantes were influential in Irish natural science, and the work undertaken there remained the standard to which many European museums aspired throughout the nineteenth century. However, the practicalities of being enclosed within the British model through funding and shared state apparatus meant that Irish museums experienced many of the same difficulties seen in the British Museum. Ireland's difficulties were compounded by the fact that, although the learned societies owned and controlled their collections, funding arrangements meant that they were subject to demands from Westminster and Dublin Castle around the promotion of culture, science and education. Museums in Ireland, and at the RDS in particular, struggled with being simultaneously Irish and British, independent and state-sponsored, private and public, as they began to form ideologies about the purposes of museums and their role in wider social developments.

The early museum: Giesecke's collection

The first half of the nineteenth century was a transitional period for natural history museums. Despite the increasing development of scientific methods, collections still tended to contain loosely organised assemblages of all sorts of things, including specimens, but also rarities, antiquities, curiosities and ethnographic items. As the practices of natural science developed into the second half of the century, natural history museums were shaped into taxonomically classified archives of specimens for study and comparison, with an increasing emphasis on educating the public about nature through the organisation of the collection. The Natural History Museum at the Royal Dublin Society followed this process, as did most similarly focused European collections. There are no extant images of the museum before the late 1880s, so following this development and forming a sense of the collections depends on manuscript records, descriptions from popular publications, and surviving specimens and objects.[35] In the early stages of the museum's residence in Leinster House, the contents of the Leskean cabinet were exhibited alongside an assortment of scientific specimens, ethnographic objects, curiosities and random interesting things. From 1813 to 1833, the museum was curated by the RDS professor of mineralogy, Sir Charles Lewis Giesecke, a German polymath who secured his position after it had been declined by Kirwan's associate Robert Jameson.[36]

By the time he arrived in Dublin, Giesecke had already established himself in two professions: in his youth he had made his reputation in Vienna's theatre world as an actor, writer and librettist, encountering eminent musical and theatrical figures, including Mozart. He left Vienna in 1799, and by 1801 resided in Berlin, where he took up mineralogy, a subject that had interested him as a youth. He became a mineral collector and dealer, making it his business to meet influential people who could further his progress in science, including Martin Klaproth and Dietrich Karsten, both highly regarded mineralogists and former students of Werner. He went to Freiberg to study with Werner himself, learning the Wernerian system of classification. Giesecke then travelled extensively, collecting and dealing in minerals as he went, proceeding to Denmark where he obtained permission from the king to study the geology of Greenland. His 1806 sojourn lasted seven years due to several misadventures, but secured Giesecke's reputation in mineralogy through definitive collections of its mineral and natural specimens, including some that were previously unknown. On his return to Europe, he was invited to Edinburgh by Thomas Allen, a banker and Wernerian mineralogist who had purchased one of his collections. Allen encouraged him to apply for the position of professor of mineralogy at the Royal Dublin Society, which had been advertised in international scientific journals.[37]

In appointing Giesecke, the society strengthened its links to the wider community of European science and culture, raising its scientific and international profile, and reinforcing the transnational dimensions of Irish science. Giesecke's duties included acting as keeper for the museum, cataloguing the mineral collections and delivering courses in mineralogy.[38] His work with Werner qualified him to shepherd the Leskean collections, and his Greenland materials became valued additions to the RDS museum. Giesecke provided an active connection to the innovative science being undertaken in Germany, and his previous career and travels had provided him with a reputation for charm and persuasion, perfect attributes for an erudite man of science in a growing and ambitious learned society.

The museum that Giesecke curated was described in a number of publications, providing us with a sense of the collections, and of the role that the curator played in its early organisation and reception. As an attribute of the Royal Dublin Society, it was portrayed in travelogues and city histories as one of the highlights of the metropolis. Limerick writer John James McGregor, in his *New Picture of Dublin* (1821), devotes six pages to acquainting the reader with the work, buildings and collections of the society.[39] After recounting a short history of the society and its personnel, McGregor enumerated the key collections associated with Leinster House, including the botanic gardens, a veterinary museum, agricultural collections, the library and fine art objects. He also mentions a chemical laboratory and lecture rooms. The natural history collection is designated simply as 'the Museum', a custom which persisted until late in the nineteenth century. Within the RDS, the term 'museum' referred to the collections of natural history, ethnographic objects and curiosities, rather than its collections of art objects. McGregor noted that the museum 'is contained in a suite of apartments, which are not considered as well calculated for the display of such an exhibition', an observation that would be repeated for several decades hence[40] (see Fig. 1.1 above).

McGregor noted that the animal and mineral collections were separate, then listed well-ordered mineral and geological holdings, with a focus on the Leskean cabinet. The animal collections he described as being less thorough, with 'few beasts and birds', though plenty of 'shells, butterflies, and beetles'. Mixed in with these items were collections of implements and curiosities from the South Seas, knife handles and a piece of crystallised iron ore, presented by Napoleon to 'Captain Usher', in reference to Rear Admiral Thomas Ussher, an Irish officer in the Royal Navy who conveyed the French leader to his exile on Elba.[41] He also cited two other museums at the society, Sir Charles Giesecke's Museum and the Museum Hibernicum Regnum Minerale, describing them as separate to the museum proper. Giesecke's reputation warranted a discrete display of his Greenland materials, and the Museum Hibernicum focused on collections of Irish minerals and fossils commissioned by the society. These were interspersed with curiosities such as large pearls from County Kerry and samples of stained glass. The entry finished with reference to the society's educational programmes, observing that lectures 'on natural philosophy, botany, chemistry, mineralogy, mining, and the veterinary art, are given at stated periods, by the different professors, to which the public are liberally invited'.[42]

The society's attributes and exhibitions were given comparable, though often abbreviated, treatment in similar volumes, such as James Brewer's

1825 *Beauties of Ireland,* written to guide tourists from England, Scotland and Wales during their visits to Ireland. Access to travel by ship and rail became increasingly easy and popular throughout the century, giving rise to a brisk trade in the literature of travel and novel experiences. Collections and museums were highlighted in books for travellers with a view to educating the reader, and to showing the visitor what was noteworthy when encountering a new city. Collections of art objects, curiosities and natural history still retained the aura of exclusivity engendered by their former status as possessions of the elite classes, so that visiting them was understood as a civilising activity with educational benefit, a way of improving oneself through participating in the conventions of gentility and erudition. These publications advertised the society's ambitions to the wider world, and they have left us with a means of seeing what the museum contained in the first half of the nineteenth century, and how it was perceived in its early form.

More specifically for a local audience, an article in the inaugural edition of the weekly *Dublin Penny Journal* in August 1832 provides detailed insight into the configuration of an early nineteenth-century museum. As in many nineteenth-century journals and newspapers, the writer is not identified; because this article was printed in the first volume of the new journal, it is likely to have been written by one of the founding publishers, perhaps antiquarian George Petrie or writer Caesar Otway. The reader was informed that the museum was 'thrown open to the public from one to three every Monday and Friday', noting that:

> [T]he civility and politeness of the Museum keeper must be extremely gratifying to everyone who visits the rooms. Everything worthy of attention is explained … you can walk from bird to beast, and from beast to reptile, and from reptile to shells, minerals, monstrosities, every thing rich and rare, ever[y] thing wonderful and curious, and incomprehensible – without an abridgement of happiness enjoyed.[43]

Though the society intended that its museum should be educational and practical, this description indicates that it was also something else. The cabinet of curiosity, the sixteenth-century precursor to the modern museum, combined natural specimens with luxury objects, rarities and specimens that were outsized or unique. They were inclined to spectacle as well as knowledge, and this tendency seemed to linger in the description of the collections at the RDS. Natural history specimens contended for attention with the luxurious, curious and monstrous, and the collections were still inclined to novelty and marvel as much as to 'the diffusion of useful knowledge'. The writer noted a range of objects, mentioning beetles, bats, mummies, tattooed heads, Greenland huts and Arabian rocks, among other things. Of particular interest was Archdeacon Maunsell's giant Irish fossil deer, standing in the middle of the room, with an image from Hart's 1825 pamphlet reproduced to accompany the text in the article.

In the late eighteenth and early nineteenth centuries, museum displays were commonly arrayed on shelves or tables, and in cases and cabinets of modest size; the plate glass that allowed for large display cases had yet to be invented. In keeping with the Enlightenment ethos of scientific experiment by direct observation, eighteenth-century museums sometimes encouraged use of all the senses to discern the qualities of an object. Keepers would frequently remove specimens from their housings, and would sometimes allow visitors to handle them. The knowledge gained by looking at collections, especially scientific ones, was to be augmented through touch, hearing and smell, sometimes even taste.[44] The *Dublin Penny Journal* indicated that the collections were close at hand, and the concentration of specimens and objects housed in the modest proportions of the domestic rooms in Leinster House suggests that the sensory ethos of the eighteenth century was still at work at the RDS in the early nineteenth century. It is easy to imagine the learned and charming Giesecke selecting a large and beautiful shell from its display on a table, handing it to a visitor while he explained its origins and significance.

The emphasis on Giesecke's attention to the visitor indicates that the social niceties of 'polite science' in the late eighteenth century were still part of the experience of visiting the RDS museum. Being shepherded around collections was a commonplace occurrence, especially as many museums were situated in converted homes. The keeper acted as 'host', guiding the visitor through the interesting aspects of the collections and conveying stories and information about the objects.[45] In early museums, the accomplishments of conversation and sociability were as important as scientific publication, with speech and personal contact accepted as legitimate means of conveying scientific knowledge, especially if offered from a reputable source. In remarking on the oral nature of British science, and the use of speech by major figures such as Charles Babbage and John Herschel, science historian James Secord notes that such men were publicly perceived as 'possessing genius or talent not so much through publications but through their persons. Their position was signalled through their status as "lions", whose presence could give intellectual depth and sparkle to a social gathering. Conversability was one of the key attributes of the gentleman'.[46] Giesecke had published in scientific journals, edited and published catalogues and was well-established as a mineralogist, but had also worked in music and theatre in Vienna, studied with Werner, persuaded a king and lived among the inuit people of Greenland. His varied experiences and scientific expertise, along with his status as an RDS professor, would have marked him out as a reliable man of science, and conversing with him about the collections may have been a significant attraction for visitors to the museum.

While knowledgeable conversation and personal contact were features of 'polite science' in the eighteenth century, the more public vehicles of catalogues and scientific publications became increasingly important means of advertising collections throughout the nineteenth century. The reputations of collections were spread by word of mouth, but also by published volumes listing their contents, and by other descriptions in print. The spreading of ideas and reputations in natural history became a mixture of personality, status, objects, speech and print, with each element adding a dimension to the dissemination of new scientific information. While generalist publications like travelogues and the *Dublin Penny Journal* satisfied popular taste, specialist publications such as scientific journals would broadcast the importance of new ideas or collections to a more focused but widely dispersed audience. Learned societies throughout Europe subscribed to a wide range of scientific journals for their libraries, and they were also distributed through personal subscriptions and booksellers. These publications were one of the most useful ways of keeping up with debates and new information, and having one's paper published in them was a mark of prestige. Throughout his time at the society, Giesecke published pamphlets and articles in scientific journals, and lectured extensively both at the society and abroad. His scholarly record furthered the society's international reputation along with his own, circulating his expert knowledge on Greenland, and introducing information he had begun to gather on the mineralogy of the north and west of Ireland.[47]

The published catalogue of a museum or collection was particularly important. The earliest published catalogue of a collection, the 1599 *Della Natura* by Italian apothecary Ferrante Imperato, was distributed across Europe, prompting scholars to study with him in Italy, and encouraging well-heeled visitors to make the journey to see his cabinet. Imperato's success established catalogues as an effective means of advertising a collection, simultaneously increasing the prestige of its owner. The catalogue became a mobile version of a collection, an easily transportable means of letting others know its contents and importance. Catalogues were especially valuable for scholars, contributing to their general knowledge about the range of available specimens and providing potential correspondents for information and advice. If the catalogues had illustrations, they were often considered as viable stand-ins for the real thing. One of the attractions of the Leskean cabinet was that it had been catalogued by Dietrich Karsten after Leske's death. The Dublin Society published an early catalogue of its own collections in 1813, including natural history specimens and antiquities along with the Leskean cabinet, so that its museum's holdings could be broadcast to other learned societies and interested specialists. The introduction to the catalogue showed an awareness of the changing systems of scientific classification, stating that 'The System is, generally, that of Linnaeus, the exception being in the Class Insecta, which is arranged according to Fabricius, with a further deviation, under the authority of Cuvier'[.][48] Its organised listings use the scientific designations of the day and detail the specimens in the collection, ranging from mammals to worms.[49]

Giesecke undertook publication of a catalogue for the Royal Dublin Society in 1832. Entitled *Descriptive Catalogue of a New Collection of Minerals in the Museum of the Royal Dublin Society, to which is Added an Irish Mineralogy*, it advertised the mineralogical collections, and highlighted Giesecke's efforts in creating a collection dedicated to Irish materials that would distinguish the society's holdings through its contribution of new evidence to established collections. The listings show that the collections of minerals spanned the globe, some clearly drawn from the curator's extensive travels in places such as Norway and Greenland, but specimens from other regions were perhaps donated or purchased. In his introduction, Giesecke emphasised the core didactic goals of the society, stating that he had based his classification on the external characteristics of minerals (rather than chemical analysis), a key aspect of Werner's system of classification, reasoning that 'beginners are generally inclined to form small collections for their private study, and this method will allow them to do so at a moderate expense'.[50] In addition to broadcasting the collections to a wider audience, this catalogue was written as an aid to those who sought to educate themselves, in accordance with the society's efforts at improvement through learning.

Under Giesecke's stewardship, the society's museum became embedded in the interlocking conventions of display, publication and scientific expertise that were evident throughout Europe. As the eighteenth century slid into the nineteenth, natural history museums became subject to an increasingly professionalised ethos. Looking at the RDS collections and the ideas that they represent shows that the early museum was not only concerned with the objects themselves but also with the growth of intellectual culture, and the social conventions that accompanied the acquisition of knowledge. The move towards scientific accuracy and organisation was still influenced by the attraction of curiosities and monstrosities that characterised earlier cabinets of curiosity, and still inflected with the courtly manners and customs of eighteenth-century science. Its bent towards practical application was a modernising factor, tying scientific knowledge into a wider project that sought to improve Ireland's economic and social character. The museum at the RDS was presided over by an erudite and charismatic keeper, a single authority developing the museum according to his interests, and attracting positive attention to the society's goals. The museum was a collection of objects that was also represented and disseminated through publications, which created public perceptions about its worth far beyond its geographic location. While the relationship between personalities, objects, text and intellectual culture remained part of the museum's character, the ways they manifested began to shift in the short term, as central government's interest in museums as an educational mechanism began to strengthen, and as the entwined structures of museums and science began to expand rapidly into the second half of the century. These factors gathered momentum at the society during the tenure of Giesecke's successor.

A new curator and the importance of display

The stewardship of the museum changed in 1833, when Giesecke passed away suddenly after dining with friends. After his untimely death, Scottish surgeon and naturalist John Scouler became the RDS professor of mineralogy in 1834. Scouler came to Dublin as a scientific generalist with active connections in Scottish science. While studying medicine at the University of Glasgow from 1817 to 1823, he had developed an interest in botany and natural history, influenced by a number of professors, including chemist Thomas Thomson and botanist William Jackson Hooker.[51] In 1823, Scouler travelled to Paris to study comparative anatomy. On his return to Glasgow in 1824, Hooker recommended Scouler to the Hudson's Bay Company as surgeon and naturalist, setting him on a path increasingly familiar to nineteenth-century naturalists with medical educations.[52] Positions on ships of trade, exploration and colonisation provided a salary while presenting opportunities for collecting foreign specimens, which helped bolster scientific reputations through lectures and publications upon returning home. Up to 1824, Scouler had acquired no qualifications through his studies, but just prior to setting sail in July that year he was 'made a Licentiate of the Royal College of Physicians and Surgeons in Glasgow, enabling him to practise medicine although he had almost no first-hand experience of any of its branches', an indication of the variable value of medical qualifications in the early nineteenth century.[53] Upon returning to Glasgow in 1828, Scouler leapt into professional life, completing his MD, securing election to the Linnaean Society, co-founding the *Glasgow Medical Journal*, and obtaining appointment as the professor of natural history and curator of the museum at Anderson's University in Glasgow.[54] The breadth and variety of his experience helped him secure the society's professorship in Dublin, where, like his predecessor, he was placed in charge of the society's museum in addition to his duties as mineralogist and lecturer.

The museum was again featured in the *Dublin Penny Journal* in 1835, not long after Scouler's arrival, in a long article devoted to the work of the Royal Dublin Society. Covering the collections in more detail, it offers clearer insight into their layout and contents. The writer began by summarising the society's overall history and activities, characterising it as a national resource and foregrounding its educational efforts, particularly the drawing schools and scientific lectures that were provided free of charge to the public. Guiding readers through the full range of the society's activities and holdings, the writer's assumptions about what they would want to know permits us a glimpse into how the RDS collections might have been perceived by the general public during a transitional phase in the history of museums and science in Ireland.

In 1835, visitors reached the museum in Leinster House by passing across a courtyard to a three-storey neo-classical facade facing Kildare Street. Upon entering they traversed two imposing halls filled with classical sculptures, casts and Irish antiquities, progressing up a grand staircase to the library and museum on the first floor.[55] The first museum room was described as containing 'a miscellaneous assemblage of curiosities', including a mummy, armour from an Indian sultan's guard, a silver brooch with an inscription in ogham, and a model of Stonehenge. A set of bronze lamas taken from a temple in Tibet was specially marked out as having caused the death of its collector, Lieutenant Boileau, poisoned by locals in retaliation for his sacrilegious act. The Irish materials in this room included 'a curious ancient Irish regal sceptre, made of iron, inlaid with gold' in which George IV had shown an interest during his 1821 state visit. There were also specimens of the glossy ibis and golden oriole, both examples of migratory species captured in Ireland, and pearls taken from the River Bann.[56] Archdeacon Maunsell's giant Irish deer was deemed 'by far the most interesting object in this room', by virtue of its size and its rarity as a full skeleton.[57] Again, the lingering ethos of the European cabinet collection was evident in the mix of objects, with ethnography, curiosities and antiquities displayed side by side with natural specimens. The writer drew attention to objects with exotic origins, as well as those that had accrued interesting stories or special status. The material in the first room seemed to have been selected for its ability to impress the visitor through rarity, status, size or antiquity, rather than to convey a sense of systematic organisation in the scientific sense.

The second room, the smallest in the museum, was described as 'dedicated to the animal kingdom'. That the zoological specimens were assembled here indicates that the scientific holdings were underdeveloped at this early stage. The systems of scientific classification employed in the 1813 museum catalogue are not mentioned here; whether they simply did not interest the writer or had been abandoned by the curator is difficult to say. Instead, the article emphasised the status of donors, or evoked well-known people or events through the presence of a specimen. The writer was most impressed that 'over one of the cases lies extended the stuffed skin of the very boa constrictor described by McLeod in his *Voyage of the Alceste*'. The large snake had been collected and kept alive by ship's surgeon John McLeod, and made famous by its lengthy portrayal in McLeod's memoir of exploration in southeast Asia.[58] Displayed in Dublin, the stuffed snake represented the allure of adventure and the unknown in addition to serving as an example of its species. A yellow-breasted martin, a large otter shot in Bray, and a chamois donated by John, archduke of Austria, were deemed the most important items in the room because they were rare, outsized or connected to a famous person.

The descriptions of the rest of the rooms were similar, showing that the logic in organising the collections centred around priorities other than the systematic application of scientific categories. The third room contained mineralogy collections and miscellaneous objects. Rather than highlighting the minerals, the writer singled out 'two very beautiful models of Chinese state pleasure-boats, made of ivory, mother-of-pearl, &c.', focusing on rarity and value rather than on the society's core scientific collections and their practical value. The fourth room was dedicated to the natural history of Greenland, populated by minerals, zoological specimens and ethnographic objects from former curator Giesecke's three-year sojourn there.[59] Though it had previously been discussed as a museum unto itself, it was now grouped with the rest of the collections. That Giesecke's collection still merited its own room again highlights the value placed on personal status, focusing on the former curator's interests and experiences as much as the scientific import of his collections. Drawing attention to the head of a walrus placed in a window, the writer notes that 'many other interesting curiosities and natural productions are contained in this apartment'.[60] The next two rooms were reached by turning right and crossing a corridor, and the writer states that 'the fifth room contains the remaining, or geological part of the original Leskean collection', as well as Greek and Etruscan antiquities.[61] The sixth and last room contained the 'Museum Hibernicum' comprising 'mineralogical and geological specimens from the thirty-two counties of Ireland', including samples of gold from a mine in County Wicklow, and augmented by antlers of Irish deer and portrait busts of prominent members of the Royal Dublin Society.[62] The closing paragraphs of the lengthy article focused on the society's educational and scientific activities, describing the drawing school, botanic gardens and mineralogy collections, and giving the schedule of public lectures along with the opening hours for the museum, botanic gardens, art collections and other amenities.[63]

Susan Pearce observes that museums have had a public function from their earliest inceptions, 'not necessarily in the sense that they have always been open to the public ... [but] in the sense that they embody and shape public perceptions of what is valuable and important at each period of their existence'.[64] She emphasises that museum objects are invested with value simply by being displayed; they indicate what is considered important or noteworthy through their visibility in official or institutional contexts. The Royal Dublin Society was one of the most influential learned societies in Ireland, and conducted its efforts at improvement and public service with a clear sense of its own authority. In making its museum available to the public, the RDS began to set the terms for what constituted valuable knowledge through the things it displayed. This sense of authority was underscored by the building itself; recessed arcades, marble corridors and statue collections evoked humanist values and classical antiquity, emphasising that the collections presented in the museum were important by virtue of having been chosen and displayed in a learned context by one of Dublin's leading civic bodies. In conveying a sense of the museum for the reader, the *Dublin Penny Journal* consistently focused on the elevated social position of donors or former owners of objects, emphasising the narratives around the objects rather than their value as representatives of scientific or cultural ideas. In the future, as the museum became more overtly systematic, the collections would continue to exhibit the tendency of highlighting rarity and status even after scientific value became a clear priority.

The idea of a national museum

As the museum grew it became a feature in more general plans for the improvement and government of Ireland. As a civic amenity with potential for scientific inquiry and education, it was among a suite of offerings from the learned societies that were supported by parliament. To encourage economic progress and civic culture, the exchequer funded a significant proportion of the Royal Dublin Society's activity on an annual basis. Starting in 1801 at the sum of £10,000 per year, but reduced to £5,300 by 1835, funding from the public purse outweighed other sources of income for the society.[65] Allocated by the Board of Trade and disbursed through Dublin Castle (after 1854 through direct oversight by the Science and Art Department), the funding supported the society's practically oriented efforts in improvement. In many ways, the RDS and the other learned societies spared the London and Dublin administrations the responsibility and expense of establishing public institutions in Ireland; museums and other public educational structures in science and art already had been created by learned societies as part of their overall missions.

Despite the sharing of common goals, the relationship between the Royal Dublin Society and Westminster, conducted through layers of intermediary bureaucracy, was sometimes punctuated by controversy. The primary source of conflict was that the society saw itself as an autonomous private members' body, while parliament and Dublin Castle saw it as answerable to the demands of the government that provided the lion's share of its funding. The society's internal governing structures caused much of the consternation. An elected central council was responsible for oversight of the society at large, and smaller committees were elected to attend to its various concerns. The Natural History Committee, for instance, was responsible for the museum and the lecture series in natural history subjects. Council and committees made decisions and conducted the business of the society, but important matters were subject to popular vote by the assembled membership, producing an 'archaic and cumbersome method of governing by general meeting' that was open to factional influences within the overall membership.[66]

Protective of its reputation and autonomy, the society was frequently resistant to outside influence or suggestions of reform while simultaneously soliciting cooperation and funding from central government. Parliamentary committees of inquiry regularly took the RDS to task for its problematic internal governance, which made long-term planning difficult, and opaque financial procedures, which made it difficult to ascertain precisely how funds were used. Nevertheless, parliamentary reports consistently recommended that the RDS should be the site of a national museum that would mimic the British Museum. This broad ambition was marred by tension around the society's refusal to distinguish between its public and private functions, or to clarify how it spent government funds, as distinguished from funds raised from its own members and activities. Records concerning the museum, such as government and society reports, as well as proceedings and minute books, depict a consistent variance between the society's stated aims to disseminate 'useful knowledge' for the benefit of the public, and an institutional culture that sometimes caused it to work at cross purposes to that goal.

Tensions between the RDS and central government surfaced publicly in March 1836, when parliament '[o]rdered, that a Select Committee be appointed to inquire into the administration of the Royal Dublin Society, with a view to a wider extension of the advantages of the annual Parliamentary grant to that institution'.[67] The inquiry was prompted by an 1835 incident in which a group of society members organised to block the membership of Dr Daniel Murray, the popular and moderate Catholic archbishop of Dublin. Murray had applied to join in advance of the annual meeting of the British Association for the Advancement of Science, held in Dublin that year; RDS members were to enjoy free access to all associated events.[68] Membership was gained through being proposed by two current members, with candidates voted on by the general membership at monthly meetings. In Murray's case, a group of conservative members appear to have banded together to block him due to his support for Daniel O'Connell.[69] Conducted amid public accusations of sectarianism and political bias, the subsequent investigation examined the internal operations of the society, highlighting its cumbersome decision-making structures and its sometimes lukewarm engagement with its public responsibilities. Chaired by RDS member (and future Young Ireland leader) William Smith O'Brien, the committee's recommendations sought to make internal operations more efficient, to increase public access to collections and resources, and to improve the society's relationships with other learned societies.

A section of the 1836 parliamentary report focused specifically on the museum, offering a window into differences between the society's ambitions and their realisation. Testimony from several quarters found the museum lacking in its role as a public resource; shortage of space, poor public access and disorganisation in the collections were highlighted as bars to the museum fulfilling its potential. The society's approach to its public duties was illustrated by the testimony of its secretary Isaac Weld, during questioning about a reduction in visitor numbers at the museum in 1833:

> One great cause of the falling off was the changing of the day [for visitors] from Monday to Tuesday. Monday is generally an idle day among the mechanics in Dublin, several of whom do not work at all on that day; consequently, so many idle disorderly people flocked in on that day, that it was determined to alter the open day of the Museum from Monday to Tuesday[.][70]

The committee asserted that the 'humbler classes of society' constituted the very public which the museum should benefit, and that it provided improving rather than idle amusement for the working classes on their free days. Weld agreed, but then complained that the Irish public lacked a sense of order, propriety, and respect for private property.[71] Mechanics' institutes, voluntary societies made up of technicians and tradesmen, were among the organisations most active in promoting self-education for their members through sponsoring lectures in science, the industrial arts and literature.[72] As the RDS supplied scientific lecturers for these efforts, a visit to its museum may well have been seen as the logical outcome of a successful lecture. Giesecke had opened the museum to the public on Mondays, perhaps to attract the very people Weld disparaged. Having been a professor of mining in Germany, he may not have been at all alarmed at having workingmen in the museum. After his death the open days were altered specifically to exclude them. In the aftermath of the Murray affair, Weld's statements reinforced perceptions among some sectors of the public that the RDS was elitist and exclusionary.

Testimony in the report presented descriptions of the museum that were less flattering than those in the *Dublin Penny Journal* of the previous year. Geologist Robert Hutton, a member of the RDS and the Royal Irish Academy, as well as of the Geological Society of London, testified that the museum in Leinster House:

> ... consists of a suit [sic] of six apartments, as unhappily devised for the purpose of displaying objects of natural history as can well be conceived; they are of limited area, they are not lighted from above, and the ceilings are lofty ... We may also remark that want of space prevents even many of the specimens which the society possesses from being displayed at all; up to this hour several boxes of specimens belonging to the Leskean collection are deposited in a lumber-room[.][73]

He continued, citing deficits in the museum's holdings, noting that 'there is no collection of Irish animals, and till lately, no separate collection of Irish minerals, nor of Irish fossils; and the collections that have been recently commenced are, it is to be hoped, only the germs of what will soon be more worthy of a national museum'.[74]

Testimony also revealed that opportunities for public access were minimal, consisting of two days per week for three hours each. Recommending that the museum and the sculpture gallery should expand their opening times, the committee admonished RDS members to consider themselves as 'trustees administering a public fund', due to the level of funding provided by the exchequer, and that the property of the society was therefore a public amenity, such that 'the public should be entitled to full and entire use of that property as at present enjoyed'.[75] In response to rectifying the deficits identified in Leinster House, the cost of building a new museum was mooted during testimony, initiating what would become a protracted negotiation around issues of financing, space and location for a new purpose-built natural history museum.

At the same time that the committee assessed the Royal Dublin Society's museum as 'defective', the British Museum was undergoing a similar evaluation;

it was also the subject of a parliamentary inquiry in 1836.[76] Great Britain's national museum received similar criticism, with issues of crowding, display, cataloguing, space and public access highlighted by the committee, in language similar to that used to describe the RDS museum, though the London collections were much larger and more complex. Robert Grant, University of London professor of comparative anatomy and zoology, provided damning testimony about the scientific value of the collections, asserting that classification, where it existed, was outdated, and that arrangement and labelling of displayed specimens was confused and partial. He noted that specimens were damaged through neglect, and that the spaces in Montagu House were dark and dusty, making organised scientific display impossible. He summarised the condition of the zoological collection as 'miserable in funds, miserable in science, miserable in materials, and its collections for the most part are without either classification or nomenclature; so that the Museum resembles more a store-house than a school of zoology'.[77] One of the most consistent observations, and most vexing to the patriotically minded members of the committee of inquiry, was the praise heaped upon the museums of Paris throughout the proceedings. The secretary of the Zoological Society, E.T. Bennett, went so far as to suggest that modern advances in natural science had only come to England with a resumption of communication with French science after the end of the Napoleonic Wars.[78]

Though both museums had been in existence since the 1700s, the emerging awareness of science and museums as improving and educational civic amenities in the early 1800s moved parliament to demand clear public benefit from the funds it expended on behalf of the British Museum and the Royal Dublin Society. Its criticisms were measured against an earnest but poorly defined sense that collections were vital to the expansion of knowledge, and that applying information gained through the study of natural science to the furtherance of industry would create economic benefits. Despite the problems it identified, the 1836 *Report from the Select Committee on the Royal Dublin Society* stated in its opening summary that:

> Your Committee are fully impressed with the opinion that it is on every account most desirable that there should be in the metropolis of Ireland a great National Museum, and that the Dublin Society is the body under whose care such a Museum could be most advantageously placed.[79]

Though this idea was already in circulation, from this point forward the museum of the Royal Dublin Society was consistently framed and promoted as Ireland's national museum by central government and the popular press. Despite the fact that it was somewhat inconsistent in its application of scientific principles, it is important to emphasise that the first museum in Ireland that carried the designation 'national' was devoted to natural science. The antiquities that are now central to Ireland's national cultural identity were not placed at the ideological centre of its museum complex until the 1930s.[80]

The concerns raised in the 1836 parliamentary reports on the RDS signalled a rapid shift from the spirit of the cabinet museum to an emergent ethos of professionalisation in both science and museums. The development of natural history museums became more crucial as the century wore on, as they were increasingly valued as national assets with educational value. It also became increasingly clear that scientific collections were bound up with a series of related developments, such as an increase in scientific publishing, the importance of catalogues and the growth of organisations such as the British Association and their determination to disseminate science as widely as possible. The early to mid-nineteenth century was a period of uneven progress from the ethos of amateur science and its catch-all approach to collections, into the taxonomically organised, professionally supervised scientific museum that was in place by the late century. The careers of John Scouler, who remained curator until 1851, and his successor, Alexander Carte, director until 1881, encapsulate some of the shifting conditions in the world of natural science, showing how they played out in Ireland, but also how they continued to be connected to international influences. The development of the museum itself was closely bound to the dispositions of its curators, and their careers trace the circumstances leading to the 1857 construction of the Royal Dublin Society's purpose-built Natural History Museum.

CHAPTER 2

Science, Education and Public Service: The Natural History Museum from 1840 to 1850

Museums, science and public service in Ireland

As natural history museums evolved from loosely organised cabinet collections into taxonomically arranged scientific storehouses, they became embedded within broadly held expectations that innovations in science, technology and manufacturing would improve the material conditions of modern life. Notions of social progress in the Victorian period were based on optimistic assumptions that rationality and reason, allied to faith and morality, would mitigate poverty, underemployment and civil unrest. Understood as civilising influences, museums and science were quickly thrust into service as useful vehicles for encouraging social improvement. The demands placed on the Royal Dublin Society's activities illuminate the ways that these expectations manifested in Ireland, with the Natural History Museum absorbing a variety of expectations even as its adherents laboured to establish it as a scientifically relevant institution. The middle of the nineteenth century was a period of profound change, and the history of the museum shows evidence for how a range of influences shaped its role as a civic and scientific amenity at a time of rapid development for both science and museums.

As a means of creating a more democratic sense of public service within the RDS, the parliamentary committee of 1836 had proposed comprehensive changes to the society's governing structures, including reorganisation of the central council and committees, changes to voting procedures and stricter reporting of its finances. Declaring itself to be motivated by 'a desire to place that Institution on such a footing as would entitle it to the entire confidence and support of the public, and render it more fully than it has yet been, an instrument in aiding the education of the people and the improvement of the country', the committee's recommendations touched on a number of areas that encouraged public access.[1] More liberal criteria for membership, the offering of free evening lectures, the extension of lectures to provincial towns, the establishment of a reading room in the library, and improved opening hours for the museum and botanic gardens were all proposed as ways of strengthening the society's civic mission. The report emphasised the society's public functions, stating that cooperation with the committee's recommendations would result in the House of Commons extending 'to the Dublin Society the same judicious and increasing liberality which has characterised its recent grants to the British Museum'.[2] The society largely complied with these conditions, agreeing that its generous funding from the exchequer meant it held its property as a public trust (but also asserting that the society itself retained ownership) and that its activities should directly benefit the Irish public. It rejected one condition: the committee had advised that the tradition of newspapers and political periodicals being made available in the members' conversation room be discontinued, as they tended to encourage political discord or 'party feeling' in what should be a neutral milieu dedicated to improvement.[3] Declining to accede to that request, the society rewrote the rest of its by-laws, largely in accordance with the findings of the report.

Assuming that it had satisfied the government's requirements, the society proceeded with its work. However, there was a sting in the tail. In late 1840, the chief secretary for Ireland, Viscount Morpeth, wrote from Dublin Castle on behalf of the lord lieutenant, Viscount Ebrington, expressing displeasure at what they saw as the society's failure to comply with the full set of recommendations in the 1836 report. Their chief concerns were the society's insistence on providing newspapers to the members in the conversation room, and lingering confusion around amended membership rules and fees. During a series of tense exchanges lasting into 1841, Ebrington tabled proposals to spilt the society into two organisations, one for the sciences and the other for arts, agriculture and manufactures, which would share common resources such as the lecture theatre and museum. When the society rejected this proposal, the Dublin Castle administration declined to renew its public funding, leaving it in financial crisis.[4]

Despite having received a healthy dose of opprobrium in the press over the exclusion of Archbishop Murray several years earlier, newspapers offered indignant support when the society's funding was withdrawn. The interventions of Dublin Castle were broadly characterised as meddling by a central apparatus that did not value Irish institutions. The lord lieutenant of Ireland was a political appointment, of no fixed term and changing with shifts in parliamentary power, so that knowledge of Irish conditions varied with the holder of the post. Ebrington held the post only once for a short period, from 1839–41, and perhaps miscalculated the level of regard for the society's work in the public arena. His withdrawal of the society's grant was poorly received in all quarters. Press accounts of the incident emphasised the public resources provided by the society, and reinforced its own assertions that it conducted itself in the interest of the country. Nationalist Thomas Davis opined in the *Morning Register*:

> The sway of a stranger has a kind impartiality in its wickedness. Here was a body consisting nine-tenths of men arrayed in favour of English supremacy. Still the curse of Swift was upon them – they were Irishmen – it was Irish in origin and objects – away with it said the centralizer, it was not managed by Englishmen – away with it said the assimilator and imperialist, it is a relic of nationality.[5]

Davis saw the work being done within learned societies as serving a vital function in the establishment of a specifically Irish identity. He lent the influence of his intellectual cultural nationalism when he saw room for common cause with the range of political and cultural views within the societies. He considered their work so important that he wrote his own plan for rationalising the learned societies, the 1845 *Institutions of Dublin*. Proposing three institutions aligned according to discipline, with art, literature and antiquities grouped together, agriculture and manufactures combined and the sciences amalgamated, Davis suggested that the extant societies place all or portions of their resources under one of the three categories, and that each new institution would have its own premises, staff and museum.[6] Though his plan was never realised, his inclusion of museums indicates their significance in political thinking across ideological divides; they were as important to the nationalist Davis as they were to the broadly unionist RDS.

Davis' support of the society was echoed in the moderate nationalist paper the *Freeman's Journal*. Praising the RDS for its employment of chemist Robert Kane, a Catholic, as a prominent public lecturer, the writer then mused:

> What will the public think then, of the furious and unrestrainable liberality of a government who having failed to dragoon the Dublin Society into a compliance with their flippant field orders, and finding that they could not assimilate this institution also into a subsidiary branch of the British Museum, come to leave the arbitration of the quarrel to – reader, who do you think? – Lord Oxmantown, – two English engineer officers, – and three professors of Trinity College![7]

Emphasising the society's independence as an Irish institution, the writer invoked comparisons with the British Museum as a feature of Dublin Castle's attempt to control the independent work being done at the RDS. The British Museum's prominence and its full support from public funds continued to highlight the half-measures being taken in Ireland, and the writer employed it as a rhetorical device in suggesting that ill-informed decisions by central government continued to undermine Irish interests. The arbitrators listed were a committee appointed to mediate between the society and the lord lieutenant, comprising British peers, military men and lecturers at Trinity College, which retained a reputation for exclusivity as a Protestant university despite having admitted Catholics since 1793. More importantly, most were men of science in some regard. William Parsons, astronomer, Thomas Larcom and John Fox Burgoyne, officer/engineers, and William Rowan Hamilton and Humphrey Lloyd, physicists, found a way to mend the rift between Dublin Castle and the society, and by mid-1841 the parliamentary grant of £5,300 had been restored.[8]

Aside from anger at what appeared to be the ill-advised harassment of an Irish learned society by a Dublin Castle interloper, the potential damage to the society's public and educational resources was central to the upset caused by the withholding of its grant, which would leave it unable to maintain its lectures and exhibitions. Though organised scientific education gained ground in Great Britain and Ireland throughout the nineteenth century, it was unevenly distributed and lacked a consistent central curriculum. As the understanding of science became increasingly important in public life, local organisations and learned societies were enlisted by central government to fashion a system of scientific education in Ireland, but policies in the United Kingdom at large ensured that the result would lack coherence. John Coolahan observes that though many European countries implemented centralised state-sponsored education systems, 'England, influenced by its prevailing political policy of *laissez-faire*, was much slower to involve the state directly in education'.[9] He argues that the development of a public education system in Ireland was an experiment in social policy, and that the establishment of a national primary school system in 1831 served political and social agendas, but that there was no plan for a consistent curriculum.[10] While primary education was necessary for providing a growing workforce with a modest level of competence in literacy and numeracy, laissez-faire economics determined that 'secondary education was seen as a concern for the middle classes, who, if they saw fit, should buy it as a commodity just like any other personal goods'.[11] Post-primary schools were private or religious concerns, and took various approaches ranging from trade apprenticeships to preparation for university. The lack of a universally accepted national curriculum meant that there could be no assumption of a standard body of more advanced knowledge across the population, hampering efforts in improvement and economic development.

The RDS sought to address this gap by providing access to areas of practical knowledge intended to be directly useful. It pioneered programmes of improvement in a number of areas, each with an educational dimension. The classes at the RDS drawing schools trained designers and architects in classical aesthetics for application to industry and building. Its Committee of Agriculture sponsored produce and livestock shows with prizes for methods that improved stock and yields. The science committees sponsored free classes in chemistry, natural history, botany, zoology and geology that served the needs of the Irish public when there were few, if any, alternatives in generalist scientific education for a wide-ranging audience. From its instalment of mechanical models in the basement of the Irish Parliament and the purchase of the Leskean collection, the society had harboured ambitions for the educational value of its collections. By mid-century, the botanic gardens and the Natural History Museum allowed keen learners to put their knowledge into action by consulting real examples of the topics covered in lectures.

The society shared in the assumptions of its European counterparts that collections and museums were vital to the project of improvement through education. Its focus on the natural sciences located its commitment squarely in the realm of the practical, leaving the 'pure' or theoretical fields to others. During the 1841 negotiations to restore its grant, the council of the RDS wrote to Morpeth in response to criticisms he had made about the society's scientific work, asserting that:

> ... the Royal Dublin Society is not, or ever was intended to be, a scientific body ... aspiring no further in the walks of Science than the gratuitous instruction of the public, and of youth in particular, in those elementary branches, more immediately connected with, and contributory to, the useful Arts; leaving to native industry, and talent, afterwards to complete a superstructure, of which it is at once our duty and pride to lay the only foundation.[12]

In outlining the society's view of its position as a 'scientific body', the council reasserted its focus on practical information and improvement, confirming that it intended its classes to provide scope for applied purposes through the 'useful arts': manufacturing, industry, craft production and design. The suspension of the grant had jeopardised these benefits, potentially leaving the artisan and middle classes with no recourse to organised practical scientific instruction.

Scientific lectures and the museum

Lectures at the RDS were reliant on the museum's collections. The origins of the lecture programmes extended back to 1800, when a report on the London Institution (later the Royal Institution) suggested that the Dublin Society had outstripped it in every way save for 'philosophical lectures'.[13] The society immediately instituted a series of lectures on mechanics and hydraulics delivered by optician James Lynch, swiftly followed by a series on mineralogy by Professor William Higgins.[14] In 1796, Higgins had already been encouraged into a short series of public lectures on chemistry by Richard Kirwan, who noted regretfully that they were attended by the middle classes or working men, rather than the audience of gentlemen he had hoped to attract.[15] In 1810, the society began to import high-profile lecturers from

England, starting with Professor Humphrey Davy of the Royal Society.[16] Organised series of scientific lectures became regular features of the society's programmes, later prompting parliament to rely on them as a means of providing scientific education in Ireland.

As the RDS developed its instructional ethos, it allowed its facilities and collections to be used for educational lectures from outside sources. Its lecture theatre was regularly engaged, usually gratis, for talks or meetings by related bodies such as the Royal Zoological Society and the Dublin Statistical Society. It also allowed individuals to deliver lectures in a private capacity. Hugh Ferguson, a graduate of the Royal Veterinary College in London, applied to the council in 1840 for permission to deliver a 'course of lectures on the horse, and on the veterinary art' in the society's lecture theatre.[17] The council determined that he should have use of the theatre and 'of the veterinary preparations contained in the Museum', directing Scouler to 'make a catalogue of the veterinary museum and have the necessary specimens put in order'.[18] The refurbishment of the materials Ferguson needed was underwritten by the society, at a cost of £15.[19] Named as the first veterinary surgeon to the lord lieutenant in 1847, Ferguson was appointed 'director-general of the veterinary department of the privy council in Ireland' in 1867, and is credited 'with having laid the foundations of a state veterinary service'.[20] Ferguson's trajectory from independent lecturer, aided by the RDS, into a state position through which he helped formalise veterinary science in Ireland exemplifies the society's involvement in supporting the development of practical sciences. Private lectures became a regular feature of the society's offerings, with the speakers routinely proposed by members, some on scientific subjects and some treating topical subjects of general interest, ranging from phrenology, to colonial postage systems, to political economy.[21]

The museum collections provided opportunity for members of the RDS to enhance their own lectures, whether delivered at the society or elsewhere, with borrowed items. There is no extant description of a procedure to be followed in borrowing specimens, but the members were apparently free in their use of the collections, with reference to objects being borrowed for single purposes scattered throughout correspondence and the minutes of the Natural History Committee. An 1848 letter to the committee 'from Dr. Scouler respecting lending or removing specimens or other articles from the Museum' indicated that Scouler was unhappy with items simply being taken out of the collections by members. The committee responded that the museum's porter 'be directed not to allow any specimen or other article to be removed from the museum, under any circumstances, without the sanction of this committee', indicating that members felt free to borrow at will.[22] This direction was quickly followed by the allowance 'that Dr. Croker King's request for the use of a single specimen from the museum to illustrate his lecture on tomorrow evening be acceded to'.[23] The regularity of requests for single specimens or access to collections for short periods of time established a pattern, showing the collections as integral to the dissemination of scientific knowledge in Dublin. An 1840 request that 'Dr. Scouler ... lend to Dr. Hart a few of the drawings of N.[atural] History, to be used by him in lecturing at the College of Surgeons' showed that differing types of materials were held in the RDS museum, and were relied upon as educational resources.[24] Through the activities of the scientifically inclined members, small numbers of objects from the collections moved throughout the scientific networks in Ireland, underscoring the museum's function as a practical resource for useful instruction.

RDS scientific lecture courses

The society's own efforts in developing lectures rapidly settled into an organised series of introductory but thorough courses in specific scientific subjects that were open to the public. Free of charge, they were held on a rotating basis, and typically offered in the late afternoon. Over a course of twelve lectures, students were introduced to the fundamental elements of a subject, delivered by an expert in the field who was employed by the society. Syllabi and details were advertised in local papers such as *Saunders's News-Letter* or the *Freeman's Journal,* sometimes accompanied by handbills displaying the details of the upcoming series (Fig. 2.1). Scouler, as the professor of mineralogy and curator of the museum, lectured in the areas of mineralogy, natural history and zoology. Botanists and RDS professors William Henry Harvey and George James Allman, also members of the Natural History Committee and TCD professors, taught courses in botany and zoology. Chemists Edmund Davy (an RDS professor) and William K. Sullivan taught chemistry, and Robert Kane (again, of the RDS) and William Lover taught natural philosophy and mechanics. The RDS lectures were popular and well-attended. In 1853, Harvey delivered two courses of lectures on botany, which were attended by 2,237 students, and Scouler taught courses of geology and zoology with

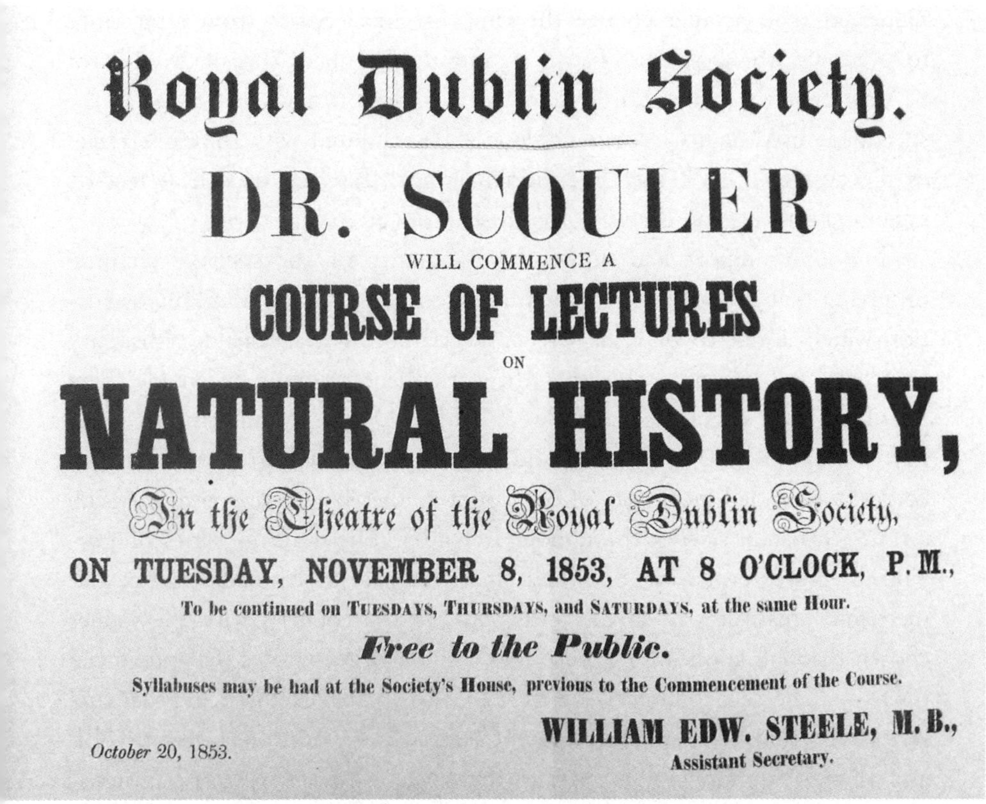
Royal Dublin Society.

DR. SCOULER

WILL COMMENCE A

COURSE OF LECTURES

ON

NATURAL HISTORY,

In the Theatre of the Royal Dublin Society,

ON TUESDAY, NOVEMBER 8, 1853, AT 8 O'CLOCK, P.M.,

To be continued on TUESDAYS, THURSDAYS, and SATURDAYS, at the same Hour.

Free to the Public.

Syllabuses may be had at the Society's House, previous to the Commencement of the Course.

WILLIAM EDW. STEELE, M.B.,
Assistant Secretary.

October 20, 1853.

Fig. 2.1 Poster advertising an RDS scientific lecture series, featuring a course on natural history taught by professor of mineralogy John Scouler.
COURTESY OF THE RDS LIBRARY AND ARCHIVES

2,343 people in attendance.[25] The RDS scientific lecture courses had become one of the few options in Ireland outside universities and colleges for undertaking a consistent educational programme delivered by trusted men of science.

Held in the lecture theatre at Leinster House, the courses were illustrated with images and objects from the collections, with the society's range of modern scientific instruments used for experiments and demonstrations. Specimens were illustrative of the subject under discussion, but were also used as visual aids to maintain the audience's attention. One of the reasons people attended lectures was to see the drawings, specimens and apparatus, without which lectures suffered. Scientific lecturing was a form of education, but also considered an entertainment, and an engaging set of visual materials could be key to the success of a lecture.[26] The visibility of lecture materials was important enough that when, in January 1849, the council of the society requested that Scouler change the time for his lectures from afternoons to evenings, the Natural History Committee replied 'that it would not be expedient to change the hour of Dr Scouler's lectures inasmuch as the specimens used at his lectures could not be exhibited with the same effect in the evening'.[27] Whether intentional or not, this also had the effect of excluding artisans and the working classes from attending.[28]

The 1836 report had noted the popularity of the society's lectures, observing that 'an institution, therefore, which supplies that kind of instruction which is not to be elsewhere procured becomes a valuable subsidiary to general education', noting that the parliamentary grant had made them possible.[29] The scientific lectures were held in Dublin, prompting the committee of inquiry to propose an addition to the society's grant so that they could be extended into more of the country, 'thereby creating and diffusing a taste for useful science throughout Ireland'.[30] The resulting series of provincial lectures began in 1838, held at the request of learned societies and mechanics' institutes in smaller cities around the country, with the venues chosen through application to the RDS. Enda Leaney notes that provincial towns were fiercely competitive in their bids to secure a lecturer, and that 127 series of lectures were sponsored by the society in 43 locations between 1838 and 1854.[31] An anonymous letter to the *Nenagh Guardian* expressed anticipation at the prospect of a provincial lecture:

> It is a source of much gratification to me ... to learn that the Mechanics' Institute have secured the services of an eminent Professor, from the Royal Dublin Society, to deliver a course of lectures on chemistry and natural philosophy, in the Court House.[32]

Provincial lectures disseminated the collections throughout the country, with provincial cities and towns benefiting from 'all the advantages for illustrations and experiment afforded by the diagrams and scientific apparatus of the Dublin Society'.[33]

The evening lecture series

The other type of lecture at the RDS consisted of evening scientific meetings in Leinster House, with men of science presenting papers on their areas of interest or research. These were also open to the public, and the evening usually comprised several individual talks. Synopses of the talks were subsequently carried in the newspapers, along with the notice that:

> All persons, whether members of the Society or otherwise, are eligible to read papers at any of these meetings, on submitting an abstract of their intended communication to the Committee of Evening Meetings, at least one week previously for their approval; and should the Committee consider the paper of sufficient interest, they recommend its publication in the Society's Reports.[34]

After 1855, selected papers were also published in the *Journal of the Royal Dublin Society*. The presentations were balanced between general popular information, subjects with economic importance and specialist scientific knowledge. Speakers presented subjects that would increase the practical scientific knowledge of the audience, such as an 1851 paper by Scouler on the principle of symmetry in animals, or an 1854 paper by George J. Allman on the artificial propagation of salmon, with specimens from the collections exhibited to the audience by Alexander Carte.[35] Some presentations at the evening meetings, however, were scientifically focused and technical, intended to present new knowledge. John Robert Kinahan, professor of natural history, presented a paper in 1856 on his studies of the types and distribution of crustacea in Port Phillip, Victoria, Australia, showing several newly discovered species of crab. His talk included a discussion of taxonomy with binomial nomenclature and detailed anatomical descriptions, demonstrated with specimens and illustrations.[36] The society's collections of scientific instruments also made an appearance, such as the occasion in 1851 when the 'meeting having adjourned to the Society's Theatre, Dr Steele exhibited the oscillation of a pendulum in proof of the Earth's rotation'.[37] The collections were integral to the evening scientific lectures in imparting general knowledge to an interested public audience, and to convey recent discoveries in natural science.

Natural science and intellectual culture

During the 1840s and into the early 1850s, lectures at the RDS provided instruction in practical science and natural history that was unavailable elsewhere. Aside from their educational value, these lectures also represent a form of intellectual culture, wherein people voluntarily presented themselves to partake in a communal exercise in self-improvement. At this early stage there were no qualifications to be gained, and there are no extant registers or records beyond the numbers of people attending each lecture series recorded in the *Proceedings* of the society. However, these figures are robust enough to show that the society's lectures began to foster a taste for natural science that would eventually fill the museum with donations, as we will see in the second half of this book. Attendance at RDS lectures, the use of images and objects to illustrate talks by men of science, and demonstrations of basic scientific principles through instruments like pendulums show a public appetite for ideas and information that would continue to grow. These events belie the notion that Irish intellectual culture was 'barren' in the mid-century, underscoring the need to revisit historical definitions of culture in nineteenth-century Ireland and to expand them out of reference to literary fiction and into the numerous areas of discovery and invention that characterise the period.

The increasing interest in science fostered by the lecture series also increased the popularity of the museum, which in turn led to the worsening of some of the issues associated with the museum's location in Leinster House. Public access to the collections for learning, an inevitable result of greater education in natural history, became more difficult as demand increased and collections grew in the six modestly sized domestic rooms it occupied. The 1836 report had advised that 'in order to form a National Museum adequate to public wants, it is necessary to provide larger accommodation … than the present rooms of the Dublin Society are capable of affording'[.][38] The minute book of the Natural History Committee for the 1840s recorded a near-constant discussion around funding, allocation of space and arrangement of the collections. A series of rapid shifts in the culture of science and museums at large from the 1840s to the 1850s aggravated tensions around the crowded conditions at the Natural History Museum, creating demands around access, arrangement and cataloguing that caused conflict among the people charged with its care. Due to an increasing reliance on museums as enhancements to education, their importance remained on the public agenda through the mid-century as they became key elements in scientific and intellectual culture. These tensions were exemplified during the curatorial tenure of John Scouler, whose stewardship of the museum was altered by broad and fast-moving developments in the growing field of natural history.

Curator's complaint: Scouler and the Natural History Committee

In January 1840, John Scouler presented his customary annual report to the RDS Natural History Committee. In detailing the previous year, he stated that his lecturing and scientific duties precluded him from maintaining the museum in the time he'd allotted for the task. He had sought assistance from geologist Frederick McCoy who, having already catalogued the Geological Society's collections, volunteered to assist at the museum in exchange for the opportunity to learn more about natural history.[39] Throughout the early part of the year, the Natural History Committee took measures to ease demands on Scouler's time, but first directed 'that a book be purchased for keeping a catalogue ... of all articles purchased or presented for the Museum – that the articles be ordered regularly, ... and the Book laid before the Committee at each meeting', which had apparently not been done previously.[40] Scouler was provided with an assistant for six months, and accounts record that McCoy was given £15 in April for assisting in the museum.[41] In March Scouler was authorised to employ someone to write labels and affix them to all the specimens in the museum.[42] These passages indicate that Scouler, who had been in charge of the museum for seven years, had not catalogued, classified or labelled the collections in any comprehensive way, nor devised a system for recording donations. It is unclear what the museum contained at this stage or how it had changed since Giesecke died, but due to the committee's mandate, from this point forward it is possible to trace the collections and their contents through ledger books, rather than relying solely on press accounts, travelogues, occasional catalogues and other partial descriptions.

The shape of the collections in the 1840s was determined by the curator, and was balanced between donations and purchases. Scouler used his ledger to record basic information about donations, for instance that in 1840 Captain French of the Light Dragoons donated a stuffed tiger, and Mr J.J. Nolan the specimen of a parrot. The entries in his ledger contained scant information with no scientific names and little indication of the significance of the donation, and often recorded only the honorific and surname of the donor. Ethnographic materials were generally classed as natural history objects in this period, and they are regular features of Scouler's donation records, with poisoned arrows, war clubs and pottery all making an appearance.[43] Even as late as 1849 his entries were still general rather than scientific, recording that Doctor Baggot donated 'an idol', RDS secretary Isaac Weld 'a section of a tree', and Sir E. Manley a 'lobster's claw'. The collections were augmented by purchased specimens from collectors or dealers, and during Scouler's tenure many of them were recorded in the end-of-year accounts in the *Proceedings* of the society. The museum's annual expenses listed entries for payments to individuals for specimens, with some names, such as James Thom, repeated across a series of years. There is no indication of what was purchased, or how it fit into the collection.

Decisions about what should be acquired were largely left to Scouler, whose records show an inconsistent approach with no apparent overall plan for creating a scientifically comprehensive collection. The acquisitions themselves had scientific value, but the society's focus on practicality and usefulness to Ireland did not appear to be among Scouler's guiding principles. For instance, though the society was eager that its museum should constitute an educational resource for Irish industry and agriculture, readily available local materials were neglected in favour of specimens from exotic locations. In March 1840, Scouler gave £10 to Captain Miller of the ship *Demerara* to collect specimens for the museum during his travels.[44] In December of the same year, Scouler denied a request from the Dublin Natural History Society for an exchange of Irish minerals because 'the Museum at present contains scarcely any duplicates of simple Irish minerals, and consequently the request of the Dublin Natural History Society cannot be complied with'.[45] Though informative local materials, easily acquired, were scant in the collections, in December 1841 the council agreed to advance '£10 to Mr. William McAuley who is about to proceed to New Zealand to enable him to collect specimens of Natural History for the Society to that value, on the recommendation of Dr Scouler'.[46] Inconsistency and the lack of a systematic approach to creating comprehensive collections, as well as a lingering taste for exotic foreign specimens over mundane but useful local ones, remained a feature of the collections for the rest of the decade.

Scouler found himself in conflict with the Natural History Committee in February 1842, when he rejected the offer of a sizeable collection of Himalayan birds, declaring the museum too crowded to display them.[47] The Natural History Committee's response highlighted the lack of space in the museum rooms and disorganisation in the collections:

> [T]he Committee would feel very desirous of obtaining the addition of the Birds mentioned … if there were sufficient accommodation for their reception … the Committee are most anxious in order to remedy this insufficiency of room … that by this means the Committee of Natural History would be enabled to display a number of collections now in the possession of the Society which are at present shut up from the public.[48]

The refrains around lack of space, poor organisation, and collections being unavailable to the public appear in committee records throughout the 1840s, continuing to echo the 1836 parliamentary report. Attempting to improve the usefulness of the museum, the Natural History Committee consistently demanded that, on the one hand, the council provide more space for the collections, and on the other that Scouler catalogue and organise the museum in more efficient ways in the available space. Its appeals met with sustained resistance from both directions.

Scouler was discontented with his position, and made no secret of the fact. His biographer E. Charles Nelson notes that 'within less than two years of his election to the professorship, he was deeply disenchanted with the post and with the Society'.[49] He had been seeking alternate employment since 1836, without success. He wrote to his mentor William Jackson Hooker that 'a situation in the Dublin Society is anything but agreeable to a man of science who retains any feelings of self-respect', and that 'I believe I repeat the feelings of every intelligent man in Ireland when I say that no one would remain with them who can remove elsewhere'.[50] Despite his displeasure, the modest number of paid positions in scientific institutions saw Scouler carrying on at the society rather than risk his income. From the 1840s onwards, the records show tension and conflict between Scouler and the members of the Natural History Committee. His dealings with the governing structures of the society reflected his discontent, and affected his approach to curating the museum. It's important to note that the ongoing conflicts between Scouler and the RDS were grounded in more than differences of personality, or disagreements about workload, although those factors were considerable. They also reflected the changes taking place in science overall in the mid-nineteenth century, when the generalist or amateur ethos in natural science began to shift into more organised structures of professional practice. As the century progressed, both natural history and museums became more specialised, and staying abreast of the changes required a willingness to learn and adapt that does not appear to have been among Scouler's goals.

Scouler was caught in a paradigm shift, one that magnified his resistance to the position he found himself in. Natural science became more demanding as its processes and procedures became regularised, and gradual moves towards professionalisation saw the ethos of the generalist amateur of the eighteenth century give way to the scientific specialist throughout the nineteenth, though this process was not straightforward. David Allen observes that in the early part of the century, the term 'professional' carried connotations of a type of servitude for money, comparing the professional man unfavourably to the aristocratic amateur who altruistically marshalled his resources for the purpose of increasing human knowledge.[51] At this time, salaried scientific employment occurred in a limited number of places, with museums and universities offering the most stable situations. By mid-century in the United Kingdom, ordnance and geological surveys, with their concentrations of geologists, naturalists and surveyors, had become established government programmes providing opportunities for trained men of science to deploy their skills. This facilitated access to science as a professional activity to the extent that most of the people employed in natural history and science, aside from those in universities and museums, worked in government-sponsored surveys.[52]

With improved opportunities for employment in science, acquisition of formal qualifications became increasingly important. Education had traditionally favoured text-based instruction in the classics, with emphasis on the acquisition of Greek and Latin, as the default curriculum for the middle and upper classes. The practical, hands-on models of teaching required by science, including experiments and collecting, had been traditionally associated with the training of tradesmen and the working classes, and were deemed inferior to any instruction based in classical texts. Early in the century, qualifications in natural science were frequently earned through completion of a medical certification, which could be extended to accommodate an interest in natural history, and then strengthened through obtaining a position as surgeon-naturalist on an expedition or military voyage. Darwin was educated in the classics at school, but went to Edinburgh to study medicine before he set out on the *Beagle* in 1831. John Scouler followed a similar course, starting his education in the classics, transferring to medical subjects and later making his way as a naturalist via his medical qualification as a surgeon/naturalist on a ship of colonisation and trade.[53] The practical and tactile nature of education in science, medicine and technology eventually gained respectability, largely replacing classical text-based studies. William Whewell's coining of the term 'scientist' in 1833, the ongoing development of science in universities and museums, and the incorporation of natural sciences into government initiatives into the mid-century helped the professional man of science to rise in stature.

As the century unfolded, the figure of the scientific amateur also began to change. The classes, demonstrations, lectures and publications offered by learned societies started to increase public knowledge of scientific subjects, encouraging participation by a wide range of people. The educational efforts at the RDS were part of wider developments to expand access to the benefits of science. In Dublin, the number of learned societies grew, and began to encourage participation in scientific activity in fields as diverse as antiquarianism, microscopy, photography and geology. The Dublin Natural History Society, for instance, was established in 1838 to promote the study of Irish natural history. Its founders kept membership fees modest, in a challenge to the more exclusive and expensive RDS, in the hope that 'every lover of the natural history of his native land should at once become a member, and lend his assistance to the development of this delightful science in Ireland, where so wide a field remains yet unexplored'.[54] In 1845 the Museum of Economic Geology was founded, partially through the influence of Robert Kane, as an educational and scientific resource with an egalitarian ethos, educating both men and women with little regard for class divides. In 1854 it became the Museum of Irish Industry, and was pressed into an amalgamated educational arrangement with the RDS in an attempt to provide comprehensive scientific education in Dublin.[55] These developments had been encouraged by the establishment of the British Association for the Advancement of Science in 1831, which aimed 'to make the cultivators of science acquainted with each other, to stimulate one another to new exertions – to bring the objects of science more before the public eye and to take measures for advancing its interests and accelerating its progress'.[56] Its annual meetings in cities across Great Britain and Ireland were heavily attended and featured the latest thinking in a range of scientific topics. Amateur science also increasingly included men in professions such as the civil service, the military or the church, who were able and well-respected naturalists, and practised science in addition to their occupations, pursuing their interests through learned societies and scientific correspondence. Ruth Barton's analysis of the language that nineteenth-century men of science used to describe themselves shows that amateurs were considered part of the community of science, and that they were welcomed into its ranks alongside professionals.[57] Amateur practitioners of natural science became increasingly numerous, skilled and specialised as the century wore on, making substantial contributions to scientific collections and publications, aiding the growth of natural history museums through the quality of their contributions.

Scouler's career at the society coincided with these changes, and his conflicts with scientifically minded members of the Natural History Committee were exacerbated by his unwillingness to address their concerns. Many members of the Natural History Committee throughout the 1840s were well-known men of science who were alert to wider changes in the field, and others were long-term RDS members who understood the importance of science in the society's overall ambitions. Robert Ball, naturalist and director of the University Museum at Trinity College, was a longstanding member who had personally assembled considerable collections of natural history; his donation of these collections to Trinity formed the basis of its museum.[58] John Hart's studies with Cuvier made him alert to the progressive research being practised in Paris, and the scientific organisation of the collections there.[59] George James Allman, professor of botany at Trinity, and William Henry Harvey, well-travelled naturalist who had written several scientific books, both served as professor of botany for the RDS, and taught courses in botany and natural history. Alexander Carte was a comparative anatomist who curated the museum at the Royal College of Surgeons.[60] These men, and others like them, formed the rotating membership of the committee, largely comprised of scientific men who were respected in their fields, and had made contributions to natural science.[61] Their differences with Scouler can be seen most clearly in disagreements over the increasingly pressing issues of classification and cataloguing, which became more significant as museums became professionalised. The Natural History Committee requested repeatedly that Scouler classify, organise and catalogue the museum's holdings, the frequency of the request indicating that it was never fulfilled. The lack of a museum catalogue became a particular source of contention, underlining the sense that the museum was not useful to the uninformed, and had become difficult to access for the knowledgeable specialist. Without one, the RDS also found it difficult to make the contents of the collections known within international circles of natural science.

Scouler wrote to the committee members in 1844, reminding them that he occupied two positions within the society, professor of mineralogy and curator of the museum, on the single standard professor's salary of £150 per annum. He outlined his contributions to the progress of the museum, asserting that he had improved the collections, and had increased the society's holdings significantly in all areas, but especially in zoology. He claimed that 'the collection of Irish shells, fishes, mollusca, crustacea, and zoophytes have all been formed by me, as is also true respecting the collection of Irish fossils'.[62] He did not say whether or not they had been classified or arranged, and there is no record of a list or catalogue enumerating or describing them. The committee appears to have been unimpressed, and tensions around creating a catalogue and organising the museum continued into the following year, apparent in an entry from February 1845 stating 'that it appears to this Committee absolutely necessary that a catalogue of the Museum be prepared forthwith'.[63]

The Natural History Committee's desire to name, order and publish the contents of the collections was influenced by a scientific environment that was becoming increasingly systematised. Accurate classification had become a standard expectation in natural history by the mid-century, as new species were being encountered regularly, and common local materials identified and organised according to scientific principles.[64] Due to the number of species being identified, consistent systems for naming and categorising them were considered imperative. The increasingly transnational character of the sciences meant that all practitioners of natural science needed to adhere to common naming systems to achieve consistency, and to ascertain whether an apparently new species had been previously identified or named. In 1842, the British Association had proposed a plan for regularising zoological nomenclature, maintaining the use of Latin as the scientific lingua franca, and branding inconsistency in naming specimens as 'evil'.[65] Correctly classified and organised collections demonstrated attention to sound scientific principles, and could legitimise an organisation in the eyes of fellow naturalists. Printed lists and catalogues of specimens and collections aided this process, allowing the named and organised contents of collections to be easily distributed for scholarly consultation, so that naming could be agreed upon and anomalies corrected. The Natural History Committee's repeated requests for systematic arrangement and cataloguing demonstrated awareness of the increasing demand for conformity to standardised scientific principles, especially as a way of showcasing the society's attributes through the exchange of publications with international learned and scientific societies.

Throughout the first half of the nineteenth century, the demands on the Natural History Museum had grown and become more complex. Giesecke had presided over a varied collection that retained some of the hallmarks of the cabinet of curiosity and was of variable scientific value. Scouler, a scientific generalist with a modest medical background, inherited the care of the collection as an adjunct to his role as professor of mineralogy. Though he had curated a university museum in Scotland, he seems to have resented his responsibility for the society's collections, viewing them as a chore rather than an opportunity to create a scientific reputation for himself and his employers. At the same time, the demands upon the museum as an educational venue and a resource for practical scientific education grew significantly. The discipline of natural history itself was simultaneously experiencing substantial changes, including demands for organised collections, taxonomical classification, and the use of consistent nomenclature among men of science. The desire to realise the society's museum as a usefully organised and scientifically rational public resource increased as the century progressed, with the scientifically trained members of the Natural History Committee consistently pressuring Scouler to name, organise and catalogue the collections. They wanted a scientific resource worthy of the society and its reputation, and sought to spread that reputation internationally. Compounding these issues was the fact that mounting demands were being made on a museum that was still housed in a former domestic residence, and that was becoming increasingly popular with the public despite continuing to suffer from issues of access and overcrowding. An 1845 report from Scouler stated that the 'museum is open to the public every Tuesday and Friday from 12 o'clock to 3 p.m. … and to students on application to the Curator'. Scouler noted that in 1842 the annual total for visitors had been 45,226, rising to 54,827 in 1843, and dropping slightly to 52,242 in 1844.[66] This indicates that the average number of visitors in three hours on each public day was 434 in 1842, 527 in 1843, and 502 in 1844. The number of people using the museum on public opening days was significant, and the five modestly sized, poorly organised museum rooms may have been crowded indeed.

The figures underscore that the society's collections were clearly in public demand. Scouler's report continued, and in defending himself against criticism from the Natural History Committee, he emphasised the issues by quoting its own observations:

> This want has been felt for some years back and alluded to in a Report from the Committee from which the following is extracted: 'Your Committee have no hesitation in stating that the Museum at present does not afford means of instruction commensurate with the number and value of objects it contains ... the specimens are too numerous for the means of displaying them, hence even when specimens are purchased, laid out, and correctly named, they have to be so crowded as to render their profitable inspection almost impossible[.]'[67]

The museum's records from the 1840s show that it was not operating in the spirit that parliament intended, as a national resource with significant public benefit. Complaints of crowded and disorganised collections had been made in 1836, and significant materials continued to be added throughout the 1840s with no clear overall plan for their arrangement, classification or labelling. Collections of Irish materials increased under Scouler's curatorship, but it is not clear whether they were available for study, or that they had been organised in any useful way. A move towards scientific rationalisation was increasingly stipulated by the Natural History Committee through its requests to have the collections arranged, labelled and catalogued. These demands were made to bring the collection into line with educational and scientific goals, but there was added pressure in the fact that the museum was becoming increasingly important in other aspects of the society's initiatives.

The museum and the School of Design

The impulse to organise the museum may also have been partially driven by its contribution to an 1849 initiative in the society's drawing schools, which since 1746 had been the primary outlet for art education in Dublin, firmly grounded in the classical fine art tradition, but also emphasising the practical application of drawing to commercial fields such as architecture and textiles.[68] The Board of Trade assumed the control and funding of the RDS drawing schools in 1849, forming a cooperative arrangement with the society and renaming the drawing schools as the 'School of Design in connection with the RDS'. The Board of Trade hired and paid the masters and instructors, while the RDS supervised daily operations, collected fees and wrote reports for the board. The students had free access to all the facilities of the society, and prizes for excellence in the various categories of study were awarded at a ceremony in the RDS lecture theatre at the end of each period of instruction.[69] The new curriculum focused heavily on the application of classical aesthetics to the processes of design for industrial and economic purposes, including manufactured products ranging from table linens to architectural ornament.[70] It also incorporated the scientifically oriented resources of the society into the programme of arts instruction in a particularly Victorian combination of art and science, forming an important innovation in Irish education that used the science collections as educational resources in ways that were not directly scientific. The new headmaster, Henry McManus, expressed appreciation for the range of the society's resources, noting that 'the School of Design possesses many advantages unknown to similar schools, namely, a museum, a rare and valuable library, botanic gardens, regular lectures by the Society's professors, on chemistry, natural history, natural philosophy, botany, anatomy, and … comparative anatomy'[.][71]

An emphasis on the marriage of aesthetics, design and natural science placed the new design school within a defining trend of Victorian culture. Aesthetics in nineteenth-century Great Britain came to have a direct relation to natural science primarily through the writings of art critic and philosopher John Ruskin, who insisted that beauty in works of art could only be achieved through the direct observation of nature, as the natural world was the clearest expression of divine perfection. Ruskin decreed that the basis of aesthetics should be grounded in a knowledge of nature that was simultaneously an understanding of God's works, and that beauty was a fundamentally divine creation rather than a preference or custom of man.[72] Ruskin asserted that in order to create truthful works of art, artists must reflect the natural world with scientific precision, insisting that 'every class of rock, earth and cloud must be known by the painter, with geologic and meteorologic accuracy'.[73] He urged the study of natural history as an essential aspect of a sound education in artistic practice, and his theories came to dominate the Victorian approach to aesthetic experience, his dictates for art filtering into architecture, design and manufacturing. Careful, direct study from nature became understood as the surest way to design objects that were beautiful, pleasing, orderly and morally uplifting, as they would be based on the principles of divine truth gleaned from the natural world.

Ruskinian aesthetics were overtly deployed in Dublin's new School of Design, where students were encouraged into the study of science as a means of creating designs which would refer to the truth of nature. Immediately prior to the Board of Trade assuming control, professor of botany and member of the Natural History Committee George James Allman called for a version of the Ruskinian aesthetic to be employed in the proposed new curriculum, in an address at the awarding of prizes to the students in the RDS drawing schools. His remarks focused on:

> ... the relation in which natural history stands to the fine arts, not only in the higher departments of these arts, but in the subordinate, though most important one, design, a relation from which will be apparent the great value of natural history studies in the creation of a pure national taste, and their consequent powerful, though indirect, bearing on the manufacturing industry of the land.[74]

The final pages of Allman's address refer specifically and at length to Ruskin's ideals, exhorting the students that young artists need not learn the 'minute scientific details of zoology and botany; but I do strongly insist on the necessity of a knowledge of the great leading truths of these sciences'.[75] Allman suggested that the development of a 'pure national taste' in Ireland would be based on an accurate translation of nature into objects designed for everyday use. It was an aspirational transfer of Ruskin's ideas from the refined area of the fine arts into the more prosaic areas of manufacturing, though John Turpin observes that many of the objects produced for home consumption were still allied to traditional handcrafts, such as furniture-making, lace-making and silverwork.[76] The intention that the design of mundane manufactured objects should be a socially improving influence was later echoed by headmaster McManus:

> The importance of design as an effective corrector of public taste is universally admitted ... The object of the school is to teach the principles of fine art and its practical application to manufacturers, and to improve taste in ornamental design ... The true object of art is to elevate and refine.[77]

William Henry Harvey gave an address at the start of his course of botany lectures in 1849, the first that students from the new School of Design would attend as part of their studies. Underscoring the argument that the artist must study nature in order to produce beautiful design, Harvey noted that 'in the decorative arts, or *ornamental manufactures*, correct form is often the essential element of beauty in the design', arguing that knowledge of structure and pattern were key to producing original and inventive new designs.[78] The inclusion of natural history studies, with reference to the collections in the museum, into the curriculum of the School of Design was seen as a boon which would provide the students of the school with the opportunity to create distinctively Irish design, with an aesthetic made more attractive and 'true' through its reference to science. After a detailed discussion of the interconnections between art, design and science, Harvey returned to the crux of the Ruskinian aesthetic at the end of his address: that intimate knowledge of nature is intimate knowledge of the divine, and that design based upon natural forms had the potential to influence the moral tenor of Irish society at large.

The rhetoric surrounding a 'pure national taste' was another means of asserting Ireland's cultural uniqueness within the confines of the United Kingdom. In the 1853 prize-giving ceremony for outstanding students, RDS lecturer and Natural History Committee member William Barker detailed the ways that the School of Design had benefited from its contact with various scientific fields, following with the assertion that:

> England and Ireland are both availing themselves of our infant institution. In England, our designs are used in the great porcelain manufactories, and Mr. Kerr, of Worcester, has given this year three prizes to our artists. In Dublin, Messrs. Atkinson, Pim, Fry, and Waterhouse have stimulated the zeal of our students by likewise instituting prizes for our students; and in Manchester, our designers are also at work, and in the lace, sewed muslin, and embroidery manufactories, many students of this school have already gained ample employment[.][79]

The students at the schools were largely drawn from the trades, artisan, working and middle classes, and it was expected that forming a sense of national identity through the creation of domestic objects would develop an aesthetic that was Irish, moral and allied to nature. This would then be passed throughout the population of Ireland and Great Britain as the students moved into various types of employment. Not only would designers have influence through the templates they created for industry, but students of the drawing schools who went on to become governesses and schoolteachers would convey these ideas to their charges, and stonemasons and plasterers would put them to use in their domestic and public works. Their study in the RDS collections, particularly in the Natural History Museum and botanic gardens, would underpin their designs with scientific accuracy and therefore with the moral strength dictated by Ruskinian aesthetic principles. The Natural History Committee's demands for clear scientific organisation of the collections, accompanied by a catalogue that would make them comprehensible, was for the benefit of the society's efforts as a whole. The use of the collections by the School of Design, and the social and moral ideals appended to the accurate study of nature's forms, as well as the school's connection to manufacturing, meant that scientific accuracy was expected by constituencies beyond the practitioners of science.

Breaking point: a mid-century shift in fortunes

Given the expectations around the museum from all quarters, it was clear to the Natural History Committee that the crowded conditions and disorganisation in the collections could not be allowed to persist. In response to its unwavering demands, Scouler replied in March 1850 that it was 'most desirable that the Museum should be rendered of use to the public and I shall gladly follow out any plan having that object in view' but showed no initiative towards formulating that plan in his role as curator, instead simply reasserting the need for more space in order to carry out any changes.[80] The pressures reached a breaking point in 1851, when Scouler and the Natural History Committee again found themselves in conflict. In February, the committee resolved, once more, that 'Dr Scouler be instructed to have a catalogue prepared and the museum put into the most creditable condition and that a sub-committee ... see the above carried out fully and without delay', and that assistants should be hired as needed to complete the task.[81] In March 1851 the committee required Scouler to formulate a plan for arranging the museum more rationally in the available space, and to specify 'the amount of additional accommodation as to cases which he may deem necessary and also the nature of the assistance he may require to enable him to catalogue and arrange the entire in a permanently useful and credible manner'.[82] The Natural History Committee had proposed replacing the flat floor cases in the rooms with tall cases comprised of compartments and drawers to house the collections of mineralogy, conchology and geology, in order to alleviate crowding while plans were progressing for a new purpose-built museum.[83] Scouler responded four days later, repeating his view that some of the collections should be consigned to storage, and stating that he had no new suggestions to make in terms of the re-ordering of the collections. As to classifying specimens and assembling a catalogue, he stated (albeit in rather unclear wording):

> At present I do not know of any one in Dublin who is qualified to make a catalogue of the Museum. I may also state that at the present when from the extent of the physical sciences naturalists almost universally confine themselves to a single department of study, and hence the care of a museum is usually divided among several curators, or if only one can be had he is not expected to be equally informed regarding the Three Kingdoms of Nature. I need not add, that my own case is no exception, and I am quite incompetent to carry on so immense an undertaking.[84]

At the monthly general meeting of the society on 19 March, the Natural History Committee submitted its report on the issues of cataloguing, arrangement and public access in the museum, including Scouler's replies to their requests. This resulted in Scouler effectively declaring himself incompetent as a curator before the assembled membership, prompting a break in the deadlock. The Natural History Committee summarised the situation for the council, including the fact that Scouler held the dual position of professor and curator on a single annual salary. They observed that when he had been hired in 1833 the demands of arranging and cataloguing the collection over time could not have been anticipated, acknowledging that the administration of the museum had outgrown its role as an adjunct to the post of professor of mineralogy.[85] In the course of their report, the committee noted that they had made inquiries into the staffing of 'other great museums', noting that they all had dedicated curators 'whose duty it is to keep the museums in permanent working order, to classify, name and catalogue the various specimens of natural history … and to be ready to afford at all times any scientific information or assistance in his power to those who, from time to time, may require to refer to the museum'.[86] The committee then proposed the creation of a permanent position of curator with care of the museum as its sole responsibility, observing that simply hiring someone temporarily to organise the collections meant that the 'museum would speedily relapse into its present condition alike discreditable and injurious to the Society'.[87]

The committee's observations demonstrate their awareness that the society lagged behind international trends in both museums and science, and that it needed a professional curator with strong knowledge of recent developments in science, but also with a proclivity for record-keeping and correspondence. Exchanges with other museums and communication with scholars and donors became increasingly important as natural history museums matured, requiring a flexible set of varied skills. The committee understood that Scouler had assumed his position at a time when a scientifically trained man of modest ability was considered capable of shepherding a general collection, and that the rapid growth and specialisation of natural science had resulted in a need for curators to have more specifically developed institutional and scientific skills. Classificatory knowledge, assembly of comprehensive catalogues, clear labelling and the arrangement of collections for teaching purposes, as well as finding ways to meet ever more forceful demands for increased public access, became factors in the management of natural history collections. Though the question of professionalisation in museums is a vexed one, and it is difficult to be specific about its progression because it happened in differing ways in various places, it is clear that by 1851 the members of the RDS Natural History Committee were seeking a professional museum curator who could create a scientifically organised collection that would satisfy the society's ambitions.[88]

At an unusually well-attended general meeting on 29 May 1851, a ballot was held among the members to choose among the four candidates who had responded to the society's advertisement seeking a curator for the Natural History Museum. The applications of Dr Alexander Carte, RDS member and curator of the Royal College of Surgeons museum, Robert J. Montgomery of the Royal Zoological Society, W.H. D'Olier Purcell, and a Mr Howse were placed before the members in attendance, including members of the Natural History Committee, Natural Philosophy Committee, Botanical Committee, and men of science belonging to the society at large. Carte won handily, securing 182 votes, with his closest rival Montgomery achieving 60 votes.[89]

Alexander Carte's first days

Alexander Carte was appointed curator of the Royal Dublin Society's Natural History Museum on 7 June 1851.[90] Originally from Newcastle West, County Limerick, he was the first Irish man to take responsibility for the museum, and the first to do so in a dedicated role with no other responsibilities. A factor in his favour was that he had already authored a catalogue of the collections at the Royal College of Surgeons in Ireland (RCSI), which he presented as part of his application for the new position.[91] Carte made his first report to the Natural History Committee four days after his appointment, and wasted no time in setting out to meet the demands that Scouler had long resisted. He began with a request to temporarily close the first two rooms of the museum so that they could be cleaned and painted in preparation for reinstalling the collections.[92] He set forth his ideas for ameliorating the cramped conditions in the museum and focusing on the scientific value of its holdings, starting with a systematic scientific organisation of the natural history specimens.

That Carte had arrived with a plan in place was no surprise. He had been elected a life member of the Royal Dublin Society in 1848, and had served on the committees of natural history and natural philosophy, as well as having contributed scientific papers to the society's fortnightly evening scientific meetings.[93] He would therefore have been familiar with the problems in the museum, and his work in the RCSI museum would have made him alert to possible solutions. His initial proposals for improving the museum included suggestions for more rationally organising the collections according to scientific principles, and ideas for relieving overcrowding. For instance, he suggested hanging ethnographic items such as shields and spears along the walls in order to create more space for specimens. As to the scientific collections, he suggested ways of organising them more efficiently while simultaneously increasing their educational value:

> It appears that the first room, being the largest of the suite[,] is best adapted for displaying the large animals, [and] it is my intention ... to commence the rearrangement of the vertebrate animals, beginning of course with the mammalia, and follow down the classification ... according to the Cuvierian system: for example mammalia in the first room, birds in the second, reptiles in the third, fishes in the fourth and so on. To a visitor even casually walking through the Museum, this may give at least an idea of the general principles of the classification of the animal kingdom, and will not preclude the invertebrate animals from being arranged in the glass cases in the centre of each room, following their classification in a similar way.[94]

A trained man of science with both local and international connections, Carte was well aware of the importance of bringing the collections into line with the fast-developing frameworks of the natural sciences. He was an alumnus of Trinity College and the RCSI, and held membership in the London-based Linnaean Society and in the Imperial Botanical and Zoological Society of Vienna.[95] He was also a member of a number of learned societies in Ireland, including the Dublin Natural History Society, the Geological Society of Dublin and the Royal Irish Academy. His expertise in comparative anatomy and his involvement with the current issues of European science equipped him to address the problems in the museum, and to propel it into a new phase. While his proposed changes were being carried out in Leinster House, the committee suggested that 'the Curator should be permitted to visit the British Museum for a period not exceeding one fortnight in order to ascertain the best mode of arranging the Society's collection'.[96] The British Museum continued to influence the maturation of science and museums in Ireland, and Carte set about developing productive relationships with its various departments.

Scouler continued in his role as professor of mineralogy while Carte pressed ahead in restructuring the museum, producing a flurry of reports for the Natural History Committee. His written requests were readily complied with, and the committee was delighted with its new curator. Records show that the first two years of Carte's tenure were characterised by vigorous action and constant contact with the committee. From June to December 1851 he was busy ordering cases and stands, having specimens cleaned, consulting with an architect over the excessive weight of the mineral cases, installing blinds on the windows, moving duplicate specimens to the curator's room for use by the RDS professors, and choosing glass for the newly constructed mahogany cases.[97] Within the committee, the latter half of 1851 was largely taken up with securing funding and selecting a site for a proposed new museum building, with debates taking place within the society as to which part of the RDS or adjoining grounds would be most advantageous.

Changes were finally underway at the Royal Dublin Society's Natural History Museum. Throughout the 1840s, the priorities of natural history and museums had been altered by a fast-developing set of factors that placed significant demands on a branch of science that became increasingly popular. The field itself became more scientifically rigorous as an increasing number of species were discovered, named and collected, and men of science laboured to construct a system for understanding the shape of life on earth and a means of communicating new information to one another and the public. The inclusion of natural history in schemes for education and social improvement placed pressures on rapidly expanding collections and on the people who shepherded them through a period of intense change. In Ireland, the Royal Dublin Society's position as one of the primary sources of popular science education for an increasingly interested public provided it with broad support when central government attempted to shape its activities, and the popularity of the museum magnified calls for it to become a credible and useful scientific resource. The use of the museum as an active adjunct to efforts in science education meant that it played a role in developing awareness of natural science in the general population, both through its incorporation into science lectures in Dublin and through the use of collections and specimens in the programme of provincial lectures sponsored by the exchequer and run by the society. Its use by art students further advanced its goals in diffusing scientific knowledge across the population. The challenges created by these factors eventually forced a change in staffing and approach at the RDS museum, and Carte was determined to direct the museum into a new phase and realise its full potential.

CHAPTER 3

The First National Museum

Growing the Museum: Carte's innovations

When Carte assumed control of the museum, he began to categorise the collections according to the wishes of the Natural History Committee, but also to the prevailing currents in European and British science. The previously unruly and confused materials were initially organised into a credible taxonomy, with specimens arranged in a clean, rationally ordered space. These changes shifted the RDS museum further away from its lingering association with the cabinet of curiosities into an increasingly modern sense of scientific display. Carte's changes began to create mechanisms for establishing order in the collections. He started a fresh register for recording donations, still extant in the museum's archives and still valued as a primary resource for identifying the historical collections. Scouler's register of donations had shown that his approach to collecting lacked scientific consistency, with most entries identifying specimens by their common names. Entries were inconsistent, and deteriorated throughout Scouler's tenure, so that some sections can only be described as messy, with blotches, mistakes and crossings-out (Fig. 3.1). Carte's new ledger book for donations was orderly, legibly written and organised. He included scientific names and classifications for as many specimens as possible, also noting any additional information, such as dates, locations and full names of donors (Fig. 3.2). He began to retain lists of purchased specimens and lists of collections sent to him by donors, and also kept the letters sent to him by way of scientific correspondence. Combined with minutes of the Natural History Committee, his documentation provides the

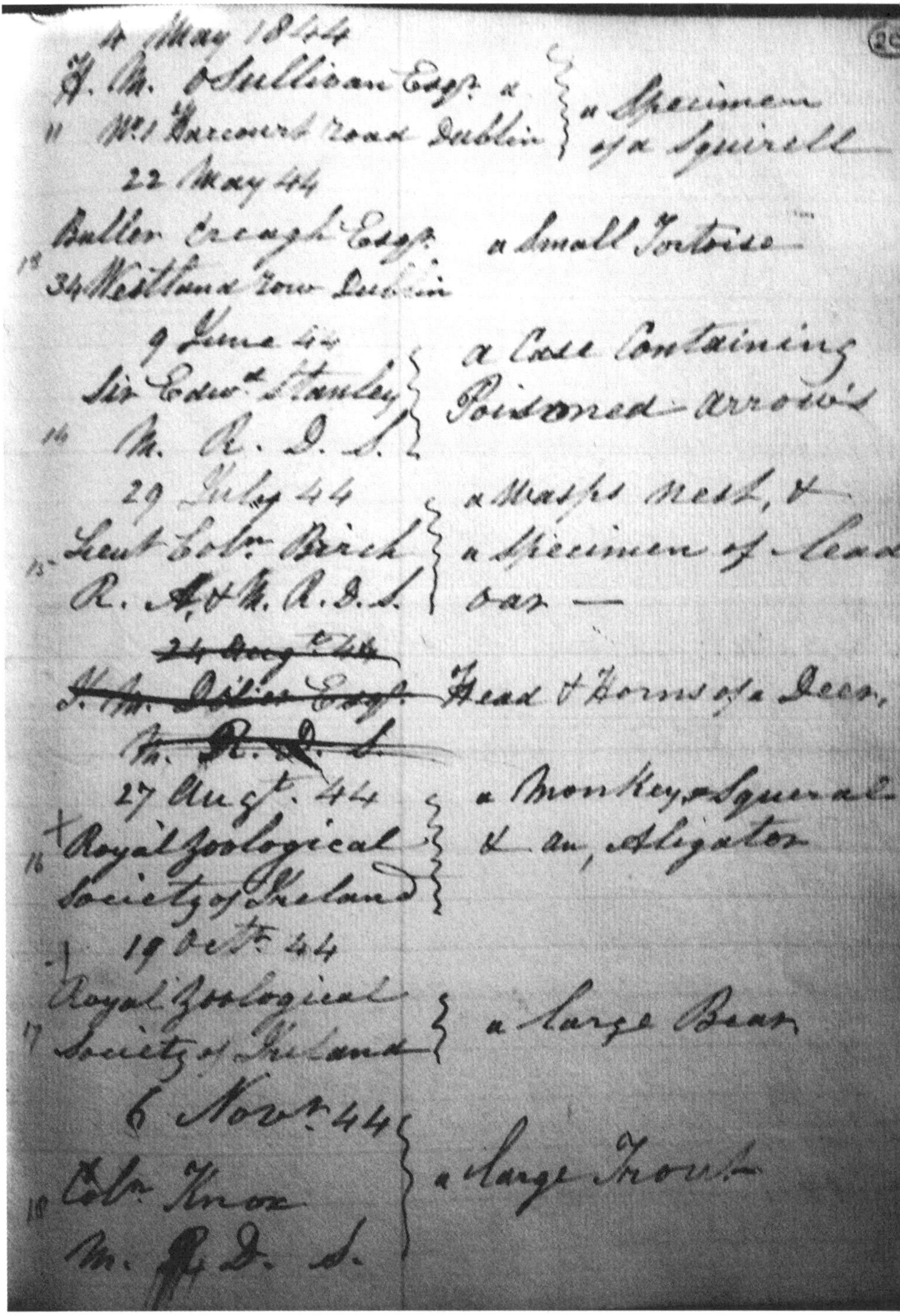

4 May 1844
J. M. O'Sullivan Esq. & — a Specimen
11 No 1 Harcourt road Dublin — of a Squirell
22 May 44
Butler Creagh Esq. — a Small Tortoise
13 34 Westland row Dublin
9 June 44 — a Case Containing
Sir Edwd Stanley — Poisoned Arrows
14 M. R. D. S.
29 July 44 — a Wasps Nest, &
Lieut Colr Birch — a Specimen of Lead
15 R. A. & M. R. D. S. — ore —
~~24 Augt 44~~
~~J. M. Oliver Esq.~~ — Head & Horns of a Deer
~~M. R. D. S.~~
27 Augt 44 — a Monkey, a Squirrel
Royal Zoological — & an Alligator
16 Society of Ireland
19 Octr 44
Royal Zoological — a Large Bear
17 Society of Ireland
6 Novr 44
18 Colr Knox — a Large Trout
M. R. D. S.

Fig. 3.1 Page from curator John Scouler's register of donations.
COURTESY OF THE NATIONAL MUSEUM OF IRELAND, NATURAL HISTORY

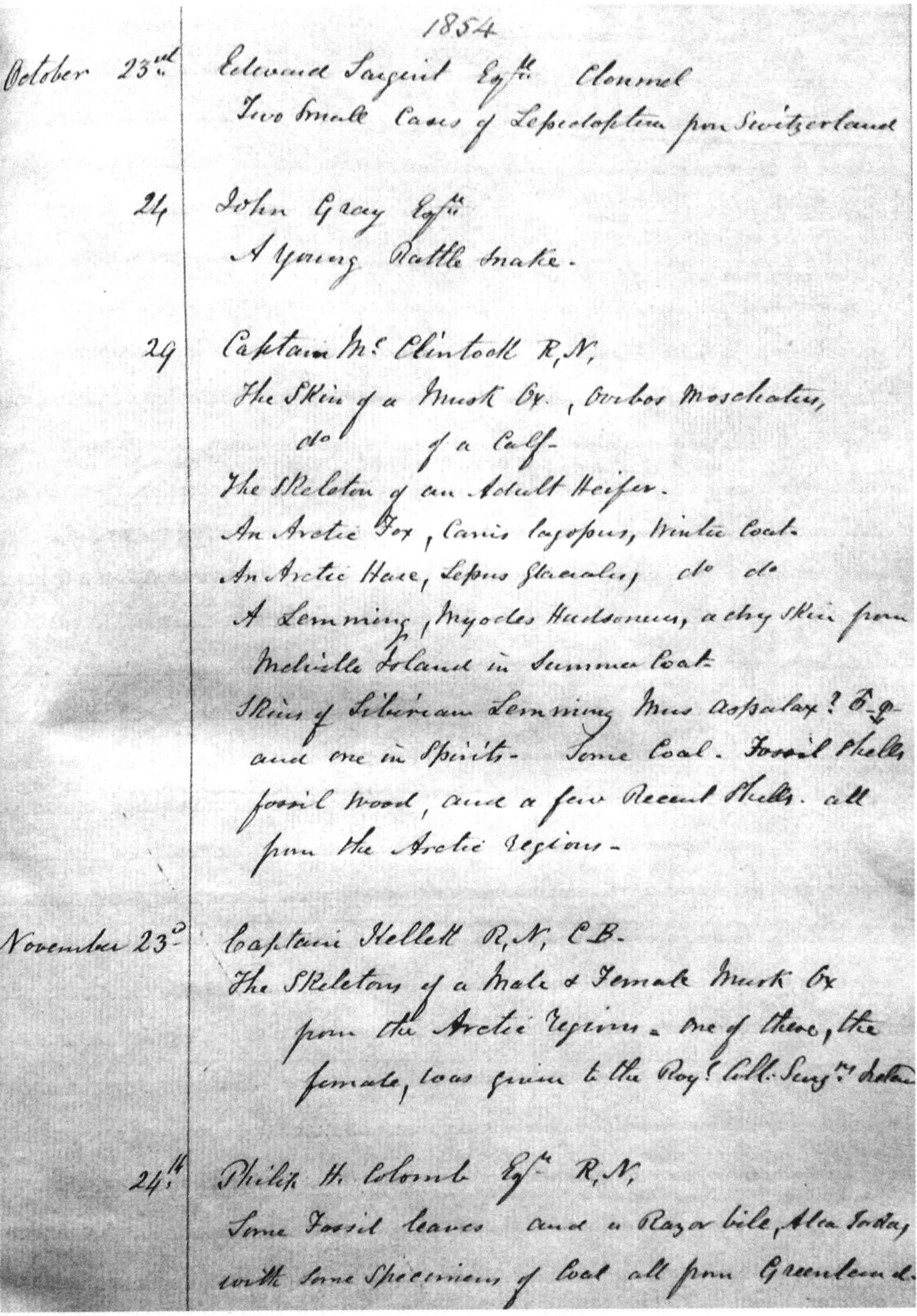

1854

October 23rd Edward Sargent Esqr. Clonmel
Two small Cases of Lepidoptera from Switzerland

24 John Gray Esqr.
A young Rattle Snake.

29 Captain Mc Clintock R.N.
The Skin of a Musk Ox, Ovibos moschatus,
do of a Calf.
The Skeleton of an Adult Heifer.
An Arctic Fox, Canis lagopus, Winter Coat.
An Arctic Hare, Lepus glacialis, do do
A Lemming, Myodes Hudsonius, a dry skin from
Melville Island in Summer Coat.
Skins of Siberian Lemming Mus aspalax? ♂ ♀
and one in Spirits. Some Coal. Fossil Shells
fossil Wood, and a few Recent Shells. all
from the Arctic regions.

November 23rd Captain Kellett R.N. C.B.
The Skeletons of a Male & Female Musk Ox
from the Arctic regions. One of these, the
female, was given to the Roy. Coll. Surgns. Ireland

24th Philip H. Colomb Esqr. R.N.
Some Fossil leaves and a Razor bill, Alca torda,
with some Specimens of Coal all from Greenland.

Fig. 3.2 Page from director Alexander Carte's register of donations.
COURTESY OF THE NATIONAL MUSEUM OF IRELAND, NATURAL HISTORY

most comprehensive written record of the contents of the nineteenth-century museum and the motivations of the people involved with it. They will appear in subsequent chapters, as we examine how the museum became a venue for the creation of scientific knowledge in Ireland.

Carte and the Natural History Committee also started to find ways of expanding the collections so that they would represent recent events and discoveries in natural history. They began by asserting the role of the society's museum as a publicly funded body with parliamentary support, taking advantage of the opportunities offered by its association with central government. Letters were dispatched to key officials, requesting a share in the benefits enjoyed by other museums in the United Kingdom. Secretary of the Treasury George Alexander Hamilton was solicited for his 'kind interference on behalf of the Royal Dublin Society with the Lords of the Treasury to obtain from them … such casts of the fossils in the British Museum as the Trustees may be possessed of, as well as any duplicates as they can spare'.[1] The committee also wrote to the Admiralty asking for 'His Lordship's attention to the claims of the Royal Dublin Society to a participation in such specimens as may be brought home in Her Majesty's Ships of War from time to time and … have a reasonable share of them assigned to the use of the Museum'.[2] The committee also applied to the 'Royal College of Surgeons London for casts of the bones of the dinosaurs and any other disposable objects of a similar class, and also to Dr Mantell for casts of the saurians'.[3] By seeking to populate the RDS collections with Gideon Mantell's important work on fossil reptiles, with replicas of objects in the British Museum, and with recent examples of species being collected by the ships of the colonial forces, Carte and the committee sought to strengthen the RDS museum by claiming an active position within the scope of British science and museums. In so doing, they would fill gaps in the collections and begin the work of creating a rational programme for acquiring a steady supply of valuable scientific material. The requests were largely successful; in September 1853, the librarian of the British Museum wrote to say that 'the casts of fossils … have been made for the Royal Dublin Society, under the instructions received from the Lords Commissioners of Her Majesty's Treasury. The three cases containing those casts have been forwarded to the Royal Dublin Society'[.][4] The museum's records also show a regular, if infrequent, series of donations from the British East India Company, as well as regular donations from the crews of military and mail ships.

In his new role as curator, Alexander Carte set to work rectifying the issues that had left the museum behind in the emerging trends of international natural science, and began planning for its future. He would be presented with challenges in his own turn when further developments in science, collecting and display continued to propel museums and science away from the spirit of the eighteenth-century amateur into an increasingly professionalised ethos. Two events in particular, the Great Exhibition of 1851 and the Irish Industrial Exhibition of 1853, would have direct impact on the Royal Dublin Society's priorities, resulting in the construction of the first purpose-built museum in Ireland. The new museum would encounter difficulties, as sustained funding for its development was not forthcoming, while it was simultaneously placed at the heart of public science education in Ireland. The irreconcilable conflicts revealed by these events would eventually lead to the establishment of a system of national education in the sciences, and to the formation of a national museum complex.

The Great Exhibition of 1851

In many ways, Ireland's national museum complex can trace its origins to the Great Exhibition of the Works of Industry of All Nations, mounted in Hyde Park, London in 1851. It was conceived to showcase advances in technology, materials and manufacturing across the breadth of the British Empire, and to encourage the use of design principles and classical aesthetics in manufacturing.[5] The plan for the exhibition was formulated by civil servant and designer Henry Cole, but was rapidly advanced when Cole managed to persuade the reluctant Prince Albert to lend his support. Once he joined Cole's cause, Albert became an enthusiastic participant, appointing a royal commission for the exhibition.[6] Albert had an interest in creating a more refined sense of taste in the manufacturing sectors of Great Britain, seeking to incorporate a classical design sensibility into new industrial processes, and an international exhibition of manufactures on a grand scale offered the potential for furthering such a goal.[7] The Great Exhibition highlighted the range of natural and human resources from across the globe, showcasing the productions of the British Empire's territories, with its sprawling displays accommodating over 14,000 exhibitors. The building was itself an advance in technology and manufacturing: an iron and glass construction covering 92,000 square metres, made possible by engineer Jeremy Paxton's innovative

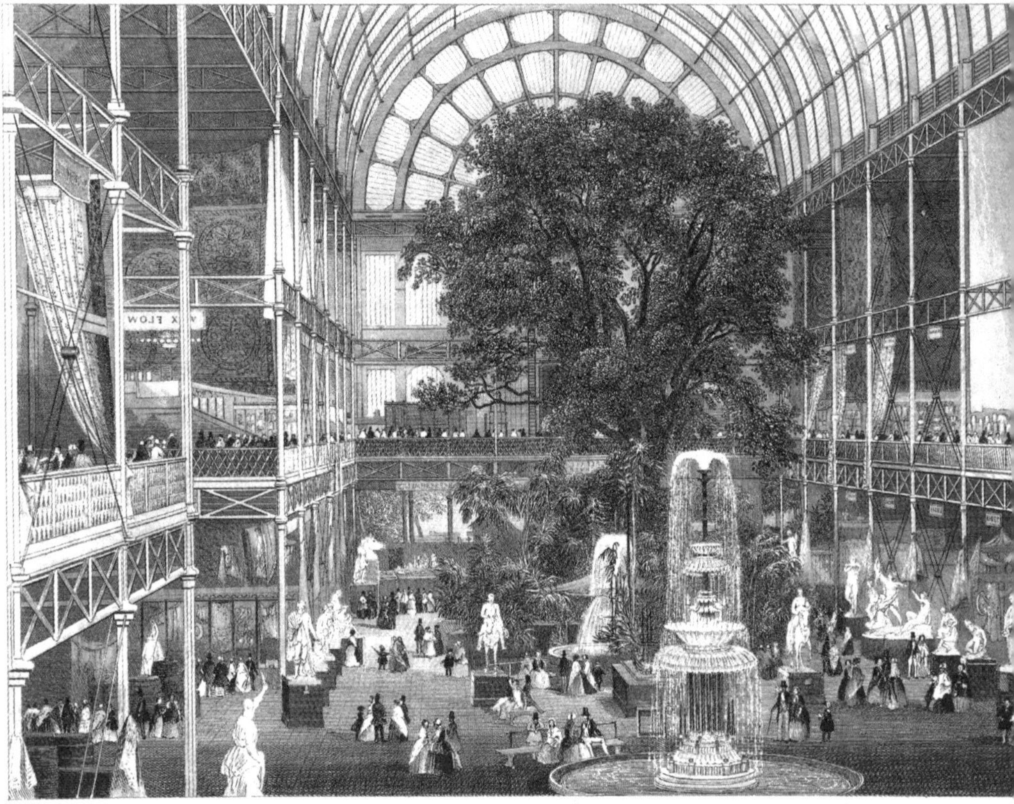

Fig. 3.3 The Great Exhibition in the Crystal Palace, Hyde Park, London: the transept looking north. Steel engraving by W. Lacey after J.E. Mayall, 1851.
COURTESY OF THE WELLCOME COLLECTION

design using prefabricated panels of cast iron and plate glass[8] (Fig. 3.3). From its opening on 1 May to its final day on 15 October, the Great Exhibition took in over six million visitors, and permanently changed the ways that exhibitions were presented to the public.

It was intended to showcase modern progress, serving as an encyclopaedic compendium of human invention, with a focus on the ingenuity of mankind in turning raw materials into manufactured objects through the application of technology. Richard Bellon observes that '[s]cience was at the very heart of this project, from its inception to its aftermath. The exhibition's organisers believed that constructing such a microcosm was the first step toward bringing productive human labour within the circle of natural law'[.][9] The committee that promoted and mounted the exhibition was filled with scientific men; eleven of its commissioners were fellows of the Royal Society, including its president, Irishman William Parsons, Lord Rosse. The sheer scale and ambition of the Great Exhibition changed approaches to creating exhibitions worldwide. As the first 'world expo', its engagement with modernity and progress realised the potential of exhibitions for imparting knowledge and expressing social ideals. The admission of large numbers of working-class visitors, a move anticipated with anxiety on the part of the upper and middle classes, changed assumptions about museum audiences when the rowdy scenes predicted by the press failed to materialise.[10] The use of rail and ship to assemble and populate the exhibition altered the ways that people thought about the geographical distribution of audiences for exhibitions, which subsequently became travel destinations in themselves rather than one of a number of items on an itinerary checklist. Above all, it fostered a taste for the new, the brash and the exotic which was to persist for the rest of the century. When Alexander Carte travelled to London in the summer of 1851 as the RDS museum was being renovated, reports on the Great Exhibition had been a prominent feature of the daily papers since April, and it is hard to imagine that he did not attend the sensation that was drawing upwards of 40,000 visitors a day from across Great Britain and Europe.[11]

The Irish International Exhibition of 1853

The potential for fashioning an Irish version of the Great Exhibition was immediately understood not by the learned societies, but by businessmen who saw its emphasis on manufacturing as a way of furthering Ireland's economic independence and bolstering its international image. On 10 June 1852, the National Cork Exhibition opened in the Corn Exchange in Cork city, but its modest size prevented it from fully realising the ambitions of the organisers. The RDS had been holding exhibitions of manufacture since 1834, and had regularised them on a triennial basis since 1838, prompting William Dargan, a society member and engineer who had amassed a moderate fortune through building roads and railways in Ireland, to approach the council with a proposition for the Exhibition of Manufactures scheduled for 1853. He suggested adapting the methods of the Great Exhibition in promoting Ireland's products and manufactures, adopting the confluence of raw materials, trade, design, manufacture, improvement and useful arts to support the goals of the society. By adjusting the scale and ambition of the Great Exhibition to an Irish context, the event would characterise Ireland

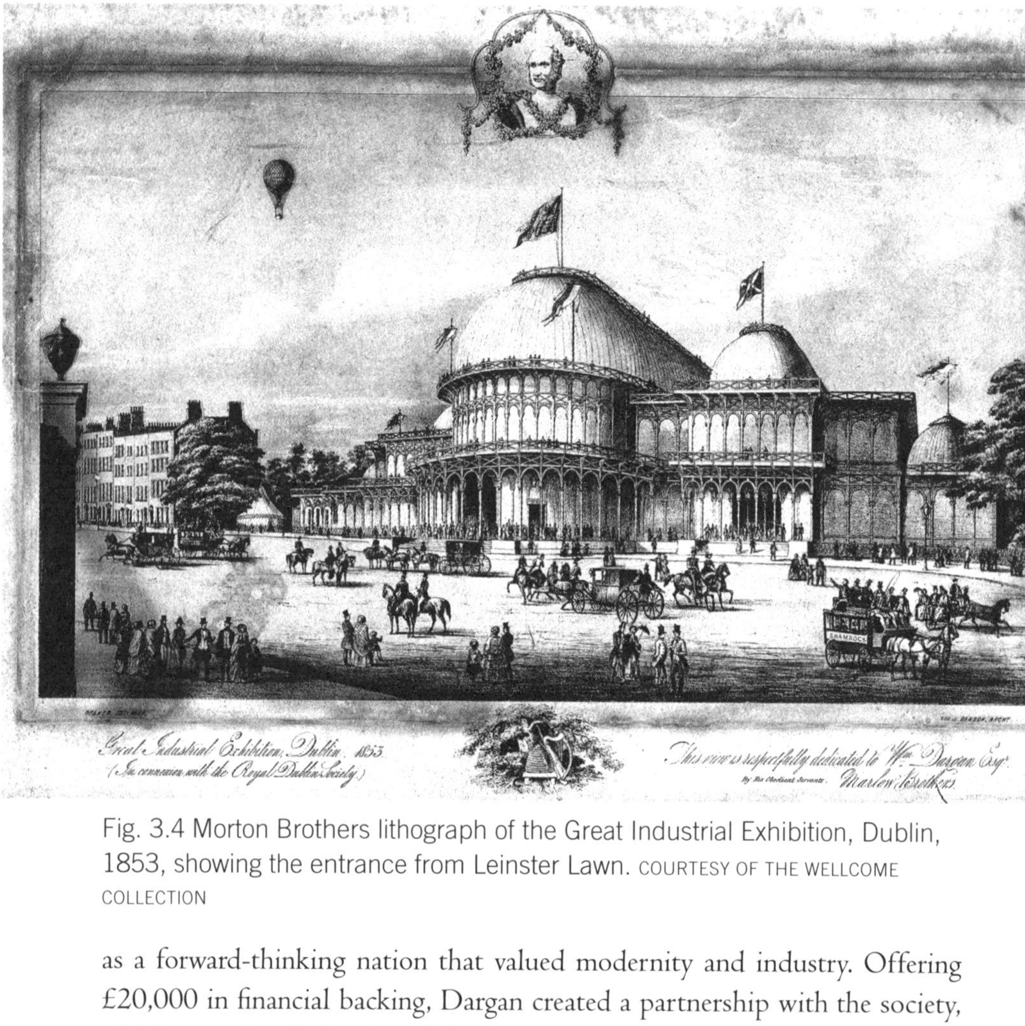

Fig. 3.4 Morton Brothers lithograph of the Great Industrial Exhibition, Dublin, 1853, showing the entrance from Leinster Lawn. COURTESY OF THE WELLCOME COLLECTION

as a forward-thinking nation that valued modernity and industry. Offering £20,000 in financial backing, Dargan created a partnership with the society, which agreed to hold the exhibition on Leinster Lawn, a large open space at the rear of its headquarters. Support from all quarters was enthusiastic. The *Freeman's Journal* immediately framed the event in terms of national pride, comparing it with London's Great Exhibition:

> [W]e feel confident that, comparing all things ... remembering that one was the work of one of the greatest Sovereigns of Europe, supported by the commercial wealth of a great commercial nation; and that the other will be the work of one man, supported by the purse of one man – a Celtic man – we believe history will pronounce the Irish Exhibition of 1853 to be the more remarkable of the two[.][12]

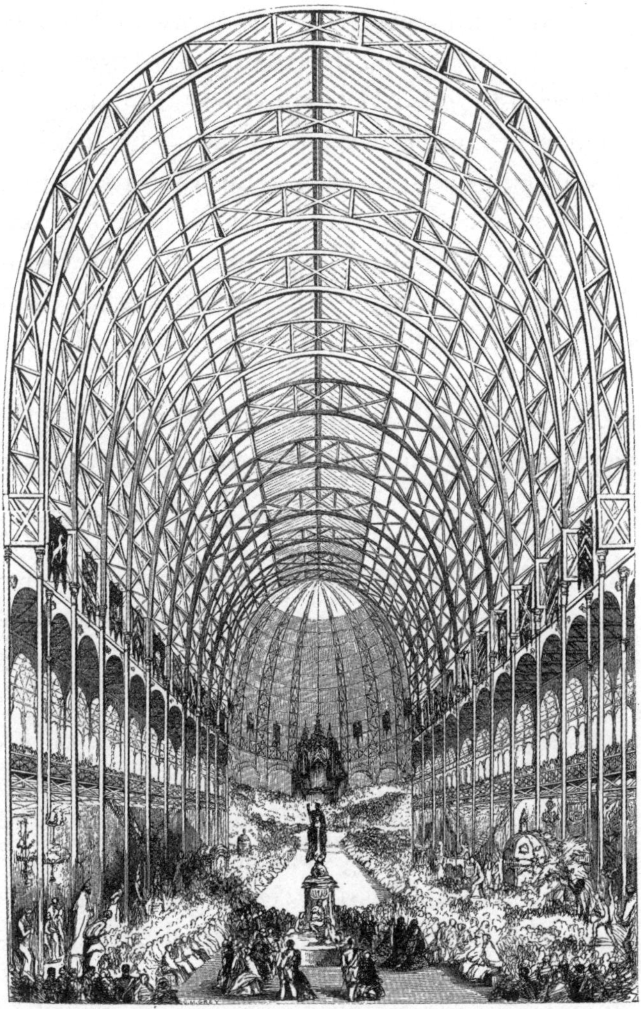

Fig. 3.5 The interior of the Irish Industrial Exhibition, showing similarities to the Crystal Palace. From *The Irish Industrial Exhibition of 1853: A detailed catalogue of its contents.* COURTESY OF THE ROYAL DUBLIN SOCIETY LIBRARY AND ARCHIVES

The Royal Dublin Society hosted the Irish Industrial Exhibition from 12 May to 31 October 1853 (Fig. 3.4). Images of the building and its interior show a conscious attempt to replicate the visual effect of Great Exhibition by mimicking the Crystal Palace, as its main building was christened. The Irish Industrial Exhibition adopted the vaulted glass ceilings, wide avenues, and arched colonnades of the 1851 building, creating a modern sense of space and light, with the aisles and display areas filled to bursting with examples of Irish industry and art (Fig. 3.5). The exhibition was patronised by the royal family, who visited Dublin from 29 August to 3 September. Queen Victoria attended each day, and the crowds swelled accordingly. The royal couple had previously visited Dublin in 1849 when plans for the Crystal Palace exhibition were taking shape in London.[13] During that visit Prince Albert had conferred with a number of the learned societies, and was no doubt happy to see the ethos of his project take root in Ireland.[14] Murphy notes that the royal couple desired an Ireland that was comprehensible to them, and that the 1853 exhibition suggested that it could be shaped through the ideals of design and manufacture that Albert promoted as progressive and forward-looking. Supporting the exhibition 'was their way of promoting an Ireland whose interests were commercial and industrial rather than atavistic', underscoring Murphy's framing of exhibitions as political as well as cultural events.[15]

In the exhibition catalogue, publisher and RDS member John Sproule asserted that 'exhibitions of different kinds have long been recognised, by the people of almost every civilised country, as amongst the most efficacious means of leading to the introduction and extension of improvements'.[16] Sproule traced the origins of the RDS Exhibitions of Manufacture to a similar event attended by Isaac Weld during a trip to France, who later proposed the idea to the society. Sproule's emphasis on the exhibition's connections to France, as well as to English examples, demonstrated that the Irish organisers were looking outward, comparing themselves to their continental counterparts and working to situate themselves within a set of modern but developing European ideals. Sproule's introduction also focused on the Great Exhibition of 1851, pointing out the change in expectations it had occasioned. In his enthusiastic promotion of Dublin, he went so far as to attribute the founding of modern exhibitions of industrial products in the United Kingdom to the triennial Exhibitions of Manufacture at the RDS, stating that 'the Industrial Exhibition may be said to have commenced, so far as Great Britain and Ireland are concerned, with the series held on the premises of the Royal Dublin Society, in this city'.[17]

The Irish Industrial Exhibition was organised and managed by a series of local committees that were heavily populated by members of the learned societies. The categories of display reflected the collections and activities they promoted, taking in everything from flax production to plaster sculptures. Natural history, though a category in its own right, was threaded throughout the exhibition in the form of raw materials like flax and silk, and in references to mining and geology. Scientific instruments, furniture and decorative items all bore a relation to natural history, either in their uses, materials or subject matter.[18] Specimens of Irish animals were on display in the exhibition hall, but not from the RDS, which let the museum stand as its contribution. The Natural History Committee opened Carte's newly refurbished museum in Leinster House to the public five days a week for the duration of the exhibition, from twelve to three o'clock.[19] The high level of public interest in the Irish Industrial Exhibition was reflected in attendance figures for the Natural History Museum, which registered 34,466 visitors for the year, whereas in 1852 it had netted only 3,008, the lower figure partly due to the museum having been closed for renovations for part of the year.[20] The success of the exhibition overall revitalised the project of building a new museum under the auspices of the Royal Dublin Society, and efforts intensified from 1853 onwards.

The 'new museum' takes shape

While Carte had been busily reorganising the Leinster House museum, the society and Natural History Committee had engaged in efforts to secure support for a new museum building. In the aftermath of the Irish Industrial Exhibition, while the glow of its success was still fresh, the Royal Dublin Society applied to the Treasury, through the lord lieutenant, for funding to realise its ambitious goal of a purpose-built natural history museum. Thomas Larcom, under-secretary for Ireland and RDS member, informed the council in July 1853 that they would receive £5,000, on the condition that the society members raise an additional £2,500 themselves.[21] As the prospect for a new museum improved with this news, the furtherance of the society's plans would come to be influenced by a new development that would also change the future of science and education in Ireland.

The success of the Great Exhibition led to the founding of a new government department, headed by Henry Cole under the auspices of the Board of Trade. In 1853, the Science and Art Department was given control over art, science and practical education in Great Britain and Ireland, funded by surplus monies from the 1851 exhibition. The new department took responsibility for overseeing the geological surveys, some learned societies, museums of science and industry and schools of science, design and art, from its administrative headquarters in South Kensington in London.[22] Within this area of the city it began building concert halls, museums and colleges according to a rationally ordered architectural plan, assembling a concentrated centre of culture and science that was self-contained. The department began to exert its influence in Ireland from 1854 as it took over the administrative oversight and funding of scientific and cultural bodies. Richard Jarrell asserts that the new department effectively controlled science in Ireland through the establishment of a centralised bureaucracy that was placed in charge of the diffuse and loosely connected system constituted by the learned societies, which now fell under the aegis of the Science and Art Department, answerable to Henry Cole and his staff.[23]

As the implications of this change were being revealed, the RDS used its newly acquired funding to commission plans for the museum building from architect Frederick Clarendon, and to contract the building to Gilbert Cockburn and Sons.[24] The exterior was planned as a neo-classical structure of modest proportions, to harmonise with Leinster House, and also to correspond to the edifice of the planned National Gallery, still in preparation and proposed for construction on Leinster Lawn beside the new RDS museum. The interior of the new museum building was designed to echo a pattern established by the Crystal Palace. The Crystal Palace 'style' used large open spaces and arched walkways to create maximum visibility of specimens and collections. With open arcades, soaring ceilings and glass roofing, this architecture proposed the possibility of visually ordering nature in one place, so that a viewer might gain a basic understanding of species and their organisation simply by looking. This style of architecture was adopted in natural history museums around the world in the second half of the nineteenth century, replacing the cramped domestic architecture of venues like Leinster House, or the modified classrooms used for university collections. The society's much-anticipated solution to the problems in the Leinster House museum was begun with a ground-breaking ceremony on 7 March 1856.[25] The event was recognised with an article in the *Illustrated London News*, reporting that the foundation stone was laid by the lord lieutenant and the event was attended by a company of the well-connected and fashionable, who enjoyed a fine spring day and a military band[26] (Fig. 3.6). Construction having commenced, the *Proceedings of the Royal Dublin Society* reported in November 1856 that the natural history section 'must be regarded by the Society as in a state of transition, the Director being chiefly and unremittingly engaged in preparing, naming and classifying the specimens' and conveying that work on the new museum was advancing rapidly.[27]

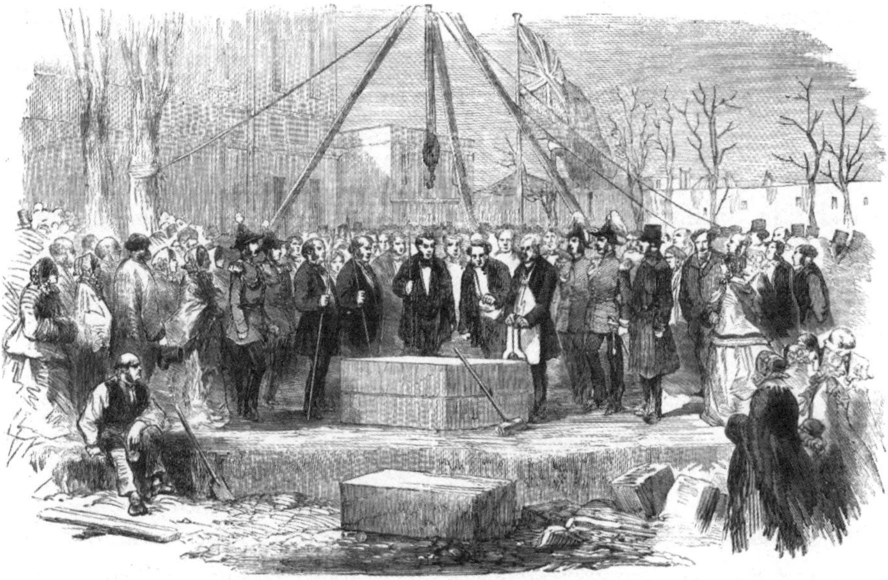

Fig. 3.6 The lord lieutenant laying the foundation stone of the new museum at Dublin, in the *Illustrated London News*, 15 March 1856. COLLECTION SHERRA MURPHY

As the RDS progressed towards its goal, the other learned societies in Dublin were also developing their museums to reflect the depth of their interests and the value of their collections. The Royal Irish Academy had relocated to larger premises at 19 Dawson Street in 1852, in order to expand the space for displaying its collection of antiquities.[28] Antiquarian George Petrie had agreed to arrange the collections in the new museum, but his work remained unfinished when surgeon William Wilde took over the task of preparing the collections in February 1857. He simultaneously planned an illustrated catalogue, which in the end ran to four volumes.[29] Wilde, both a scientist and antiquarian, chose to use a taxonomical arrangement in the reorganisation of the collections, its principles drawn from natural history. Trinity College was in the process of constructing a new geology museum, designed by architects Thomas Deane and Benjamin Woodward, who adopted the principles advocated by Ruskin in their design. The building itself was a testament to the marriage of geology, natural history, aesthetics and economics. The beauty and utility of Irish marble featured in its interior, and carvings of native Irish plants, made from life by John and James O'Shea, decorated the surfaces.[30] The Museum of Economic Geology, founded in 1845 and run by former RDS lecturer Robert Kane, was established to mimic the Museum of Economic Geology in London. In 1854 it became the Museum of Irish Industry, with a focus on mining, manufacturing, raw materials and practical education, and was the only museum in Ireland run directly by the state.[31]

These museums, attached to stable and influential organisations, had been able to take advantage of a changed landscape in the aftermath of the Great Exhibition. Smaller museums did not fare as well. The 1857 annual report of the Dublin Natural History Society noted that it struggled to advance its museum, its finances having been drained during the famine years, and its building rental and publications taking up a large portion of its spending. It was a fully voluntary society, supported by modest membership fees and donations, and its council expressed distress that collections focusing wholly on carefully identified and arranged Irish material, some of it rare or unique, were hampered in their care and display by lack of resources.[32] Many of its members and officers were men of science attached to larger institutions in various capacities, who expressed a desire to focus sharply on Irish natural history for its own sake in a way that was not possible in their professional capacities, but they also appear to have been unable to supply the material stability that such collections required.

The motivation for renewed activity in Dublin museums can be traced to the aftermath of the 1851 and 1853 exhibitions, but those with scientific mandates were spurred on by another looming event. The learned societies had banded together to propose that the annual meeting of the British Association for the Advancement of Science be held in Dublin in 1857. When the request was accepted, Dublin's intellectual institutions mounted a concerted effort to represent the city in the best possible light as they prepared to host the yearly scientific extravaganza. The societies cooperated with one another to show their attributes to advantage, organising public events and private gatherings, as well as aiding one another with details and arrangements. Trinity's new geology museum was to be unveiled during the event, as were the newly arranged collections at the Royal Irish Academy. The construction of the Royal Dublin Society's new natural history museum was rushed to meet the meeting's August 1857 deadline, and several important events were scheduled to be held there. The society committed more of its own funds, resolving 'to allocate a portion of the unappropriated balance, standing to the credit of the Society, to the completion of the building'.[33] Members were also approached to contribute personally, as the RDS had been elected to host a scientific *conversazione*. British Association *conversaziones*

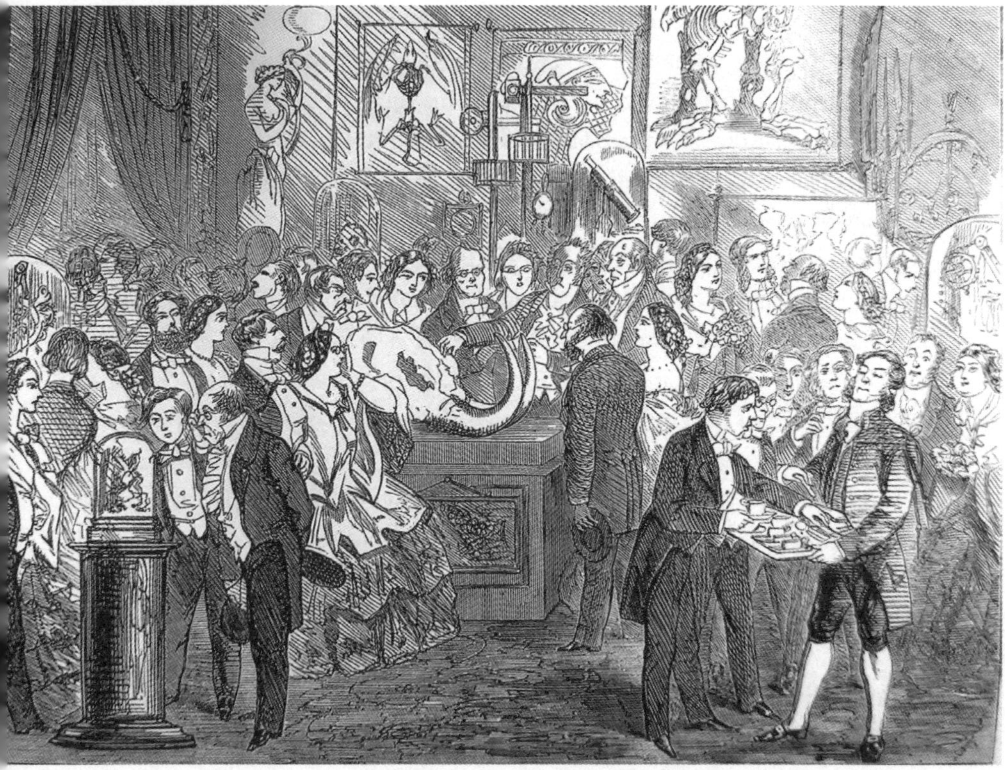

Fig. 3.7 'A Scientific Conversazione', in George Augustus Sala, *Twice Round the Clock: Or the hours of the day and night in London*, 1859. COLLECTION SHERRA MURPHY

were a vital aspect of the annual meeting, social occasions where science and leisure combined. These events were keenly anticipated and typically crowded with a combination of savants, amateurs and the socially prominent in attendance, usually with a large contingent of women.[34] Scientific *conversaziones* were lively affairs, with all manner of instruments and specimens available for inspection, where science could be explained in a 'setting that was, in effect, halfway between a lecture and an informal conversation'.[35] Their popularity is indicated by their inclusion in journalist George Sala's examination of London social life, *Twice Round the Clock, or the Hours of the Day and Night in London,* which takes readers into the various entertainments and activities of the city. He marked 11 p.m. as the hour of the scientific *conversazione,* with an image depicting a fashionable gathering in a museum setting, socialising with food and wine among the specimens and scientific instruments (Fig. 3.7).

Conversation was an important feature of Victorian science, and Secord argues that an emphasis on 'great deeds' and influential individuals in the history of science is 'inappropriate to understanding a period when people differing in gender, rank and depth of expertise not only talked about science, but in doing so contributed directly to its making'.[36] For the members of the British Association, a *conversazione* was an important vehicle for the exchange of ideas and scientific debate, as well as for the forging and renewal of social ties. A sparkling and engaging evening was essential, and cities hosting the British Association competed with one another in contriving the most interesting gatherings. Mindful of its reputation, the council of the RDS resolved that 'the character and influential position of the Royal Dublin Society should be maintained in a worthy manner; and that, with this view, a subscription, of not less than 5s. from each member, be set on foot, for the purpose of defraying the expenses of the *conversazione* to be given to that body on the Society's premises'[.][37] With this decree, the council made the members personally responsible for the success of an event that would ultimately reflect on their society.

The Natural History Museum inaugurated

> Judging from appearances up to the present, the meeting in Dublin promises to be one of the most successful and brilliant reunions of the Association that has ever taken place. A very large number have already taken out members' and associates' tickets, and fresh arrivals from England, the Continent and the provinces are hourly expected ...[38]

From Wednesday, 26 August to Wednesday, 2 September 1857, the assembled mass of the British Association for the Advancement of Science descended upon Dublin. The enormous week-long event involved science and spectacle in equal measure, and the learned societies combined forces to demonstrate that Dublin's networks of knowledge were primed to offer a stimulating gathering for their international counterparts. Association meetings followed a standard format of scientific papers during the day, public lectures and socialising in the evenings, interspersed with social occasions large and small. Meetings and proceedings were held at Trinity College and the Rotunda during the day, with evening *conversaziones* at the Royal Dublin Society, the Royal Irish Academy and Trinity College. There were also afternoon promenades at the zoological gardens and botanic gardens, and various events at Dublin Castle and in private homes.[39] Excursions into the Irish countryside, guided by leading men of science, rounded out the week. Dublin's social and scientific networks operated in concert to impress a veritable who's who of British, Irish and European science.

The Dublin press supported the efforts of the learned societies, with the *Freeman's Journal* providing extensive and positive coverage of the occasion, and the staunchly nationalist *The Nation* confining its normally critical stance to good-natured taunting of the visitors, and praise for the event.[40] The conservative *Dublin University Magazine* went so far as to assert that in recent years, Ireland had 'learned much; she has awakened from a dream of petty independence, to cast her lot heartily with the sister island; she has given up agitation for industrial rivalry'.[41] Murphy's assertion that exhibitions of art and science were used in mid-century as a means of political persuasion is again germane here. During the 1857 meeting, that notion took on a layer of complexity in that Irish men of science, regardless of political or religious affiliation, used the occasion to assert the unique qualities of Ireland within the overall context of British science. The intellectual elites of Dublin made a concerted effort to mark themselves as simultaneously Irish, scientific, loyal, independent and progressive in the aggregate effect of their conference papers, which used the event to promote a specific image of Ireland. They 'represented a nation with abundant resources and significant economic potential, with a sense of the unique richness of its own past and a desire to demonstrate Ireland's attractive qualities to a central administration more accustomed to focusing on famine, rural unrest and the threat of rebellion'.[42]

The new Natural History Museum of the Royal Dublin Society was inaugurated as part of this concerted effort, with its gala *conversazione* held on Thursday, 27 August. The paint on the walls was barely dry, as the builders had worked until Monday night, leaving little time to arrange the collections for the high-profile event.[43] Though the museum was open, it was far from finished; the upper floor had been fitted with displays, but the ground floor had no exhibits and the interior walls were unfinished and without display cases. Gaslight had been installed, however, and the unfinished ground level had been disguised and decorated as a refreshment room. With the incomplete building 'fitted up temporarily for the occasion' and the upper floor used as the 'principal room', the *conversazione* at the RDS museum was a stylish party attended by Dublin's social and scientific elite, with guests including 'the nobility and the gentry, the dignitaries of both churches, the judicial bench, the learned professions, men eminent for their literary and scientific achievements, merchants, manufacturers … there was scarcely a man of note in Dublin at this season who was absent'.[44] The interlocking networks of science, administration, trade, the arts and religion which made up the intellectual culture of mid-century Dublin were present at the launch of the new museum as Dublin's pre-eminent citizens played host to their international counterparts.

Unveiling the new Natural History Museum as part of the British Association meeting meant that the RDS could showcase its collections and raise the profile of its activities in the eyes of the international scientific community, and that Carte's work in reorganising and classifying the collections would be presented to the assembled scientific elite. The best description of the exhibitions during the opening gala comes from the *Freeman's Journal*, which noted that the displays were arranged by Carte. They appear to have been balanced between local materials and international collections, reflecting the scope of the society's holdings. Some were chosen to emphasise the society's promotion of practical science, such as display cases showing edible crustacea and molluscs that were pointed out as 'being instances of what might be done in the way of economic zoology'.[45] The exhibition also showcased prominent collectors or recently discovered materials, and drew from the holdings of members and associates to round out the displays. Carte included his personal collection of Kiltorcan fossils, well-preserved ferns from Kilkenny that were a popular subject of contemporary study. Diagrams and images of natural history, 'with which the walls were covered as closely as in a picture gallery', were lent by prominent Irish men of science Robert Kane, Joseph Beete-Jukes, Samuel Haughton and William Henry Harvey.[46] Scientific books from the RDS library lay on tables beside 'philosophical' or scientific instruments from the society's impressive collection. The Arctic specimens donated by well-known Irish explorer F. Leopold McClintock, RN, featured prominently, as did the contributions of staff-surgeon William Carte, made while on duty during the Crimean War. Their donations were related to topical events straight from the pages of the daily papers, as well as being of scientific interest. The *Freeman's Journal* consistently pointed out the quality of the science on display, foregrounding the sterling reputations of the donors and participants in the exhibition. Declaring the event a triumph, the writer opined that 'the president and members of the British Association will not soon forget the interesting evening that they passed beneath the roof of the first national museum that was erected in our island'.[47]

'In a state of abeyance'

In the aftermath of the British Association meeting, the 1857 annual report of the Royal Dublin Society contained a long and detailed discourse on the new Natural History Museum, highlighting that the interior remained a shell due to lack of funding to complete it. Central heating and ventilation had not been installed in the rush to finish before the British Association meeting, and the glass roof leaked and admitted too much light into the building, making viewing difficult and damaging the specimens. The floors had yet to be finished, and the supply of cases was woefully inadequate for the size of the collections.[48] The old rooms in Leinster House were still being used as a museum, remaining crowded and unsatisfactory. The report included a letter from Carte affirming that the bulk of the museum's holdings were still unavailable to the public, and that the donors to the collections were being poorly served in the existing state of affairs.[49] In January 1860 the RDS council asked that the Natural History Committee 'report to the Society at its next meeting the present state of the New Museum, and what works and funds are required to complete it, so that it may be open to the public as speedily as possible'.[50] The committee responded that 'owing to the defective state of the roof of the New Museum which admitted water during the late snow, and also owing to the want of proper ventilation and heating of same, they cannot approve of transferring the valuable collections intended to be placed therein', estimating the cost of repairing and finishing the building at £5,085, with heating and ventilation at an additional £800.[51]

The society petitioned the Science and Art Department for support, pointing out in 1861 that the museum continued to suffer from lack of funds, protesting that 'this department is the only public establishment of its kind in Dublin, and is in fact named in the Act of Parliament 17&18 Vict.c.99 as the National Museum'.[52] Making comparisons with the level of funding enjoyed by the British Museum, the society requested that parliament extend similar consideration to the 'Irish National Museum' and that its support would be 'completely in accordance with the spirit of the period, whereby the Society may be able to open a source of public instruction too long, comparatively, neglected'.[53] The press again came to its aid, noting that a national resource was languishing with no apparent plan for its completion. In September 1862 the *Irish Times* reported that the 'beautiful new Museum of Natural History ... has been almost in a state of abeyance for some years, for want of funds to complete the internal arrangements, and to classify and place in cases the magnificent collection now in possession of the Society'.[54] The society's pleas were met with silence, and it carried out parts of the work on its own as finances allowed. From 1861 to 1865, the records and annual reports of the society and the Science and Art Department record a consistent series of requests for funding, accompanied by descriptions of work taking place on a piecemeal basis. Repairs were made to the roof, heating and ventilation were installed in 1862 and floors and small cases fitted on the ground floor in 1864, with each bit of work prompting closures and re-openings of the museum. Attendance figures fluctuated accordingly, but still showed that the museum was in public demand, ranging from nearly 21,000 in 1862, to just over 10,000 in 1864.[55] The collections were gradually moved from Leinster House as work progressed and the committee felt the collections would be protected.

Carte and the committee carried on their work in the museum to the best of their ability under imperfect conditions. The scientific activity at the RDS continued as Carte and the Natural History Committee continued with their programme of collecting, rationalising, classifying and cataloguing the specimens and objects. Carte's salary had been doubled from his starting wage of £122 in 1851 to £250 per annum by 1858, reflecting the society's recognition of the importance of his work.[56] John Scouler departed for Scotland in ill health in 1862, and his position as professor of mineralogy was assumed by physicist and mineralogist Robert H. Scott.[57] The RDS continued to strengthen its scientific reputation through the publication of papers delivered at its evening lectures in the *Journal of the Royal Dublin Society*, which it exchanged with numerous learned societies internationally. The journal also publicised lists of species in the collections, and encouraged donors by highlighting their donations in special listings, using information drawn from Carte's ledger book. Carte continued to grow his network of donors and correspondents, which ranged around the globe and provided a steady stream of specimens and information. An increasingly comprehensive collection of Irish materials, many of them donated, began to position Ireland within the ever-developing picture of the distribution of species across Europe. Though its physical housing was unfinished, the museum had made the conceptual shift into a modern centre of natural science by adhering to scientific principles and actively participating in networks of expanding knowledge. As the scientific work of the museum carried on, the society let the Science and Art Department know that it was ready to mount fully comprehensive exhibitions for the public as soon as it could secure funding to complete the works in the museum. The exasperation of the council was expressed in its annual report for 1863, which ended with:

> Notwithstanding the interest which the public continues to manifest in this Society … the Council cannot but feel it to be very discouraging to those who gratuitously devote their time, knowledge, and experience to the management of an institution of acknowledged public utility, to observe that while means are not wanting to establish and maintain with commendable liberality kindred and neighbouring institutions, the funds which are absolutely required merely to complete the Society's Departments are, notwithstanding repeated applications, still unsupplied.[58]

Aside from seeing itself as having been abandoned by the parliament that had so long supported it, the society's frustration at the state of affairs during the 1860s also had its roots in decisions made by the Science and Art Department in 1854. Upon its arrival in Ireland, the department had attempted the rationalisation of science education by compelling the Royal Dublin Society and the Museum of Irish Industry into a cooperative relationship, whereby the scientific lectures and educational elements of each were combined under a common Committee of Lectures, administered by the department. The new arrangement endeavoured to satisfy the need for basic science education for the general public, and to provide more intensive instruction for those who desired scientific education for employment or advancement. The new arrangement established 'a short course of twelve lectures, termed popular, at the Royal Dublin Society, and a distinct long course at the Museum of Irish Industry [MII], termed systematic'.[59] The RDS lectures remained free of charge, and systematic lectures at the MII would allow for examinations at the end of the courses, incurring a modest fee. The RDS provincial lecture series were also transferred to the Committee of Lectures, and a system of examination established, so that people outside Dublin could avail of the same educational opportunities as those in the city.[60] The teaching staff, formerly employed by the RDS, were transferred to the new department, receiving the title of professor of the Science and Art Department, and situated 'as pertaining equally to the Royal Dublin Society and the Museum of Irish Industry, the courses of lectures being given partly in the theatre of one institution, and partly in that of the other, and illustrated from the collections in both museums'.[61] These changes were resisted strenuously by the RDS, which had remonstrated 'against the assumption of this society's inability to discharge its educational trusts, as heretofore, implied by the transfer of those important functions to other hands'.[62] That the museum, central to the discharge of its educational duties under the Committee of Lectures scheme, was now being neglected by the very government that had engineered this tricky situation was a bitter pill for the society to swallow. By 1864, however, change was afoot as science education in Ireland became the focus of two parliamentary committees, which also closely examined the role of museums as public resources.

Museums and scientific education

Amalgamating the educational efforts of the society and the Museum of Irish Industry was neither smooth nor comfortable. As the scheme played out over time it became clear that the arrangement should be re-examined, which came in the form of two assessments from central government. One, an 1862 report on the system of scientific instruction in Ireland, and the other an 1864 select committee that scrutinised the scientific institutions of Dublin, resulted in wholesale changes to the existing systems of scientific and technical education in Ireland. These events also prompted a public debate about the use and meaning of museums in education and culture as government sought to define what they were for and how they should be utilised. Though they treated similar questions and bodies of information, the 1862 and 1864 reports reached radically different conclusions, and the debates they engendered contributed to the eventual removal of national collections from the hands of Irish learned societies.

The testimony of men of science and the conclusions of their government interlocutors made it clear that museums and collections were central to the ongoing development of natural science in Ireland. Reports and testimony stressed that the specimens and objects held within museum collections were considered inherently valuable to the educational functions of the Royal Dublin Society and the Museum of Irish Industry, and therefore essential to any effort in rationalising a system of scientific education. Their uses and distribution were topics of debate because meeting the government's educational goals was deemed impossible without them; specimens, objects and collections were tactile manifestations of the abstractions in scientific texts and lectures, and they aided in clarifying the structures of natural science. The summaries and testimonies in each report indicate the ways that collections were used and considered, emphasising their value at every turn.

In October 1862, the *Report upon the Royal Dublin Society, the Museum of Irish Industry and on the System of Scientific Instruction in Ireland* was completed. Its authors were four established members of the administration: Richard Griffith, head of the Valuation Survey of Ireland, Francis Blackburne, a judge who was a member of the Privy Council of Ireland and former lord chancellor, Charles E. Trevelyan, controversial civil servant, and J.F.D. Donnelly, a rising star in the Science and Art Department with a passion for technical education. Their report summarised the convoluted system devised by the Committee of Lectures, and explained the complications arising from having one cohort of lecturers serving two institutions, teaching similar subject matter at differing educational levels for varying audiences in different venues. This system of teaching included the Science and Art Department's 'pay by results' system of examination where educators earned extra pay for successful exam results, an additional layer of bureaucracy. The report highlighted the importance of collections throughout, stating in the opening summary that the 'industrial portion of the Museum of Irish Industry is a practical application of the natural history collections exhibited by the Royal Dublin Society', and that the 'facilities for study are decidedly diminished rather than increased by dividing such varied arrangements of similar objects between two museums'.[63] Their prevailing view was that simplifying the complex arrangements meant that the museums must be merged, asserting that 'by concentrating our means and efforts on one museum, it may be rendered more complete and attractive than if two museums had to be maintained. More people therefore are likely to come to one museum than two, and they are likely to get more instruction from it. It is more economical to have one museum than two'.[64]

The debates around how many museums for the teaching of science should exist in Dublin centred on the motivations of their own adherents; the advocates of the RDS argued that a large general museum would serve all, while Robert Kane, on behalf of the MII, argued that a smaller, quieter museum in addition to a large general one offered more profitable opportunity for study. Samuel Haughton of Trinity College, long-time member and staunch supporter of the RDS, summarised one strand of thinking, opining that 'we want a museum in Dublin, with a large general collection for popular purposes ... I could not hesitate to express my opinion that the Dublin Society is the proper place for a public collection'.[65] Kane, unsurprisingly, differed in his view. His summary of the purposes of the Museum of Irish Industry was that it sought to 'teach the scientific principles involved in the various branches of industry, the uses to which raw materials are applied, the various processes through which they pass and ... the actual condition of the arts of manufacture in this country, England, and elsewhere. All the specimens are arranged with this view'.[66] He drew a distinction between museums for practical learning and museums for educational recreation, arguing that maintaining two museums may better facilitate focused study by serious students; he referred to London and Paris as examples, especially comparing the generalised collections at the British Museum with the tightly focused collections at the Geological Museum in Jermyn Street.

Despite Kane's best efforts to convince them otherwise, the committee's recommendations in the 1862 report were that the two museums and their educational programmes should be amalgamated and placed under the auspices of the RDS for the sake of efficiency and consistency. The summary and some of the testimony made much of the fact that the Museum of Irish Industry was a relative newcomer, and noted that:

> The Society is supported by a large constituency, residing in every part of Ireland and representing every Irish industry; all that takes place in connection with the Society, therefore, speedily becomes an object of general interest, and secures an amount of cooperation which cannot be expected in the case of more isolated institutions.[67]

While allowing that some aspects of the society's governance remained deeply flawed, the report recommended the consolidation of public science education into the structures of the RDS. However, any discussion of the society's museum as a comprehensive educational facility was notional at best, since the ongoing lack of funding meant that it remained incomplete, and was far from being fit to fulfil the expectations being heaped upon it.

The issues raised and conclusions drawn led swiftly to the 1864 *Report from the Select Committee on Scientific Institutions (Dublin)*, which examined the scientific bodies in Dublin that received support from the exchequer. This included the RDS, the Royal Irish Academy, the Museum of Irish Industry, and the

Royal Zoological Society. It strongly countered the primary conclusions of the previous report, especially taking umbrage at the proposal to reassign the publicly funded collections and educational functions of the Museum of Irish Industry into the hands of the RDS, a private members' body, decreeing that there was 'not the slightest ground for stating that the collections of the Museum of Irish Industry and the Royal Dublin Society are similar. The transfer of those of the former to the latter place would be a great scientific blunder'[.][68] The 1864 report also disagreed that the educational experience at the two places was broadly similar, pointing out that RDS members continued to grant themselves a level of privilege that was at odds with the ethos of a fully public and educational institution. Of the lectures at the RDS, it observed:

> The lectures delivered at the Royal Dublin Society are of less practical utility than they otherwise would be to students who are not members, on account of the privileges which members and their families reserve to themselves of occupying the portion of the theatre close to the lecture table. This must always prevent real students from attending there ... they cannot conveniently examine the specimens, study the disposition of the apparatus, or ask explanations of the professors.[69]

Having re-examined all the scientific institutions of Dublin, the committee concluded that the RDS, as a private body, should not have primary responsibility for programmes of public education in the sciences. The committee agreed that there was 'nothing now in the circumstances of Ireland which renders it expedient that the technical and scientific instruction given in that country, at the expense of the State, should be entrusted to the management of a body of private gentlemen, rather than to a public scientific institution, as in England'.[70] This statement, a core conclusion of the 1864 report, was in many ways the end of the undisputed reign of the learned societies in Irish science and culture.

The committee emphasised that the Museum of Irish Industry, having been founded by the state for a specific purpose in 1845, was a public institution funded by public money, and declined to amalgamate the museums into one larger institution. Its solution was the establishment of a Royal College of Science for Ireland that would assume responsibility for the delivery of scientific education that had previously been administered by the Committee of Lectures, and that would expand and formalise science education as a state-sponsored initiative. The Committee of Lectures was disbanded, and all public teaching functions were removed from both the RDS and the MII. When it was founded in 1867, the Royal College of Science for Ireland was placed into the Museum of Irish Industry's St Stephen's Green premises, and the MII was subsumed into the new college under Kane's direction. The educational programmes of the RDS were left diminished but intact, retaining the resources that had made them valuable in the past with the exception of the scientific lecture series.

Completion

The loss of the lecture series was perhaps offset by the fact that the 1864 report prompted a break in the deadlock over funding for the Natural History Museum. In May 1865, it was announced that £3,000 of the £4,500 in the parliamentary estimates of the Royal Dublin Society were earmarked for the works in the museum, and the tendering process began. The works commenced in June 1866, again undertaken by Cockburn and Sons.[71] The minutes of the Natural History Committee during this time read as a compendium of the workmen, materials, craft skills and practical decisions that went into constructing a nineteenth-century space for scientific display. In 1866 heating and ventilation were upgraded, and in 1868 a horizontal glazed ceiling was installed under the pitched glass roof to suffuse light and prevent leaking. Cases were built against the walls, and desk and table cases began to be installed throughout the rooms. Due to the extensive works being undertaken, the museum was closed for the entirety of 1867, and alternated between opening and closing during 1868. When the museum was open, times were expanded to four days a week, and for the first time on 6 May 1868, was opened on one evening per week as well. In consequence of the new arrangements in the museum, the Natural History Committee suggested that it was 'desirable that an accurate return should be kept of the visitors. For this purpose, the Committee recommend that a turnstile with a numbering-index be placed at the entrance'.[72]

In his reports to the Science and Art Department for 1867 and 1868, Carte detailed the ongoing progress in the collections, highlighting expansions into new areas and the development of existing ones. His improvements to the scientific value of the museum continued unabated despite the ongoing works in the building. Staffing finally reflected the museum's transformation into a professionally minded natural science establishment, with the hiring of a permanent taxidermist, Robert Pride, and two full-time assistants, entomologist William F. Kirby and naturalist A.G. More, as well as two porters to look after the building. Mineralogy professor Robert Scott left to become the head of the new Meteorological Office in London, and was replaced by mineralogist J. Emerson Reynolds. In reports and publications Carte highlighted materials that increased the scientific value of the holdings, such as the fruits of a collecting excursion made by More and the chair of the Natural History Committee, William Andrews. The pair travelled the southern half of the country collecting marine specimens, increasing the holdings in native species of fish, sponges and zoophytes such as hydroids and anemones. Carte also emphasised a new and extensive collection of mosses, lichens and fungi that had been purchased from the society's reserve funds. The collection had been arranged and classified by experts from across Europe, and it opened a new area of study within the museum. Carte announced that 'the entire collection, which may be considered the most complete in Europe ... will serve to form the nucleus of a general herbarium, long a desideratum in the institution'.[73] This was where some women in Irish science would begin to fashion professional careers in the latter part of the century, with botanist Matilda Knowles and zoologist Jane Stephens most prominent among them. In 1868, Carte and Reynolds undertook a tour of museums in Paris, Strasbourg, Heidelberg, Darmstadt, Frankfurt, Bonn, Leyden and Brussels to ascertain their approaches to collecting, display and management, and to form relationships with curators at European natural history museums.[74] All these developments point to the museum becoming more resolutely scientific under Carte's guidance, and many of his initiatives continued to bear fruit well into the future.

After the period of construction and improvement, the museum finally re-opened in February 1869. Attendance showed that the institution had been missed, and that the public were hungry for a glimpse of the finished venue. Figures for the year stood at 31,915, with 19,003 of those attending during the Wednesday evening hours.[75] Based on the success of evening openings, the RDS council moved to investigate the possibility of extending to two evenings a week. That change was made in 1870, and attendance leapt to 103,237.[76] Despite the efforts of the RDS generally, and Alexander Carte in particular, to render the museum a useful and viable public resource, it was perhaps inevitable that decisions were taken to transfer all important collections from private to state control. In the wake of successive government reports attaching importance to collections as essential public resources, the private/public nature of the collections held by the learned societies became problematic in an increasingly professionalised world.

In this regard, the completion of the museum amounted to more than finishing the building and rationalising the collections and displays. The most persistent factor preventing the Natural History Museum from becoming a fully professionalised public resource was that it was still within the direct purview of a private members' society. Regardless of the long relationship built with parliament and the good intentions of the society and the Natural History Committee, the museum could not achieve equal status to its counterparts in the rest of Europe and Great Britain unless it became a fully functioning public resource. The first step in this direction was taken in 1866, when the Council of Education issued a minute paper that finally separated the funding for the Natural History Museum, the botanic gardens, the library and Leinster Lawn from the general finances of the RDS, asserting that these important amenities should be clearly funded through public means, as were their counterparts in the rest of Great Britain.[77] Effectively, this meant that the cultural assets that the state had so long relied upon would still be administered by the RDS, but that the financial arrangements for them would be entirely separate from the society's other activities, so that its problematic decision-making mechanisms and idiosyncratic use of funds would no longer concern central government.

It was a division that eventually led to a wholesale separation. The Dublin Science and Art Museum Act of 1877 announced the establishment of a national museum that would be built on land owned by the RDS, and that would include a national library, roughly aligned along the South Kensington model. The Natural History Museum, the botanic gardens, the RDS Library and all the society's collections were taken into state control for the sum of £10,000, and were to form the basis for a national collection.[78] The exceptions were scientific books and periodicals, publications of other learned societies, and the works of art in Leinster House, which remained with the society. While the 1877 act is widely understood as the mechanism by which the collections of the Royal Irish Academy and other learned societies were also subsumed into the national museum, it was written solely in reference to the Royal Dublin Society, laying out the legal basis under which the amenities that had so long been supported by government would now come under its direct control. Carte and his staff followed the museum, becoming employees of the Science and Art Department. Carte remained as director until his death in 1881, when his assistant More assumed the mantle of curator. As the state assumed control of art and science in Dublin, the separation of collections from the Royal Dublin Society and the Royal Irish Academy in particular meant that the amateur networks of knowledge that had pioneered collections and made them central to Irish intellectual and cultural life had given way to the establishment of a fully professional and public museum complex in Ireland.

By this time, it had been nearly sixty-five years since the Royal Dublin Society named Charles Lewis Giesecke as curator in 1813. Natural history museums had changed significantly, shedding the spirit of the cabinet of curiosity as they became increasingly professionalised, and the development of natural science as a field began to demand accuracy, organisation, clarity and consistency. Natural science itself became more complex as a largely amateur ethos developed into a complex set of professional roles and disciplines, but was still supported by legions of dedicated amateur collectors. Major occurrences like the establishment of the British Association for the Advancement of Science, the success of the Great Exhibition, and the foundation of the Science and Art Department had profound effects on the development of museums, science and education in Great Britain and Ireland. The Royal Dublin Society's Natural History Museum was at the centre of this process in Ireland, where the national museum complex had its deepest roots in a scientific collection, rather than the collection of antiquities that now serves as a global representative of Irish culture. While there are no surviving images of the museum's interior in the period we have examined, a glass slide dating to about 1883, two years after Carte's death, shows the collections on the ground floor as a well-ordered and scientifically organised space, created by the director and his staff from the chaotic displays he inherited upon taking up his position (Fig. 3.8). This image conveys a sense of what the museum contained shortly after being taken over by the state, and is a representation of the scientific ideas of the day as interpreted through the material in the collections. Crucially, it also shows that the current popular notion that this museum has not changed since it opened in 1857 is incorrect.

The institutional history of the museum shows that a range of factors affected how it was seen by governing structures, the scientific community

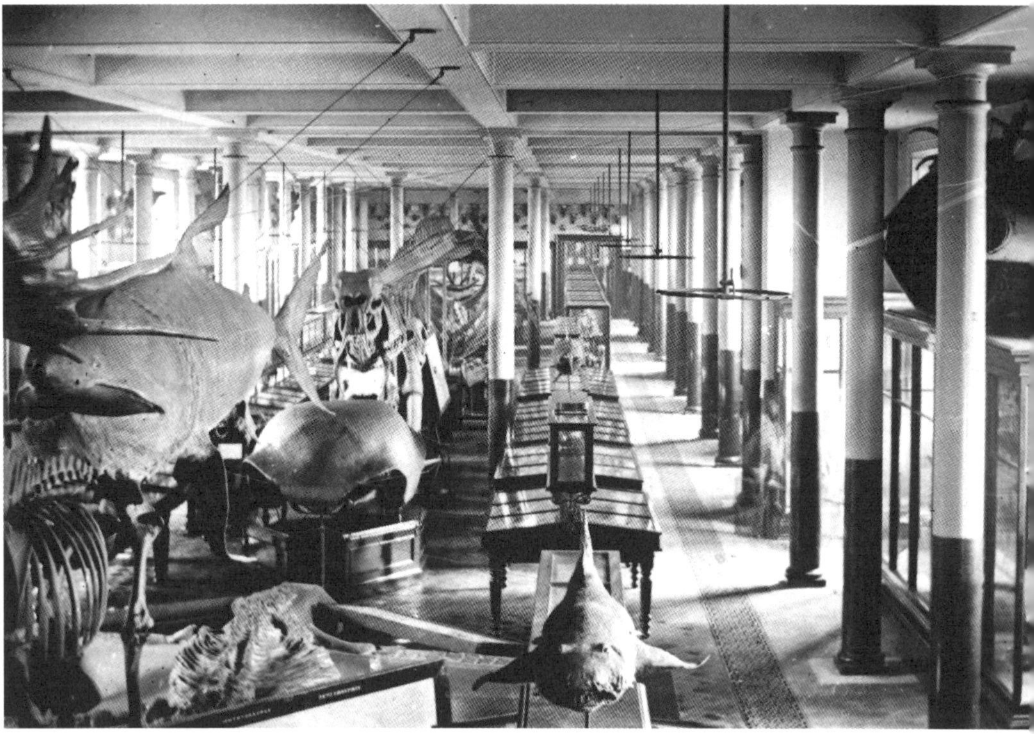

Fig. 3.8 The ground floor of the Natural History Museum, *c.* 1883, just after Alexander Carte's death. COURTESY OF THE NATIONAL MUSEUM OF IRELAND, NATURAL HISTORY

and in the popular arena of the press. Aside from the value of its collections and its contributions to natural science itself, its usefulness ranged from a venue for self-improvement, a resource for organised scientific education and even as an adjunct to education in the arts. Importantly, it was assumed by its adherents to have an important role in the formation of a specifically Irish intellectual culture through its various uses, whether in objects from the collections being used to illustrate lectures around the country, or through its influence on the designs of artisans reflecting Ireland's natural beauty. Through its various operations, the Natural History Museum may be seen as an intrinsically cultural institution, and one that helped to create the culture of science and museums in Ireland. Its activities in the nineteenth century and its place in public culture again belie the idea that Ireland in the mid-Victorian era was culturally barren; it is simply the case that culture was busily unfolding itself in areas removed from the corpus of literary fiction.

The RDS natural history collections were the nucleus around which central government gradually arrived at a plan for a Science and Art Museum in Ireland. Those collections were largely created by an array of people who pursued natural history at various levels of engagement, from casual donors to men of science who used their study of the collections to place Ireland within a wider context of European natural history. Period sources show that a range of people both contributed to and utilised the museum, and that its value and purposes were understood at a variety of levels, as people who engaged with natural history in the Victorian period ranged from amateurs to professionals. Most significantly, the RDS Natural History Museum, under the guidance of Alexander Carte, became the centre point of a network of interconnected scholars and naturalists who shared information, connections and institutional affiliations, which they employed to create new scientific knowledge out of the specimens found in the collections. Their contributions created important foundations in Irish natural science, but many of them are still not widely known or appreciated outside their fields of study. The next section of this book will examine their contributions, and look at the origins of the collections that made much of their work possible.

PART 2

Scientific Knowledge and the Uses of the Natural History Museum

The previous section of this book traced the early institutional history of Dublin's Natural History Museum, examining its development from a transitional eighteenth-century collection that retained the hallmarks of the cabinet of curiosity, into a scientifically oriented nineteenth-century natural history museum. Because its development was driven by a range of expectations around its role as a public amenity and educational venue, it was perceived and used in a number of ways by differing groups of people, each with ideas about what it was for and how it should be utilised. The next three chapters will consider the museum as a configuration that moves beyond the confines of a building and a tangible collection, focusing on its wider existence as a point of convergence for people, things and exchanges. From casual donors of scientific material to professional men of science who used the museum as a resource, its functions spanned the rungs of a telescoping ladder of science and intellectual culture. It became a central point in a network of communication between people with broadly common aspirations, which they expressed in various ways. From this point of view, the museum as a whole became an object that people used to think about the world and its configuration. They also employed it to demonstrate civic pride, build social capital and contribute to the development of new scientific information. It became a point of common reference as people debated and discovered new ideas and structures in nature, and attempted to grapple with what they meant and how they fit into existing bodies of knowledge.

CHAPTER 4

Building the Collections: Participation in Natural History in Nineteenth-Century Ireland

Donors and natural science in Ireland

Throughout the first half of the nineteenth century, parliamentary committees produced reports offering earnest generalisations about the importance of the collections at the Natural History Museum. The 1836 report on the Royal Dublin Society asserted that continental museums were open to 'every class of society' and that 'the lowest classes do in very great numbers enjoy that advantage', concluding that access to museums 'tends to improve the opinions and feelings of the humbler classes of society'[.][1] While declaring their usefulness in enhancing the moral and intellectual condition of the Irish population, these publications contained little detail about what was actually held in collections or why they may have produced such an effect, perhaps assuming that the benefits of science and museums required no explanation. Careful reading in the museum's archival records lends texture and depth to these generalised assertions, presenting us with details about how different people understood the collections and interacted with them. Donation lists, letters, scientific papers, newspapers and other primary sources show that natural history was a lively focus of public interest in nineteenth-century Ireland, clarifying the vague assumptions in official documents.

One of the most important things that these sources make clear is that donations from the public were essential in building the collections at the Natural History Museum. Carte relied heavily on a network of contacts and associations to encourage contributions, noting in an 1861 report to the Science and Art Department that 'were it not for the liberality which the Society has always experienced from the public, as evidenced by the extent and value of their donations, it would not be possible to maintain, much less extend, the collections of the Museum'[.][2] He employed several strategies for encouraging donations, but the most successful was the insistence that donors were publicly credited for their contributions. Carte put his register of donations to good use in compiling lists for publication in the *Journal of the Royal Dublin Society*, crediting donors by name, detailing their donations and sometimes commenting on their scientific importance. Selecting some of the contributions for display in the museum provided further encouragement. Alberti notes that collectors often sent specimens to museums because they wished to make contact with well-known men of science, or perhaps have their contributions included in displays and publications.[3] A named specimen on display in the museum was a form of scientific social capital, fulfilling a desire for validation of one's contribution to the public good. A letter to Carte from a regular donor who sent a sparrow hawk shot on his farm expressed that 'I expect shortly to see him set up in one of your glass cases'.[4] While central government had decreed that the Natural History Museum was the first Irish museum, the donors made this a concrete reality by shaping the collections through their own interests and participation.

Information about donors takes on clearer meaning when examined through the wider frame of natural history in the Victorian period. The nineteenth century was the zenith of natural history, and its discoveries were features of an emerging field that continually signalled change. The sciences generally had 'assumed tremendous significance in the second half of the century as every theory, and every new discovery, seemed to contain huge implications for all facets of human life. Interpreting, and arguing over, the social, political and religious meanings of scientific ideas became the focus of intellectual life'.[5] Natural history in particular had shifted some of the fundamental conceptions of humanity's relationship to nature, as its evidence called into question the age of the planet itself and revealed the complexity and longevity of the life forms it supported. The general population was informed about these developments in a range of ways, including 'public lectures and scientific demonstrations, textbooks, atlases, dozens of popular magazines and pamphlets and even the literature of science fiction provided hosts of learners with insights into the discoveries of science'.[6] Magazines such as *The Zoologist* treated natural history specifically, while more broadly focused publications such as *The Weekly Review of Politics, Literature, Science and Art* placed science into a generalist context for wide distribution. Specialist journals such as the *Annals and Magazine of Natural History* published scholarly articles for a more learned audience. Books for all levels of interest repeated this pattern. William Henry Harvey's *The Sea-side Book* (1849), for example, introduced neophytes to the species of the shoreline in Ireland and Great Britain, while his carefully researched *The Genera of South African Plants* (1838) established the scholarship of South African botany. Enthusiastic attendance at events such as the society's evening lecture series and the British Association for the Advancement of Science increased the visibility of science in the public eye. Scientific lectures and demonstrations were widely available, and were advertised in the newspapers as well as throughout learned societies. One could hear a lecture on science in places as diverse as a mechanics' hall, a ladies' luncheon or in the lecture theatre of the Royal Dublin Society.

Considering these factors alters the way that we can think about the history of the museum, and its place in the history of science in nineteenth-century Ireland. The history of science in Ireland has tended to skirt around the Natural History Museum, as it offers no apparent watershed moment in Irish science, no grand discovery that has attracted international acclaim. The tendency to think about the history of science as a series of conceptual leaps forward made by brilliant individuals obscures patterns that do not fit that model. From the perspective of the 'great thinker/great deeds' version of history, the activity at the Natural History Museum in the nineteenth century may seem disparate, messy and inconsequential. The museum's records, however, show a participatory model of natural science that relies on involvement from a wide range of people, and that slowly and over time adds up to the formation of scientific knowledge, a consequence of slow burn rather than big bang. Understanding its significance requires patient sifting of information, and following the connections between the people and things that allowed the museum to be a haven and conduit for people who wanted to participate in natural science in Ireland.

These observations can be clarified through a related field of study, the sociology of scientific knowledge (SSK), which looks at the practice of science as a social structure. Historian of science Andrew Pickering notes that SSK insisted 'that science was ... social all the way down to its technical core: scientific knowledge itself had to be understood as a social product', noting that this was to be accomplished 'through studies of real science, past and present'.[7] He emphasises that the process of constructing scientific knowledge requires a social dimension, for instance in the lab work of theoretical sciences such as astronomy and physics, where groups of people interact as social units to produce scientific knowledge, bound by the rules and ethics of their fields of inquiry. There is equal value in applying the general principles of SSK to the more prosaic activities of nineteenth-century natural history, where the social dimensions of scientific activity are important in understanding how people communicated with one another, how they exchanged information and how they interacted with the museum, illuminating the place of natural science in Irish intellectual culture. Across the social spectrum, from working-class ornithologists to aristocratic fossil collectors, people contributed to the museum, often eliding strict class divisions while bound by common interest. Divisions in the echelons of knowledge were equally porous. At a basic level, the practices of natural history were similar, whether one was a weekend shell collector or museum curator. Increasing one's specialisation into fields such as comparative anatomy or palaeontology, as well as publishing studies and results, separated dedicated men of science from generalists, but the levels of expertise in natural science remained permeable, and contact between practitioners at differing levels was commonplace as they exchanged specimens and information.

Sociologist Bruno Latour offers a useful way of thinking about the material in the museum's archival records. He urges researchers to resist automatically assessing their findings through the accepted or predetermined theories of their fields and instead to 'follow the actors', or observe the actions of the people being studied before deciding how to assign meaning to their interactions. Latour asserts that a 'good account is one which traces a network'.[8] Rather than evaluating people and their activities through fixed fields of knowledge, he suggests that we allow the webs of contact between people and things to govern how we begin to understand them. Though he is proposing to alter some of the ways that sociology is conducted as a discipline, his exhortation to write social accounts by paying attention to the connections between people and things is valuable in revealing the historical relevance of the Natural History Museum. The primary materials relating to the museum show a version of natural science and museums in Ireland which has not yet been explored. It reveals a network of interactions that only becomes visible through following donations, specimens, letters, memberships, publications, images and people through their interactions with one another. The importance of the Natural History Museum rests not only on the aspirations heaped upon it from official quarters, but also in its significance as an expression of the complex and interconnected nature of period intellectual culture. The primary materials for the museum trace a network of associations between individuals and small groups that largely disregards the 'great thinker/great deeds' model, showing instead a sustained cooperative effort among people who valued securing Ireland's place in the field of natural science, or who wanted the museum to be successful and respectable, a worthy representative of national aspirations. While tracing these connections in minute detail would be tedious, showing their general shape by using the museum as a nucleus demonstrates how it behaved as the central node of a rich and active network.

Following these connections also suggests that the museum has been overlooked in both Irish history and the history of science partly due to the perceptions of elitism surrounding the RDS, and its notional association with the goals of the Anglo-Irish Ascendancy. Science historian James Bennett, among others, has aligned the practices of Irish science in the period with the political objectives of the Ascendancy, linking it to the Victorian administration's desire to shape Irish society through the promotion of education and the application of scientific principles to social issues:

> [Nineteenth-century] science seemed a particularly appropriate tool to architects of social reform because of its supposed cultural neutrality, its claims of distance and independence from faction and sectarian interest. ... That claim was not accepted in Ireland, or at least it was suspect. One problem was that it was simply the case that science was already located in Ascendancy culture as a matter of social and educational fact.[9]

His assertion is demonstrable, but primary materials show that the situation in natural history was more complex. The exceptions were notable, and the wider intellectual environment in which the Natural History Museum developed throughout the century was characterised by a range of factors with enough variety to make sweeping statements problematic. For instance, that most (but not all) Irish men of science were of Protestant background does not automatically translate into alignment with the aims of the Ascendancy, though preference in education and employment remained a factor in social, and therefore scientific, relations. Protestant men of science from dissenting or nonconformist sects were not uncommon in Ireland's scientific circles. Giesecke, for instance, was a Lutheran, and botanist William Henry Harvey was a Quaker.[10] Geologist Samuel Haughton was the son of a Quaker merchant, but was raised within the Church of Ireland.[11] Geologist and artist George Victor du Noyer was a Huguenot.[12] Defining science in Ireland as firmly located within Ascendancy culture also does not take into account that some of the most important contributions to the study of Irish natural history were made by men of modest social status, well away from the advantages claimed by members of the Ascendancy. The study of migratory and coastal bird species was advanced by Mayo farmer Robert Warren, and the first significant study of Irish butterflies was undertaken by shipping clerk Edwin Birchall.[13] The RDS Natural History Committee counted businessmen, amateur naturalists and medical practitioners among its members. While Ascendancy culture may have been the driving force behind signature events like the construction of Lord Rosse's monster telescope in 1845, the Anglo-Irish gentry made limited contributions to natural history in Ireland; fossil dealer William Willoughby Cole (the earl of Enniskillen) and geologist/botanist James Talbot (Lord Talbot de Malahide) were exceptional in their consistent engagement with natural history collections. It is clear that the RDS as an institution had been founded firmly within Ascendancy culture in the eighteenth century, but records for its museum show that the range of people involved with the organisation had shifted by the 1850s, with the mercantile and middle classes firmly embedded within the membership.

Donors to the museum present us with a snapshot of public interest in natural history in Ireland at a time when science, education and museums were experiencing rapid change, creating context for consistent demands from the political administration that the museum should be accessible and useful as a public resource. They show that natural history was practised by a range of people, with women, ordinary citizens and casual collectors contributing alongside those occupying professional positions that demanded scientific expertise, such as military medicine and missions of exploration, or geological surveys. Some donors sought to add to the corpus of knowledge about Ireland, and to link that information to the unfolding assessment of global populations of species. At the same time, smaller donations from amateurs and individuals show that natural history was an aspect of civic culture in Ireland. Carte made it clear that donations were welcome from all, regardless of their level of scientific knowledge, and through these means both grew the collection and promoted the importance of the museum.

Who donated to the Natural History Museum in the mid-nineteenth century?

The importance of the collections at the RDS Natural History Museum resided not only in the physical objects which filled cases and storage spaces, but also in the act of collecting, the ways in which it was accomplished and the conceptual activity it signified. Collecting specimens in this period may be broadly classified as anything from picking up unusual garden insects to assembling comprehensive sets of fossils describing a geological region. What people thought worthy of collecting, how they went about it and why specific things made their way to the museum suggest the range of ways that the Irish population understood natural history. The people who donated material to the Royal Dublin Society's museum assumed that they were contributing to the public good, and often specifically for the benefit of Ireland. In soliciting donations, Carte was known to couch his requests to Irish contacts abroad in language that invoked a sense of Irish identity, citing the 'desire to have in the metropolis of Ireland a Museum worthy of the country'.[14]

Variable levels of public engagement with natural science meant that donations to the museum varied accordingly. A casual interest in natural science might generate single donations of unusual or curious specimens such as white blackbirds or deformed birds' eggs. More systematic collection was taken up as a hobby or polite accomplishment, and a donation to the museum was the logical end result of an improving pastime. For some, this pastime led to involvement at the level of the dedicated collector, who specialised in an area of interest and sought to create comprehensive collections in that field; donations and a desire for information brought these donors into the museum's orbit. The donors recorded in the first five volumes of the *Journal of the Royal Dublin Society*, spanning the years 1855 to 1870, demonstrate the range of participation in natural science during the mid-century.[15] Drawing categories is always problematic, but the records of donations show that people's motivations for donating fall into some general trends, providing a snapshot of the donors and the collections in mid-century, just before and after the building of the 'new' museum in 1857. Though many donors could be placed in more than one category, the divisions drawn here give us a working template for seeing how people thought about the museum, and show that the categories of amateur and professional science were a factor in the growth of collections, but more malleable than might be expected.

The differences between amateur and professional science in the nineteenth century are a source of debate, but Ruth Barton's close attention to the language used by men of science themselves shows that professionalisation in the form of paid positions was not vital for participation in Victorian scientific networks. Her analysis of the language employed by these men in assessing the contributions of peers shows that terms such as man of science, votary, worker, labourer and cultivator were employed to designate inclusion in the community of scientific discourse.[16] The stereotypical figure of the 'gentleman amateur' could be included in these descriptions, as could anyone who occupied a paid position, but by mid-century they also took in anyone who regularly pursued scientific activity and participated in scientific networks. Barton notes that the term amateur was in limited use, deployed primarily to describe the student or beginner.[17] However, an 1858 letter to Carte shows wider usage, hinting at the popularity of natural history as a leisure pursuit. Robert Nutall, an Irish doctor working in San Francisco, had responded to Carte's request for specimens with the admission that he harboured 'a holy horror of amateur collections usually altogether without value except in the eyes of the inexperienced and infatuated creatures who make them', and asking for guidance in making his own contributions scientifically valuable.[18] Nutall's description suggests that unfocused amateur collections were common enough to be understood as a passing reference, and perhaps not limited to beginners, but assembled by people whose knowledge remained rudimentary.

In the history of Irish science, Bennett has determined that 86 per cent of Irish men of science in the 'nineteenth century were professional in the sense that they were in paid employment directly related to science. Some of the

14 percent of amateurs were university professors holding chairs in non-scientific subjects'.[19] His focus on paid employment ties science in Ireland to political frameworks, asserting that 'the very high incidence of professional careers reflects the degree to which the scientific enterprise was controlled by public institutions and through them by a central administration', highlighting the impact of the Ordnance Survey and the Geological Survey, as well as the Royal Dublin Society and Royal Irish Academy.[20] While the central administration may have controlled the institutional context for natural science, museum records and manuscript sources show that, in addition to paid professionals, there was strong involvement with the Natural History Museum from people who do not fit within Bennett's categorisations because they were not scientific professionals, and are therefore not visible in the context he examines. Some of them made significant contributions to Irish natural science and to the growth of collections, and were valued as men of science and fellow travellers by their professional counterparts.

The categories of donors drawn here are informed by Barton and Bennett, but also show that participation in natural science in mid-century Ireland was wide-ranging, crossing the divide between amateur and professional, and examples of specific donors and donations give detail and depth to the abstractions in official reports. Two overarching categories capture general attitudes; casual donors and regular donors behaved differently, and approached the museum with differing intentions. Within these general groupings two more detailed categories present themselves. The collections of the Natural History Museum benefited from the posting of Irish men around the globe, employed in roles attached to the colonial expansion of the Empire. They donated to the museum as they collected natural materials during their travels, making both casual and regular donations. Their contributions show the relationship between natural history and colonial activity, tracing the links between Irish men in the crown services and the development of natural science in Ireland. Close examination of period sources also shows the emergence of a more concentrated cluster of Irish men of science, who were well-informed and had regular contact with the museum. As well as donating carefully classified and analysed materials, these people made sense of the collections through writing, publishing and speaking, transforming them from raw material into a form of scientific knowledge. The museum as an institution was enhanced and, in many ways, defined by the combination of effort from each of these constituencies.

Casual donors

Casual donors do not fit comfortably within categories of scientific interest, but appear to have been motivated simply by finding something unusual and deciding that the Natural History Museum was the place it should be housed. The aggregation of these small acts of donation shows that the museum was present in the public consciousness, and that people generally understood it as a venue for participation in natural science. Small donations from members of the public, with no apparently consistent interest in science, are scattered throughout the records of both Scouler and Carte. What constituted scientific material for these donors reveals interesting glimpses of the public perception of natural history in the mid-century. For instance, specimens that were deformed or exceptional arrived in a small but steady stream: in 1858 James Kelly sent an enormous duck's egg, F. Jones donated a white mole in 1856 and in 1857 a man identified simply as Keily, Esq. sent a live locust.[21] Items commemorating significant events also made their way to the collections. In 1856 John G. White sent a 'piece of carbonised matter taken from the ruins of Covent Garden Theatre'.[22] The Theatre Royal at Covent Garden had spectacularly burned to the ground in March of that year, an event covered prominently in the press. Other single donations were more in the spirit of scientific endeavour: Joseph Jackson donated a collection of rocks from the United States, James O'Neill sent copper ore from New Zealand and William Fosbery a specimen of the death's-head moth.[23] Though these donations were not necessarily of individual scientific value, they suggest that the act of donation to a civic institution was valued by members of the general population, and that the donors understood the value of scientific collection. Donations of unusual specimens and curios also indicate that the ethos of the cabinet of curiosity remained part of the public perception of natural science well into the period during which it was becoming more taxonomically focused and systematic.

Members of the RDS with no particular interest in science, but who wanted the society's museum to be noteworthy, donated in ways which differed sharply from the scientifically oriented members. These casual donations again illuminate the range of understanding about the purposes of the Natural History Museum, even from within the organisation that owned it. From the 1830s to the 1850s antiquarian objects, curiosities and ethnographic materials were common donations from the overall membership, and the natural history collections seemed to be the place that members thought to deposit anything they found strange, rare, prodigious or historically significant. As was generally the case in the nineteenth century, ethnographic materials were thought of as being firmly in the realm of natural history, as they represented exploration and its encounters with non-European populations. Ethnographic materials were collected as ways of studying and classifying the differences among the world's people, but sometimes also as souvenirs of military action, and they appear in the museum's records throughout the century alongside specimens of zoology, mineralogy and geology. In 1856, RDS member George Macdona donated 'two quivers, twenty-two arrows, two bows, two shields, one churn, one rattlesnake, one centipede, one tarantula, and an arrow-point used prior to the introduction of iron into Texas'.[24] Contributions from non-scientific members took on a more considered scientific character as Carte continued his programme of rationalising the collections and publicising their contents. Businessman Walter Sweetman sent two black-headed gulls, and a pelican that had escaped from the zoo and was shot near New Ross, County Wexford. Edward Dombrain contributed a warbler, and Robert Tuohill donated two small collections of reptiles. Well into the 1860s, however, these more scientific trends were still occasionally accompanied by donations of Roman tiles and Chinese umbrellas.

Given that donation to the collections was a largely male-dominated activity, it is worth noting that women appear regularly, if less frequently, as casual donors who made modest contributions. Women sometimes contributed to the collections through the intervention of a male family member or a member of the RDS, but more often under their own names. Casual donations from women were highly variable in their engagement with science: Mrs Murphy sent a large and deformed hen's egg, Mrs Kirby sent a queen ant and scorpion from India and Miss Hamilton sent specimens from Nicaragua, including snakes, nests, a turtle and the ear bones of a manatee.[25] Priscilla (listed as Mrs Henry) Sherrard of Thorndale, Drumcondra sent specimens of coal, fossils, a pied blackbird and a barn owl at various times.[26] She wrote to Carte in 1868, to say that:

> Finding that the Dungarvan Society have given up all intention of forming a museum and wishing to dispose of my little collection do you know anyone who would be likely to purchase it as I would prefer selling it case and all ... there are also a few minerals given me by Sir Charles Giesecke.[27]

Sherrard was the daughter of Edward Evans, JP, of Gortmerron House, Tyrone, and was married to architect Henry Sherrard, secretary of the Wide Streets Commission and an RDS member, so was a woman of social standing.[28] Her donations and the description of her 'little collection' indicate that perhaps she was one of 'the inexperienced … creatures' so despised by Nutall, but also that she was alert to the importance of collections and donations. Some women's donations defied period expectations that ladies' collecting activity should centre on flowers, ferns and shells: Miss Woodruffe sent a great anteater in 1859, Lady George Hill donated two fallow deer skins and a set of antlers in 1861 and Susan Scott sent a roe deer from Scotland in 1867.

Women's donations to the RDS museum provide a corollary to reports of women's attendance at the society's evening lectures, and their consistent participation in the Science and Art Department's education programmes. The 1864 *Report of the Select Committee on Scientific Institutions* had complained that the RDS lectures tended to reserve the best seats for members and their families, but it is not hard to imagine that women like Priscilla Sherrard were among them, and some were more than disinterested observers. Women were also prominent during the public events at the Dublin meeting of the British Association for the Advancement of Science in 1857. From its inception the association had been happy to include women in social events such as *conversaziones* and evening lectures, but in its early years had mixed and reluctant policies on the admission of women to the sectional meetings where the serious science took place. From 1850 women's access to events both social and scientific had been secured, and 'ladies' tickets' became a valued source of income for the association.[29]

The extant literature around the participation of women in natural history in Ireland suggests that they gained little ground in professional positions until after the 1890s, when evidence of publishing and professional careers grew sharply.[30] The museum's records indicate that perhaps their earlier contributions were made in less visible ways. The minutes of the Natural History Committee show that in 1853, Mary Baker was paid £6.2.6. for stuffing birds.[31] In 1852, the *Proceedings of the Royal Dublin Society* noted that in the recently held scientific examinations held through the School of Design, Louisa Brady had emerged as the top candidate in chemistry, natural history and botany, and women frequently excelled in the scientific classes held under the Committee of Lectures scheme.[32] An 1865 letter from Royal Irish

Academy librarian Edward Clibborn sought Carte's assistance in securing posts as governesses for two young women, relaying that they had won prizes in their science studies at the Museum of Irish Industry where 'they took all the premiums at Sir R. Kane's in botany, chemistry, etc. … in fact, were they boys, not girls, they might stand for fellowships or cadetships or any other sort of ships'.[33] While women appear to have been primarily casual donors in the mid-century, their consistent presence in the networks of science suggests that further archival study might change our understanding of their role in citizen science in Victorian Ireland.

Regular donors

Sources show that people who donated to the collections on a regular basis tended to be more scientifically informed than casual donors. Some were scientific amateurs, some were RDS members and others were established men of science, but all were alert to the educational and scientific purposes of natural history museums. Ranging across a social spectrum, there was strong participation from people in commerce and medicine, and more modest contributions from farmers and landed gentry. As might be expected, professional men of science were also regular contributors. Dedicated amateurs and scientific professionals were equally represented in Carte's published lists in the society's journal and annual reports, aiding his goal of encouraging participation through valuing donors' contributions, no matter the social status of the donor. As they appear regularly, these people are the 'actors' whom Latour suggests we follow, and their contributions confirm that natural history as a scientific pursuit elided strict boundaries of class, education and profession, again calling into question the idea that science in nineteenth-century Ireland was the sole province of the privileged. Their relationships to one another and the significance of some of their activities will form the basis of subsequent chapters, as they demonstrate that the development of natural science in Ireland was a collaborative endeavour, the result of an interconnected network.

Members of the society's Natural History Committee were, unsurprisingly, regular donors to the collections. The membership comprised businessmen, medical professionals and legal practitioners in addition to men of science. They were a driving force behind the growth and funding of the museum, and the minute books of the committee's meetings provide one of the key resources for tracing the minutiae of its development as it unfolded. The committee members understood Carte's ambitions, working alongside him to transform the museum according to emerging scientific standards and the ambitions of the RDS. The membership changed across time, but some names appear consistently throughout Carte's tenure. John Rathborne, owner of a candle-making company founded in the 1400s (and surviving to the present), donated a range of zoological specimens, ranging from exotic monkeys and toucans to local moths and birds.[34] John Good was a long-serving member of the RDS Natural History Committee, but is visible in the historical record primarily through his contact with others rather than in his own right. He is listed in a Board of Works report from 1850 as having owned two cutters that operated as trawlers in Dingle, County Kerry, but were registered in Dublin.[35] Dr William Frazer, another committee member, credits him with providing specimens of and information about a rare shell, collected while plying his Dublin trawlers in Dungarvan, County Waterford. Frazer's paper on the shell, published by the Natural History Society of Dublin, indicated regular contact with Good, implying that he owned a number of trawling vessels.[36] His work in the fisheries and his interest in natural history generated regular donations of species found in the sea, from fish, to crabs, to the skull of an orca. Andrew A. Dunlop was a long-term member of the committee who contributed zoological specimens from India, Penang and locations in the East Indies, suggesting that he was being sent material from the region by contacts in the civil or military services.

Landed families who were not members of the gentry were also regular donors. Phineas Riall, a justice of the peace from a landed banking family, began to contribute zoological materials, mostly birds, in the mid-1860s from his residence in Old Conna, Bray, County Wicklow.[37] Sandford Palmer leased a large farm in Tipperary from the earl of Portarlington, and sent a range of specimens including horns, a rat, a sparrowhawk and other zoological material.[38] He corresponded intermittently with Carte, and one letter records his donation of the skeleton of a chestnut horse, 'a very great favourite of mine'.[39] Edward Waller, a corresponding member of the RDS and another landowner from Tipperary, was a barrister and noted amateur naturalist with a specialisation in molluscs. He presented papers to the British Association in 1867 and '68, marking him out as a labourer for science, who was valued for his contributions to an overall body of knowledge. His regular donations were scientifically valuable, such as his 1870 donation of 'twenty-two rare species of British mollusca, taken off the Shetland Islands'.[40] Landed proprietors were among the original audiences for the RDS collections, and they remained important to the museum as it developed and changed over time.

Medical men were also regular donors to the museum, and though it might be expected that they would contribute material related to comparative anatomy or other aspects of their professional activity, their contributions were often from other areas of interest. Dominic J. Corrigan, a Catholic doctor who specialised in heart and lung diseases, sent fish taken in Irish waters, including the first Irish specimen of the tadpole fish, and specimens of birds from Florida and the Himalayas. Robert Battersby, MD and deputy inspector-general of hospitals, sent fossils, shells and fish. Eye and ear surgeon William Wilde was a widely travelled collector and member of the Royal Irish Academy, who contributed a toucan, birds from China and snakes from Hong Kong to the RDS museum. Many of the medical men who contributed to the collections did so from their positions within the crown forces, where they combined their scientific skills with their impulse to study natural history. They will be discussed later in this chapter.

There are two women in the records who might be considered as regular donors. Though modest, their contributions again indicate that women's participation in natural history in Ireland prior to the turn of the twentieth century may be found in unconventional places in the historical record. A Mrs Nangle of 11 Percy Place, Dublin, appears in Carte's lists as having donated a small series of *Balea fragilis*, a land snail, from County Down. The focus on a specific species suggests more than a casual interest, but there is no more information about her.[41] The other woman who might be classed as a regular donor was Mrs Thomas (Helena) Townsend, an amateur collector of shells who sent marine specimens from the area surrounding her home in Smithville, Skibbereen, County Cork, and from nearby Lough Ine. Townsend was from an influential family, the daughter of a former deputy governor in Baltimore, and the wife of Commander Thomas Townsend of the Royal Navy.[42] The Townsends were a large landed family, with the main family seat located in Castletownshend, not far from Helena Townsend's residence. She regularly sent specimens, usually large scallops, from 1856–61, some of them organised into series, and in 1858 she sent a list of local species she had observed.[43] In an undated letter to Carte, she wrote, 'I am here on the brink of the sea – the waves are high and the weather wild, nothing has been thrown on the sands but seaweeds in abundance – any heap of such I have turned over in search of shells but in vain', going on to say that she hoped to hire men to help her dredge in Lough Ine.[44] Her donations and single letter in the archives place her outside the category of the casual donor and into the status of a focused amateur with a consistent interest in a range of species defined by her locale.

Landed gentry from the Ascendancy classes were infrequent donors to the collections, but there are notable exceptions. James Talbot, Lord Talbot de Malahide, was one of the small number of men holding hereditary titles who were active in natural history in Ireland. Talbot was an antiquarian with a strong amateur interest in science, and a member of several learned societies that promoted natural history.[45] He was eager to make connections between fields in natural science and the possibilities they presented for understanding the past. For instance, his presidential address to the Royal Irish Academy in 1866 cited the study of astronomy in helping establish a chronology for the Battle of Clontarf, a case of science enhancing historical knowledge.[46] Malahide contributed birds and fossils to the collections. Mervyn Wingfield, Lord Powerscourt, was another titled member of a landed family who contributed to the museum, and who communicated with Carte about scientific matters and acquiring specimens for his residence at Powerscourt House in Enniskerry, County Wicklow. He contributed specimens that were shot on his property, such as deer and otters, as well as animals that he acquired on hunting trips.[47] Another prominent titled donor, William Willoughby Cole, Lord Enniskillen, was a scientifically knowledgeable fossil dealer with an international reputation, who had extensive contact with Carte. He is listed in the *JRDS* as having made a single donation of a fossil nautilus, but his interactions with the museum were richer and more complex than such a modest entry might indicate. He will feature in the next chapter as part of an interconnected network of scientific fellow-travellers.

Regular donors were the lifeblood of the collections, and the representative examples above are merely indicative of the people who contributed steadily to making the museum an active and viable scientific resource. Considering them confirms that a range of people across a social spectrum in Ireland thought that natural history collection was a worthwhile activity, adding nuance to the generalities proffered by official reports and central government. While there is a healthy body of scholarship on natural history as a leisure activity in Great Britain in the nineteenth century, there is still work to be undertaken in the history of Irish science, and the museum's records indicate the richness held in archives.[48] Many of the people examined thus far provide potential for investigating natural science as an aspect of intellectual culture in nineteenth-century Ireland, and the following groupings provide further scope for in-depth consideration.

Natural history and colonialism in the collections

Repeating a pattern observable around the globe, the collections at Dublin's Natural History Museum are rich in materials that were gathered in the pursuit of empire. The global explosion of natural history in the mid-nineteenth century was deeply entwined with the colonial activity of the European states, which embedded collecting and classifying nature into their methods for colonising territories and peoples.[49] John M. Mackenzie notes that museums contributed to the ways that colonial powers organised new information about the world, turning the unknown into the familiar and creating an archive of knowledge as specimens and objects arrived into collections.[50] Demands for useful information about climate and natural resources rendered the gathering of scientific information a necessary element of the expansion of the British Empire in the nineteenth century. The Admiralty and the Royal Geographic Society (RGS) included the collection of natural and ethnographic materials into their instructions for missions of exploration; the Admiralty's 1849 *Manual for Scientific Enquiry* and the RGS's *Hints to Travellers* served as practical guides to collecting and recording scientific objects and observations.[51]

Natural science in Ireland benefited from this activity through Carte's claim on a portion of the material sent home by missions of exploration and conquest, but also from donations by Irish men serving within them. The history of natural history in Ireland is complicated by the fact that 'Ireland's relationship to the British Empire has been the subject of much confusion and controversy'.[52] Joe Cleary points out that the empire itself was a complex and messy affair, consisting of 'a heterogeneous collection of trade colonies, protectorates, Crown colonies, settlement colonies, administrative colonies, mandates, trade ports, naval bases, dominions, and dependencies'.[53] The number of people needed to control and maintain its power across the globe was substantial, and Irish men took advantage of the prospects for employment offered by the Empire's various services and bureaucracies.[54] By and large, the history of nineteenth-century Ireland has focused on the conditions and effects of the crown's control in Ireland, making the participation of Irish men in the pursuit of empire in other places a problematic detour in 'the mythic march of the nation'.[55] There has been some examination of museums and empire in Ireland, most notably around similar material in the Belfast Museum collected in the early nineteenth century.[56] In Dublin, the significant number of donations that originated from colonial service has added a level of complexity to the museum's history, perhaps shedding some light on its absence from standard historical sources.

Donations to the RDS Natural History Museum from Irish men deployed in the various surveys, missions of exploration, military and civil services were made firmly within the context of empire. Full treatment of the rich and complex relationship between the natural sciences in Ireland and their connections to empire is beyond the scope of this volume, but the donations to the museum begin to illuminate areas of Irish history and science that warrant further exploration. For the donors who sent materials from their postings, the Royal Dublin Society museum, with its highly visible public profile, seemed the logical choice for depositing collections made in the course of their duties. Donations from members of the military and civil services comprised a wide variety of materials, ranging from zoological specimens, to ethnographic materials, to items of historical import. As with other donors, these men held varying ideas about what might be valuable in a collection of natural history. Casual collectors sent things that they thought interesting or unusual, as did their civilian counterparts. Amateurs with an interest in science collected broadly, attempting to create bodies of material representative of natural history in the area where they were posted. Collectors with scientific expertise took advantage of their foreign postings to enlarge the museum's holdings with focused donations in their personal areas of interest or proficiency, or from areas of natural science in which they thought the museum might lack specimens and examples.

Donations were most often scientific in their intent, but the lingering spirit of the curiosity cabinet brought in varied types of objects. Occasionally, tokens or trophies of victory over conquered populations during wars or colonisation were sent by officers associated with the action. The first volume of the *JRDS* lists a donation from 'Col. H. Hope Graham, 59th Regiment (India), lock and key of the Eastern Gate of Canton, taken by the 59th Regiment on 29th December 1857'[.][57] Graham was a commander in the British force sieging the city of Canton during the second of the Opium Wars, inflicting significant damage in a bid to secure the lucrative opium trade for British companies in China, and to expand it despite Chinese opposition.

The battle for Canton was widely covered in the popular press and in military gazettes.[58] Notice of this object in the *JRDS* linked the collections directly to the ethos of imperial military intervention; it was also advertised in the *Freeman's Journal* as being on exhibition during the society's evening scientific meeting on 26 November 1858.[59] Such a display would not have been universally commended; in February 1858 the *Freeman's Journal* had printed a scathing letter from RDS member James Haughton deploring the brutal treatment of the citizens of Canton during the attacks.[60] Military action also brought donations of antiquities and cultural artefacts; in 1866 the *JRDS* listed a donation from Major General Cunynghame of 'a glass lachrymatory, an earthenware lachrymatory, a glass bottle or urn, broken; an earthenware bottle – all taken from the tombs at Kertch, Crimea'.[61] Arthur Augustus Therlow Cunynghame had commanded a force of Turkish soldiers holding the fortress at Kertch during the second year of the Crimean War, and later made this donation while he was a commander in the north of Ireland, assisting in countering Fenian activity in 1869.[62] The removal of cultural material from vanquished populations for display in European museums was a signature component of imperial control in the nineteenth century, making these types of objects directly indicative of the problematic relationship between museum collections and the exercise of power. Though donated as objects of historical importance, they also stood as markers of military triumphalism, ways of exhibiting a nationalistic sense of pride in the dominion over territory and people. The foregrounding of these materials in Carte's register and in public notices complicates the museum's history, and shows that in its heyday it was more than simply a 'dead zoo', and was at least marginally allied to the overt display of imperial power without reference to science.

This extended into the donation of ethnographic materials, as military men with limited scientific experience sent material they thought descriptive of the local populations they encountered during their missions. In 1856 Lieutenant John Hutchinson of the HMS *Herald* donated 'a collection of war implements, dresses, &c &c from Feejee and the Esquimaux', and in 1857 Captain Rochfort Maguire of the Royal Navy sent '3 skulls of Esquimaux, 1 pair of snowshoes and a case of arrows from the Mackenzie River'.[63] From the other side of the world, MD Charles Egan sent 'two skulls, one of a Kaffir, the other a Hottentot', along with bird skins and a snuff box.[64] Donations of ethnographic material, which included human remains, were regularly made to the Natural History Museum into the later nineteenth century. They served to place the understanding of non-Europeans and their cultural practices into the same conceptual territory as the organisation of new species and their habits, and were used as scientific evidence for Victorian concepts of race and for creating hierarchies of value for non-European societies.[65] The bulk of ethnographic material donated to the Natural History Museum was gathered in the course of exploration, survey, mapping or military action, taken as part of an information-gathering exercise that underscores historian Benedict Anderson's assertions that the Victorian reliance on the museum, the map and the census formed pivotal aspects of the ways that colonial powers measured, defined and represented the people and regions they took under their control.[66]

Some of the donations made by non-scientific military men were of scientific value, though they were often accompanied by other types of material. In 1856, Captain Cookman, a member of the RDS attached to the 99th regiment in Beggars Bush barracks, donated 'British fossil shells and specimens of Iron ore from Wexford', while Major C.R. Butler of the 20th regiment sent 'a Russian helm, sword and fuse-box from the Crimean war; a Chinese umbrella; 68 bird skins, [and] a bottle of snakes from Canada' in 1857.[67] From time to time, a member of the services contributed a specimen that became scientifically significant; Lieutenant Edward Trevor Dunne, of the 24th regiment, Royal Hospital sent Carte 'a living specimen of the mud fish (*Lepidosiren annectens*) from McCarthy's Island, Gambia', in 1858.[68] A poorly understood species, its arrival prompted a period of study and the publication of a scientific paper by medical lecturer Robert McDonnell, MD, who had also received one at the same time from a friend in the Royal Navy. Carte and McDonnell undertook joint observations and anatomical studies, which were presented to the society's evening scientific meeting, then published in the *JRDS*.[69]

Irish men with scientific experience found opportunities to pursue their interests through employment in the British Army and Royal Navy. Since 'the armed forces, especially the Royal Navy, played a significant part in British science, and ... naval science was "Big Science"', requiring considerable resources, it is not surprising that men who sought to incorporate their scientific interests into their careers might choose military service in the absence of other professional outlets.[70] Missions of exploration and survey required scientific expertise, and drew scientific men, both amateur and professional, into their ranks to gather specimens and data. Latour has argued that collecting evidence and information in a distant locale for transfer back to a centre of imperial power requires that 'the "things" you gathered and displaced have to be presentable all at once to those you want to convince and who did not go there'.[71] In order to gather and transport bodies of evidence, 'you have to invent objects which have the properties of being *mobile*, but also *immutable, presentable, readable,* and *combinable* with one another'.[72] He terms these objects 'immutable mobiles', objects that do not change, but that can be moved and transferred, then used as reliable representations of a place, its environment and its inhabitants, emphasising that consistency was required so that meanings and interpretations would be stable and uniform.[73] The collection of specimens, and their written descriptions, became part of this overall exercise, operating in concert with other types of evidence like maps, charts, log books and drawings to convey a full and apparently objective assessment of any new place. Irish men of science in the crown services were part of this process as they collected, recorded and reported their observations in the course of fulfilling their duties. They also collected and researched on their own behalf, and their donations to the museum place Ireland within the well-documented relationship between empire and natural history.[74]

Medical professionals in the armed forces were steady and prolific donors to the museum, carrying the tradition of the surgeon-naturalist further afield as the empire expanded. As was the case with their civilian counterparts, they often donated according to specialist interests outside their medical practice. Their scientific training focused their approaches to collection and identification, so that even modest donations tended to be scientifically valuable, adding to the extant body of information in specific fields of investigation. Carte listed an 1861 donation from Dr Lyall of the HMS *Plumper*, consisting of seventeen bird skins and a small collection of insects from the Georgia Straits and Fraser River region of northern Canada.[75] The *Plumper*'s mission was to establish the ocean boundaries between British and United States territories in the northern hemisphere, assigning colonial ownership through mapping the globe. David Lyall was attached as surgeon to the *Plumper*'s surveying mission, but had had a long career in the Royal Navy as a surgeon-naturalist specialising in botany. He had collected in the Antarctic, New Zealand, the Arctic and the Mediterranean.[76] He was therefore well aware of the kinds of material that would be considered scientifically useful, and that would describe the fauna of the area within the official record.

During the Crimean War, Staff Assistant Surgeon William Carte made a focused collection for the Natural History Museum. Carte was already embedded into the scientific networks of Dublin; he was a member of the RDS, was a licentiate of the Royal College of Surgeons in Ireland, and had served as curator of the RCSI museum.[77] His Crimean collection consisted of birds, shells, insects, mammals and fossils.[78] He presented a paper on his collections and experiences to the RDS evening scientific meeting, which was subsequently published.[79] A narrative account filled with descriptions of local botany, zoology and geology, with observations on geography and weather, it was a broadly drawn scientific portrait, creating a context for the materials he donated by relating the ways that the physical conditions of the region had influenced the pursuit of the war. He devoted special attention to the success of the hospital he worked in, attributing its admirable recovery rates to the composition of the stone upon which it was built, which he credited as providing a particularly dry substrate that discouraged disease.[80] He also described the climate, geology and landscape in terms of their advantages and disadvantages to troop movements and deployment, applying the principles of natural history to their ramifications in waging modern warfare.[81]

In his assessment of the region's flora and fauna he focused particularly on a hamster he designated as *Hamster cricetus*. Declaring it as poorly represented in scientific literature and collections, Carte described its anatomy and habits, represented it with illustrations, and sent it to the museum as an uncommon specimen that would perhaps worthy of further study.[82] He also compiled lists of species, their habits and habitats, and provided charts of meteorological observations. The extent to which this collection was bound into the military activities of British forces is hinted at in his description at the start of the list of shells, which 'were collected chiefly in the vicinity of the Green Hills Battery, during leisure moments in the trenches'.[83] Carte's paper and collections placed natural science into the middle of battle, where the geopolitics of the 'balance of power' at issue in the Crimean War were also used as an opportunity to further scientific knowledge. Carte's paper drew parallels between battle and science, stating that 'I may be permitted to say, that could we divest our feelings of the horrors necessarily attending a state of warfare, much unlooked for good has been the result of the late campaign', citing friendships which were 'brought about by a similarity in scientific pursuits', listing other officers with whom he shared information and collections during his appointment.[84] Carte's collections were highlighted in the *Freeman's Journal* during the opening of the Natural History Museum in 1857, the year after the war had ended, still fresh in public memory.

The collections at the Natural History Museum also benefited from materials gathered during voyages of exploration, which were not always military per se, but sought to identify places where advantages might be had for the empire, and were often conducted with the acquisitive spirit characteristic of the nineteenth-century expansionist zeitgeist. The most copious and well-known donations were made by Captain (later Sir) Francis Leopold McClintock, a naval officer from Dundalk, and pioneer of polar exploration techniques. McClintock participated in four Arctic journeys to search for the lost expedition of Sir John Franklin, in 1849, 1851, 1852 and 1857.[85] McClintock's last voyage of 1857–9 found documentary proof that Franklin had perished on 11 June 1847.[86] McClintock was a keen and able naturalist. On each of his polar journeys he kept careful records, diaries and environmental readings, returning with volumes of meticulous measurements. He also recorded information on weather patterns, geographical features, animal life and native peoples, as well as compelling narratives of his crew's experiences on the ice. McClintock was responsible for mapping large sections of the Northwest Territories, previously uncharted by the western powers; during his time in the Arctic, his surveys of the coastline provided the Admiralty with information for detailed maps of the region.[87] His donations of fossils, birds, eggs, mammals and botanical materials added significantly to the scientific knowledge of the fauna in the Arctic regions.

McClintock also served as commodore-in-charge at Jamaica from 1865–68, a period of unrest during which the Jamaican Assembly was dissolved and the island came under direct rule from Great Britain as a crown colony. He continued to send specimens to the museum, accompanied by detailed letters from his posting in Port Royal, describing species that were new to him and including small sketches and measurements.[88] The longevity and regularity of his contributions was perhaps due to the friendship that he and Alexander Carte had developed. An 1866 letter invited Carte to Jamaica to collect fish, where McClintock promised him 'pot luck', joking that 'if a man put himself up to it he would be richly rewarded with an immense variety of the inhabitants of the deep. Who knows but you might hook up a Fenian or two, they seem to have skedaddled out of Ireland. If Stephens has turned merman no doubt you will find some of his followers amongst the coral islets off Port Royal'.[89]

The museum's collections also benefited from donations by Irish men of science working in scientific surveys, particularly ordnance and geological surveys, which were by definition required to gather specimens and information. Mackenzie points out that these surveys were frequently allied to the creation of infrastructures such as roads and railways, particularly in colonial centres, and took advantage of the disruption of the landscape to gather data and specimens.[90] Geologist Thomas Oldham, who had headed the Geological Survey of Great Britain and Ireland, was appointed head of the Geological Survey of India in 1850. Oldham sent modest but valuable donations to the museum as he set about establishing the scientific basis for geological study in India.[91] One of Oldham's staff members, Irish geologist Valentine Ball, was a member of the RDS and a regular contributor to and correspondent within Dublin's natural science community. His father Robert Ball had founded the Dublin University Museum through the donation of his own extensive collection.[92] Valentine Ball was therefore aware of the value of museums and collections in the pursuit of building knowledge, and engaged in the systematic collection of specimens in addition to his survey work, distributing them among various organisations. His strategic donations are alluded to in an 1867 letter to Carte: 'I send you the zoological specimens I have collected during the past season. Last year's collection I sent to Wright [E. Perceval Wright, director of the Dublin University Museum] but the present one consists chiefly of birds' skins for the mounting and exhibition of which I conceive your museum possesses greater advantages than T.C.D.'[93] Ball's letter goes on to say that he'd given the rarest of his collections to the Indian Museum in Calcutta, suggesting to Carte that if 'you really wish to increase the number of your Indian specimens you had best send me whatever you may have and I shall undertake to get you good value in return for them. I have the assurance of Dr Anderson (the curator's assistant) in this matter'.[94] Ball's collections and correspondence are representative of the ways that men of science in colonial posts helped shape the role that collections played in the international exchange of scientific information. They also show a specific example of the exchanges that became commonplace between museums in European cities and those in the colonies, which contributed significantly to the global distribution of scientific information.[95] Ball's donations in particular, distributed among various museums, and his willingness to facilitate exchanges between institutions, indicate his heightened appreciation of the importance of collections, and his desire to distribute the evidence he gathered as widely and fairly as possible. His contributions to the development of Irish museums reached their apogee in 1883, when he was named director of the recently established Dublin Science and Art Museum.[96]

The foreign civil service was also a rich source of donations to the museum. The ambitions of the empire were underpinned by legions of clerks, barristers, judges and other professionals who formed the administrative mechanisms necessary for the functioning of imperial power. As educated middle-class men, a number of them harboured an amateur interest in natural history, and contributed to the museum from their postings around the globe. Among the most prolific was Sir William Jeffcott, second son of a merchant family in Tralee, County Kerry, who was educated in law at Trinity College. Jeffcott began his civil service career in Australia, where in 1843 he was appointed judge of the Supreme Court at Port Phillip.[97] In 1849 he was appointed recorder of Singapore and Malacca, and was knighted in the same year.[98] Jeffcott was responsible for helping reform the court system in the Straits Settlements, and was remembered in his obituary as a devoted public servant who had also contributed to improving education and alleviating poverty in his jurisdiction.[99] At the time of his unexpected death in 1855, he was a regular contributor to the museum's collections and donated materials from across his jurisdiction, which required travelling long distances from Singapore to Penang.[100] Carte's 1855 report on the progress of the museum lists donations from Jeffcott in most of the categories of species in the museum's holdings, including a panther, geckos, snakes, insects, sponges, corals and ethnographic objects.[101] The range of the material indicates that he was attempting to send materials that were broadly descriptive of the range of life on the peninsula where he was pursuing his profession as a judge. Carte expressed his regret at Jeffcott's death, lamenting that 'the natural sciences have lost an enlightened patron, and this Society a zealous and indefatigable friend'.[102]

Civil servants who donated to the museum were usually British or Irish men in foreign postings, but one, William Thomas March, clerk of the crown of Spanish Town, St Catherine, Jamaica, was a native Jamaican, a free man of mixed race (listed as a 'mestee' in local records) who sent significant donations of material to the Dublin museum, to Harvard and to the British Museum. He was also a correspondent of botanist William Hooker, director of Kew Gardens.[103] March's areas of expertise were botany and ornithology, and throughout the 1850s and '60s he sent specimens of Jamaican birds to the Natural History Museum. One of them, a rare petrel that had not yet been scientifically described, prompted Carte to write a paper for the Zoological

Society of London notifying it as a new species, naming it *Pterodroma caribbaea.* Carte's paper quotes liberally from March's correspondence, crediting him for information about the bird and its habits, and the known instances of its sighting or capture.[104] March is listed in the *Proceedings of the Royal Dublin Society* as an honorary member of the society from 1854, an honour granted to those who had made notable contributions to the goals of the society. His contributions and Carte's paper will be examined in more detail in Chapter 6.

The evidence in the primary sources for the Natural History Museum illuminates the ways that the collection and donation of scientific material was threaded through the colonial services, both civil and military. Donation records show that material was received from sources as disparate as men on mail ships in the West Indies, infrastructure engineers in Nova Scotia, commanders in India and legislators in Australia. While the military services promoted 'big science' as a means of gathering data for understanding and controlling territory and people, the men who worked in these services, from commanders to clerks, participated in small acts of scientific collection in a personal capacity. They sent the results of their activities to the museum, underscoring Jean-Marc Drouin and Bernadette Bensaude-Vincent's assertion that 'since the field of investigation extends all over the world, professional naturalists have long been aware that they need the help of well-disposed volunteers to collect rocks and fossils, reports on birds' migrations, and similar phenomena'.[105] The men in military service were particularly well-situated to assist in the process of natural history collection as a means of building knowledge, and their individual acts, pursued across time and geography, aided Carte in building a varied, credible and useful collection.

Scientific donors

The Natural History Museum also benefited from focused donations by men of science, increasing the scientific reputation and focus of the collections. Some were paid scientific professionals, and some were dedicated naturalists employed in other contexts. They included scientific men of international repute, members of the Natural History Committee, and members of other learned societies. All of them collected, studied, wrote, lectured or published. They knew one another, whether personally, professionally or by reputation, and often collaborated to conduct analysis of the collections in order to contribute new information to the growing corpus of scientific knowledge.

Their areas of speciality meant that the museum received scientifically valuable material from expert sources, and could rely on their expertise in making sense of collections. While this group of people formed a network of scientific activity that will be the emphasis of the next two chapters, their individual contributions also form part of the history of donations to the museum, so they are included here to give a sense of how they differ from other donors. Four people will stand in here as representative of the types of scientific donors who contributed material to the collections.

Men of science in the small number of paid positions in Ireland were important to the museum, as they were colleagues and fellow-travellers who collectively defined the scope of natural science in Ireland. Professional scientific educators were central to this process. Chair of geology at TCD and long-time member of the Natural History Committee Rev. Samuel Haughton was ubiquitous in the networks of nineteenth-century science. From within his academic position he pursued a range of interests, comprising geology, mining, palaeontology and animal physiology, and was a promoter of the Irish language.[106] He contributed fossils to the collections, analysed and wrote about donations from others, and corresponded widely with men of science. Haughton was a stalwart of Irish natural history, and his name recurs throughout the archival records. In another educational context, zoologist John Robert Kinahan held a paid position as lecturer for the Science and Art Department in zoology and botany, delivering courses under the Committee of Lectures schema described in Chapter 3.[107] He was also a medical professional and member of the Natural History Committee, and was prominent in networks of natural history, writing extensively on a variety of subjects but maintaining a personal interest in crustacea.[108] He had travelled to Australia and Peru as medical officer on a ship, held offices in several learned societies, and was an active researcher, credited with identifying new species and providing clarification when he thought identification or descriptions of extant species were unclear.[109] He donated focused and scientifically organised collections of crustacea from his travels and from his work in Ireland, some of them new species which he named and described for the scientific record.[110]

Important contributions were also made by men of science who were employed in other professions but were scientific experts in their chosen fields of investigation. Entomologist Edwin Birchall belonged to a Quaker business family in Leeds; he worked first for his family, then in shipping firms in Dublin and Liverpool before returning to Leeds, finally retiring to the Isle of Man.[111] He developed a wide-ranging amateur interest in natural history, but is remembered for his focused work on Irish lepidoptera; he published the first comprehensive catalogue on Irish butterflies and moths in the *Journal of the Natural History Society of Dublin* in 1866, though he had been working on Irish species since the mid-1850s.[112] His work extended previous efforts by the Rev. Joseph Greene, a TCD divinity student who had published a partial list of Irish species in 1854, before relocating to England where he pursued his career as a clergyman and maintained his reputation as a lepidopterist.[113] Despite the surge of interest in natural history generally, Irish moths and butterflies remained relatively unexamined until Birchall took notice of them and began to exhort English entomologists to look to Ireland for new species, and for ones which had seemed to disappear from England. He published several lists in the *Entomologist's Monthly* magazine, asserting that 'owing to the almost entire absence of local collectors, our knowledge of the Lepidoptera of Ireland is still in a very unsatisfactory state … there are about a dozen Irish counties, comprising almost the whole of Ulster, into which even the wandering Lepidopterist has scarcely penetrated'[.][114] In 1857 Birchall made 'a valuable donation to the cabinet of Lepidoptera, including two fine specimens of *Erebia cassiope* lately discovered by him in Ireland', referring to the mountain ringlet, a British butterfly which was extremely rare in Ireland, with only seven examples currently held in collections, two of which are Birchall's donation to the Natural History Museum.[115]

Much of the activity in mid- to late nineteenth-century Irish natural history centred around determining precisely what species were extant in the country, when, where and in what number and frequency. Gathering such a body of information required observation over time within a defined geographical area. Robert Warren, a farmer who was also a dedicated ornithologist and general naturalist, contributed substantially to the knowledge of sea birds and their migratory patterns in Ireland, as well as to the study of Irish birds generally and to the zoology of his local area. Warren leased over 130 acres in Sligo, situated on the estuary of the River Moy on the Sligo/Mayo border with access to the Atlantic.[116] The location of his farm presented him with extensive opportunities for collecting and observing both local sea birds and migrant populations, establishing Irish occurrences of previously unrecorded species. He contributed regularly and often to collections; in addition to the RDS museum, he sent specimens to the Natural History Society and Queen's College Cork, and live birds to the Royal Zoological Society.[117] Warren contributed lists, papers and notes to the *Proceedings of the Natural History Society of Dublin*, the *Proceedings of the Dublin University Zoological & Botanical Association*, and later to the *Zoologist* and *The Irish Naturalist*, but never to the *Journal of the Royal Dublin Society*. He communicated regularly with the Natural History Society of Dublin, of which he was a corresponding member, and his relationship with Carte was possibly due to their shared membership in that society rather than any sense of allegiance to the RDS.

Following the actors

The donors to the Natural History Museum were diverse, but were united in their desire to contribute to an Irish institution that was part of an increasingly confident impulse to establish a clear sense of identity by gathering evidence and displaying it for the public benefit. Collections of local materials served to foster greater understanding of Ireland's physical makeup and natural resources. International collections added the museum to a widely dispersed and fast-developing professional milieu of natural science in Europe. These factors provided the museum and its adherents with the opportunity to position Irish science within an international context while strengthening its networks at home. As pursued through the learned societies, natural history was one of a number of fields that stimulated the creation of a specifically Irish cultural identity, and that were also bound up with wider European ideals. Antiquarianism, for instance, began to record and preserve the monuments, artefacts and texts that today form the foundation of Irish cultural heritage, and which represents Irish identity internationally. Natural philosophy, a field of study that contained a range of nascent disciplines, gave rise to the study of chemistry, which was used to further the understanding of Irish soil and the composition of the land itself. The emerging practice of statistics, then defined as the gathering of economic and social data, attempted to use scientific methods to ameliorate social problems by analysing the causes of famine, poverty and disease. The learned societies that explored these disciplines supported one another through a consistent engagement with emerging ideas and a generalised desire that Ireland should contribute to novel developments alongside its continental and North American counterparts. In this atmosphere, participation in natural science became a cultural activity in itself, perhaps driven by a desire to be involved in the sense of discovery occasioned by new information arriving from across the globe, new inventions that seemed to appear daily, new modes of travel, dress and entertainment that changed the experience of daily life. Rather than being the 'most culturally barren' in modern Irish history, this period was rich in social, scientific and intellectual culture that evinced a sense of modernisation and change.[118]

The abundance of new species arriving into Europe from other parts of the world was an exciting development, revealing the dizzying array of natural forms in ways that had not been possible before. The arrival of new species, displayed at the museum, in the botanic gardens and at the zoo, perhaps encouraged people to look more closely at the natural world immediately surrounding them. A vogue for creating collections of local species saw amateur collectors gathering insects, ferns, shells, leaves, minerals and other widely available materials as a means of participating in science. Alongside material arriving from far-flung places, collections of local material became a desideratum for smaller museums as they strengthened their scientific reputations. Edward Forbes, mid-century zoologist and lecturer, asserted that 'when a naturalist goes from one country into another, his first enquiry is for local collections. He is anxious to see authentic and full cabinets of the productions of the regions he is visiting'.[119] Local materials descriptive of Irish natural history, displayed in an organised and competent fashion, had long been cited in official reports as being desirable in the RDS museum, and Carte's programme of rewarding donors by publishing their names and sometimes displaying their donations helped progress this goal as the century unfolded. Both international and local collections made through donations meant that Irish people became active participants in creating the shape of natural science in the nineteenth century.

Alexander Carte was able to harness the general popularity of natural history in the mid-nineteenth century towards the cause of enriching his museum. By publishing lists of collections and distributing them through the society's *Journal*, which was sent to about 250 learned societies around the world, he was also able to create alliances with similar organisations at home and abroad, creating opportunities for collaboration and exchange.[120] In organising the museum and preparing it for growth into the next phase of its existence, he drew upon prevailing currents in science and popular culture. Natural history was popular and public, but also increasingly scholarly and specialised, and this combination of factors guided Carte's plans for the museum as he sought to create the publicly accessible and scientifically credible museum so long desired by the Natural History Committee and central government.

One of the most important conclusions deriving from examining how people interacted with the museum is that it shows that natural history was a facet of public intellectual culture in Dublin in the mid-nineteenth century. The combined efforts of the Royal Dublin Society, central government, the popular press and the Natural History Committee had created a public profile for the museum that had fixed it in the public consciousness as the place where natural materials belonged. 'Following the actors' through their donations to the museum lets us see that natural science was undertaken at varying levels by a cross-section of the population, and that the Natural History Museum had a distinct and visible public profile, reflecting the ways that science was entwined with wider developments in the Victorian period, variously pursued as leisure, education, data-gathering and political statement as well as a scientific endeavour. During the vagaries and setbacks to the museum's building and funding, Carte continued to collect, exchange, correspond, organise and analyse, creating the best possible collection he could in anticipation of being able to finally display it in a completed building worthy of its status as the national museum.

CHAPTER 5

COLLECTIONS INTO KNOWLEDGE: SCIENTIFIC USES OF THE NATURAL HISTORY MUSEUM

Interconnected: men of science in learned societies

NATURAL HISTORY COLLECTING in the nineteenth century attracted a wide range of people, who in turn filled European museums by donating specimens and materials from all over the world. Collections in themselves, however, are simply aggregations of objects until they are placed within a context that explores how and why they are meaningful or valuable. The staggering number of natural history specimens in nineteenth-century museums needed to be identified, classified, catalogued and organised in order to be understood as scientific information within the unfolding understanding of the structures of life on Earth. While donations provided the raw material of collections, transforming them into scientific knowledge was the purview of a small but interconnected group of people who studied them, turned them into evidence by writing or talking about them and then communicated the information to their peers and the wider public. As the storehouses that held the largest numbers of specimens and employed trained professional staff, natural history museums tended to be at the centre of this process, and Dublin was no exception.

The transformation of natural history collections into organised scientific knowledge was undertaken by people who were connected by their common interests, often forming alliances through their involvement with organisations. Dublin was home to numerous collections other than the Natural History Museum and the Museum of Irish Industry. In addition to its well-known holdings in antiquities and ancient manuscripts, the Royal Irish Academy held collections of bones, fossils and ethnographic material.[1] The Geological Society of Dublin (from 1864 the Royal Geological Society of Ireland) held collections with strong correlations to the core mineral and geological holdings at the RDS.[2] Dublin University (Trinity College) housed the Dublin University Zoological and Botanical Society, which had a museum with a broadly based natural history collection, as well as the geology museum that was opened in 1857 in the same week as the Natural History Museum.[3] The Queen's Colleges and the Royal College of Surgeons in Ireland had collections and museums for teaching and study.[4] The Natural History Society of Dublin formed a museum focused strictly on collections of Irish materials. The Dublin University Society merged with the Natural History Society in 1864, further strengthening its influence.[5] Like the RDS, these societies held meetings where papers were read, published scholarly journals and advertised their collections to a wide range of national and international fellow-travellers.

These organisations were populated by Ireland's men of science, who served as staff in some and as members in others. Most were involved with more than one simultaneously, and many also belonged to high-profile societies outside Ireland, like the prestigious Royal Society or Linnaean Society, or London-based organisations like the Geological Society or Zoological Society, as well as learned societies throughout Europe. Through shared interests and involvement with a number of organisations at the same time, people from different societies and backgrounds formed a strong network of interlocking personal and scientific relationships that shaped the development of both museums and natural science in Ireland. Alexander Carte placed himself at its centre, acting as a conduit for people and information, creating a hub for this growing network within the then most visible and well-established museum in Ireland. The natural history correspondence files in the National Museum of Ireland archives show that throughout the 1860s and into the 1870s Carte used his position as curator to facilitate communication and exchange between men of science who could interpret collections and articulate their importance for a broader audience.[6] While Scouler, perhaps wilfully, had interpreted this task as too much for one man, Carte's actions suggest that he understood the value of a network of like-minded colleagues working together as a body, regardless of attachment to a particular institution or area of study.

The ways that men of science in Ireland might have crossed paths with one another are represented in Table 5.1, which gives a sense of the complex interrelationships in Irish natural science. It shows a representative sampling drawn from a much larger network, and the people chosen for inclusion demonstrate the potential for communication among men of science in Dublin through shared membership in societies. The contents are drawn from membership lists of five Irish learned societies with a focus in natural history, along with fellowship in three important London-based societies: the Royal Society (FRS), the Linnaean Society (FLS) and the Geological Society (FGS). From 1857 to 1870, the names shown here appear repeatedly in the sources for natural science in Ireland, as well as in the records of the museum. These people also represent many of the categories of people who donated to the museum: military men, civil servants, businessmen, medical practitioners, landed gentry and professional men of science. Two of the things that particularly stand out among this group are the number of people in Carte's orbit who were responsible for their own museums and collections, and the number of them who assumed positions of responsibility within one or more organisations.

People dedicated to the promotion of natural science in Ireland formed a kind of super-society among themselves, in some ways independent of the goals and priorities of the organisations they belonged to. They used the resources of their organisations to advance the growth of science in Ireland by acting collectively, and also by pursuing their individual interests through multiple venues. From the exemplars in this table, William Andrews is perhaps one of the best representatives of the interconnectedness of the men of science within Carte's orbit. He was an active member of all five Irish societies, serving as an officer in three of them. He was a long-term member of the Natural History Committee at the RDS and a society stalwart, assuming more responsibility the longer he remained, even travelling to London to testify to a parliamentary committee on the society's behalf.[7] He simultaneously served as president of the Natural History Society, of which he was a founding member, where he chaired meetings and supervised

Member	Royal Dublin Society	Royal Irish Academy	Natural History Society Dublin	Geological Socie of Dublin
Agassiz, Louis		Honorary	Honorary	
Allman, George J.	Natural History Committee	•	Corresponding	
Andrews, William	Natural History Committee	•	President; Vice-President	Vice-President; Co
Baily, William Hellier			•	•
Barker, John, MD	Natural History Committee	•	Council	Council
Carte, Alexander, MD	Director, Natural History Museum	•	Vice-President	Vice-President; C
Du Noyer, George Victor		•	Corresponding	•
Enniskillen, earl of (W.W. Cole)	•	•	Corresponding	President
Frazer, William, MD	Natural History Committee		•	
Good, John	Natural History Committee		•	Council
Griffith, Sir Richard, LL D	Natural History Committee		•	Vice-President; Co
Harvey, William Henry, MD	Natural History Committee	•	President	•
Haughton, Rev. Samuel, MD	Natural History Committee	Committee of Science	President; Vice-President; Council	•
Kinahan, John Robert, MB	Natural History Committee President; Council	•	Hon. Secretary	Council
Larcom, Thomas A., RE	•	•		•
McClintock, Sir Francis Leopold	Honorary		•	Honorary Fellow
McDonnell, Robert, MD	•	Committee of Science	•	
Montgomery, Robert J.	Natural History Committee		Hon. Curator	
Powerscourt, Lord (Mervyn Wingfield)	•		•	
Scott, Robert H.	Mineralogist			Secretary
Talbot de Malahide, Lord (James Talbot)	Vice-President	Vice-President	•	President; Council
Warren, Robert			Corresponding	
Wright, E. Perceval, MD	Natural History Committee	Committee of Science	•	Secretary

Table 5.1 Learned societies as scientific networks in mid-nineteenth-century Ireland

n University gical and nical Association	Profession or Affiliation	FRS	FLS	FGS
sponding	Biologist; Geologist; Curator, Museum of Comparative Zoology, Harvard	•	•	•
	Former lecturer RDS & TCD; Regius Professor & Keeper of Natural History, University of Edinburgh			
	Naturalist; Former head of the Irish Fisheries Company			
gical Committee	Geologist; Curator of fossils, Geological Survey of Ireland		•	•
gical Committee	Lecturer Science & Art Dept; Curator, Museum of the Royal College of Surgeons in Ireland			
President, gical Committee	Licentiate of the Royal College of Surgeons; Director, RDS Natural History Museum		•	
	Artist & Geologist, Ordnance & Geological Surveys			
esponding	Landed gentry; Private museum at Florence Court; Dealer in fossil fish	•		
	Licentiate Royal College of Surgeons in Ireland; Zoologist; Botanist			
	Owner of fishing fleet			
	Geologist; Civil engineer; Commissioner of general survey & valuation			•
	Professor of Botany, TCD and RDS; Curator of Botanical Museum, TCD	•	•	
-President; gical Committee	Professor of Geology, TCD; Curator of Geology Museum	•		
ncil; Zoological mittee	Zoologist; Botanist; Lecturer, Science & Art Dept		•	
	Engineer; Chief Undersecretary for Ireland	•		
	Royal Navy commander; Arctic explorer; Naturalist; Cartographer			
ogical Committee	Civil surgeon Crimean War; Anatomy lecturer; Medical supervisor Mountjoy Prison	•		
	Secretary, Royal Zoological Society Dublin			
	Landed gentry; 7th Viscount Powerscourt			
	RDS Professor of Mineralogy; Meteorologist Met Office, London			
	Landed gentry; Antiquarian; Geologist	•		
esponding	Farmer; Naturalist; Expert on Irish birds			
. Secretary	Curator, Dublin University Museum, Professor of Zoology, TCD		•	

the delivery and publication of scientific papers.[8] In each of these positions, he was involved with collections and museums, and in working with people across the social spectrum of natural science in Ireland. He chaired meetings, donated to collections, authored scientific papers and was an expert on salmon, who wrote some of the first scientific papers on fisheries in Ireland.[9] He delivered scientific talks and published in the journals of the RDS, the Royal Irish Academy and the Natural History Society, as well as being cited in newspapers for his work on salmon populations.[10] Andrews appears repeatedly in minutes, reports of meetings, scientific papers and in the press, showing that he was part of an extensive network that relied on both scientific and social ties to build a body of information about the natural history of Ireland. Most importantly, he marshalled all these elements into building a body of scientific information around the life cycles of fish in Irish waters, intending to contribute to sound policies for the husbandry and economic viability of Irish fisheries.[11] He is also an excellent example of a dedicated man of science whose efforts contributed to the general progress of natural history in Ireland both in his studies and through his administrative and collegial expertise, but who did not generate a ground-breaking discovery or technique, and has thus been largely forgotten in the history of science in Ireland.

Many of the men on this list were scientific professionals in the modern sense; they engaged in collecting, teaching, researching, writing and curating collections as paid professional activities. Samuel Haughton, William H. Harvey and E. Perceval Wright all had teaching and curatorial responsibilities within Trinity College at the same time as they were members of all the other Irish societies. Harvey had been appointed keeper of the herbarium in 1844, and was named as professor of botany at Trinity in 1856; he had previously taught botany at the RDS.[12] He lectured for the Science and Art Department, and wrote volumes of both popular and professional science.[13] He was a lithographer who made his own images for illustrating his books, at the rate of one per week from 1856.[14] He was a lifelong friend of celebrated botanist William Jackson Hooker, and in 1866 died of tuberculosis at Hooker's house at Torquay, on the Devon coast.[15] Wright, Trinity's professor of zoology from 1858 to 1869, succeeded Harvey as professor of botany and curator of the herbarium, and was also curator of the Dublin University Museum.[16] He had been an original member of the Dublin Microscopical Society, which held meetings in his rooms at TCD, but was later subsumed into the Natural

History Society of Dublin.[17] Haughton, a polymath who became chair of geology at Trinity in 1851, was also curator of the geological collections during 1856–7 when the new geological museum was being built.[18] Haughton published throughout the journals of the learned societies on a number of topics, served on committees and was a ubiquitous presence in the networks of scientific activity in Dublin. All three of these people had served on the RDS Natural History Committee, as well as holding positions within the other societies.

Carte's career presents perhaps the strongest example that networks of people constructed natural science in nineteenth-century Ireland. Prior to arriving at the RDS museum, he had studied at the Royal College of Surgeons in Ireland and Trinity College. He had curated the RCSI museum, where his predecessor was John Hart, and his successors were William Carte and John Barker; all three were influential at the RDS and active in both medicine and natural history.[19] He was a member of a number of societies both national and international, and maintained contact with a range of people across the spectrum of natural science. His work at the RDS appears to have been characterised by a willingness to value scientific contributions from people with varying levels of expertise. His donations programme certainly suggested this, but his wide membership and activity within other societies, his correspondence and the records of his interactions with other museums suggest a man who used his position for the benefit of the field as a whole. He appears to have been generous with his time and expertise, and was ubiquitous in his presence in the networks of natural science in Ireland. The rest of this chapter, and the next, will look at Carte and some of his colleagues, showing that they extended the significance of the museum beyond the confines of buildings and cases of specimens, into networks of people who worked together across institutions and geographical boundaries towards common goals.

Carte as a conduit for information and exchange

From the mid-century forward, natural history museums were dependent upon their curators as the authorities around whom their purposes were aligned. Equally, the institutional weight of the museum's reputation provided curators with a unique status due to the position they occupied. The museum and the curator became a dual configuration, each reinforcing the other, and while 'specimens lent status to collections, what was particularly crucial was the relationship between curatorial authority and the collections'.[20] Natural history museum curators combined personal relationships, professional contacts, scientific knowledge, publication, exhibition and the interpretation of collections as part of their positions.[21] Carte's curatorship spanned the wider context of the mid-century shifts in scientific culture, a time when the ethos of professionalism was becoming the norm, and curators were tasked with creating scientific meaning within their collections, rather than simply listing and displaying their contents. Curators became professionals specifically suited to and chosen for the role, rather than assigned the care of a museum as a supplementary duty, as had been the case with Giesecke and Scouler. Alberti notes that the museum was distinguished from other, similar sites by 'a combination of credibility, authority, and expertise' and that the museum as a site put the curator's work into an authoritative context.[22] He observes that:

> [T]he authority of the museum did not stem solely from personal expertise, but relied also on the credibility afforded to individuals in a particular venue, which depended on a distinct relationship between person, place, and thing. Credibility, then, was built on trust, character, and patronage within particular localities and spaces. Curators spoke with authority because of where they worked.[23]

Carte's training in medicine and comparative anatomy, his previous curatorship of the Royal College of Surgeons museum, his record of publications and talks and his involvement with scientific organisations all granted him the status of an authoritative man of science, allowing him to become the hub around which the activity of the Natural History Museum revolved. That the RDS enjoyed significant support from central government, especially for its museums and educational efforts, underpinned the authority of Carte's position. The museum's correspondence files show that he was considered a valuable source of information and expertise, and his value to other scientific bodies is represented by the records of his talks and publications. He spoke at the British Association, the Royal Geological Society of Ireland and the Natural History Society of Dublin, and had papers read at the prestigious Royal Society and the Zoological Society of London. He authored several pieces of research establishing or confirming new species, and was an expert on the giant Irish deer.[24] Despite his contributions, he has been poorly recorded in the history of Irish science. Though the biographical information around Carte is somewhat spare, his scientific output and the traces of his activities suggest that he was trusted and esteemed due to his position, but also due to his inclination towards cooperative and collegial relationships.

Correspondence and the museum

Carte's influence can be discerned by looking at the correspondence addressed to him in the museum's archives. The letters reflect his position of authority, and at the same time demonstrate the ways that social and professional positions were navigated in networks of natural history as people from varying backgrounds and levels of expertise communicated with one another. It is important to note here that it is unclear whether the letters in the museum's archives are the complete record of Carte's correspondence. In the nineteenth century, official materials such as minute books and letters addressed to the society were conserved as permanent records, but correspondence between individuals often was not. This was not uncommon in the period; Comerford notes that in 1868 the long-serving undersecretary for Ireland Thomas Larcom 'took his own papers with him on leaving office, as was then still the general custom'.[25] That Larcom's papers now rest in the National Library of Ireland is not because their preservation was official policy. The records of the Natural History Museum seem to have been subject to similar conditions, and it is possible that some of Carte's letters were kept at his home, and have since been lost.

As with casual donations, a number of the letters addressed to Carte were single communications from people seeking information, making donations or offering collections for sale, their regularity suggesting that the general public saw the museum as the place where such requests were to be directed. Andrew Morgan, the lighthouse keeper at Carlingford, addressed Carte in correspondence simply as 'Sir', and wrote to inform him 'that I have a very rare bird it is a white crow that I got stuffed, and I wish to know if it would be purchased in the museum'.[26] In contrast, J. Reed, obviously an acquaintance, informed 'My dear Carte' that he was sending a dove from Wexford to the museum by Wicklow rail, 'one such as I never have seen here before. As it may be rare I have shot it for you'.[27] George Freeman of Enniscorthy wrote to seek information on a fossil deer that had been found in his locale, in preparation for a paper he was writing for a local scientific publication.[28] Commander Richard Mayne of the HMS *Eclipse* conveyed that 'I was in the H.M.S. Plumper during her last commission when she was supplied by you with various stores for nat. hist. purposes', requesting that Carte provide him with more supplies for his new commission, so that, should the opportunity arise, he might continue to collect for the museum.[29] Carte was approached by friends, acquaintances and strangers for a wide variety of purposes, and was regularly called upon to provide information, access and to act as an intermediary.

Anne Secord has examined the role of social position in scientific correspondence, noting that exchanges between scientific correspondents 'had to satisfy the same criteria as other aspects of scientific practice', and that differences in social position were navigated through the development of 'an almost formulaic mode of correspondence, which served to establish the trustworthiness of a writer proposing an exchange of specimens, books or ideas'.[30] People who wrote to Carte seeking his assistance as a scientific contact and acknowledged expert, but who were unknown to him, took a number of approaches to establish themselves as reliable scientific correspondents. In 1859, Adam White introduced himself:

> I dare say my name is unknown to you, I have been for 23 years an assistant in the Zoological Department of the British Museum, and must be known to some of your friends, if Mr. Haliday, or Professor Jukes, or Dr. Kinahan, or the late Wm. Thompson of Belfast, or Mr. Baily be in that list.[31]

White used the formulaic strategy of establishing his own institutional credentials, and then invoking common contacts as a means of initiating correspondence in the absence of a formal introduction, or recommendation from a mutually trusted contact. In rare letters from a woman, Susanna King of Suffolk addressed Carte as 'respected friend', writing four times about two collections of shells she had arranged and labelled, wishing to sell them to the museum using her friend Thomas Chandlee of Waterford as intermediary, invoking a local contact as assurance of her capability.[32] Requests for all types of information from strangers were a regular feature of Carte's work, exemplified by a letter from Howard Saunders of Surrey, who wrote that his friend A.W. Crichton suggested that Carte might be able to provide 'information respecting the present breeding-haunts of the Golden and Sea Eagles', as he would be visiting Ireland and wished to collect eggs, previously having had to pay handsomely for the ones already in his collection.[33]

Regular correspondents and donors, especially those who were also members of learned societies, phrased their letters in a manner that suggests the familiarity of ongoing contact. They adopt the tone of exchanges among equals, addressing 'Dear Carte' or 'Dear Dr Carte'. Frederick Foot of the Geological Survey went straight to the point in one letter, which begins 'Dear Dr Carte, Do you care about worms?'[34] Others were alerting Carte to the arrival of donations, such as Robert Warren's dispatch that he had sent an Iceland gull from Castlebar; the shipment also included a green sandpiper for the Natural History Society collection, which he asked Carte to send on to taxidermist Richard Williams.[35] The circle of his communication was closed when the *Proceedings of the Natural History Society of Dublin* recorded that R.P. Williams announced the donation of a green sandpiper from Warren.[36] That Warren felt free to ask favours of Carte indicates that their contact was mutually beneficial, and Warren's letters were friendly, sharing personal news as well as observations about nature from his farm, suggesting social ties as well as common scientific interest. Letters from men of science within Carte's circle were likely to contain similar requests for favours or information. The repetition or frequency of such interactions within the group of people around Carte again underscores that the model of 'great thinker/great deeds' in the history of science does not describe the ways that natural history progressed in Ireland. Rather, a constant flow of small acts between people of modest scientific status steadily built up knowledge over time, and these relationships sometimes migrated into the international context as Irish men of science dispersed into positions around the globe.

For instance, an 1867 letter from F.W. Hutton from New Zealand thanked Carte for having sent him scientific papers; his writing suggests that he had recently relocated there, and was feeling isolated from the latest information. Hutton's letter mentioned David Moore, curator of the RDS botanic gardens, for whom he was collecting specimens, as well as Robert Scott and E. Perceval Wright, all mutual friends or acquaintances. Hutton made the intriguing comment that he was 'glad that the liberals had got a victory in the Nat. Hist. Society – things will go better now, I hope'.[37] Moore had been elected as president in 1866, replacing Rev. Samuel Haughton of Trinity College, and in 1867 businessman Robert Callwell succeeded Moore as president.[38]

Outside official records of society proceedings and scientific papers, it can be difficult to discern how new ideas in science, such as Darwin's theories, affected relationships between scientific fellow-travellers, but tensions may be glimpsed in correspondence between friends. Haughton had been among the first men of science to publicly criticise Darwin after publication of *On the Origin of Species* in November 1859, and his biblical reading of natural history as an expression of the divine mind was at odds with others in Dublin's scientific networks, such as zoologist Wright and geologist Joseph Beete-Jukes, supporters of Darwin.[39] Dublin's men of science took views somewhere along the spectrum from theistic interpretation to scientific materialism, which they expressed in letters and conversation. Alexander Melville, professor of natural history at Queen's University Galway, had made cautionary comments about Darwin after the presentation of an 1859 joint paper by Carte and surgeon Robert McDonnell on the *Lepidosiren annectens*, in which they sought to determine whether the animal was a fish or an amphibian. During an ensuing discussion, Melville declared that the *Lepidosiren* was an 'antidote to the doctrines coming into fashion regarding transitional forms' and that it mitigated against the adoption of Darwin's theories.[40] RDS mineralogist J. Emerson Reynolds, in a letter to Carte while he and William Andrews were on society business in London, wrote that 'I hope Darwin doesn't catch hold of you and make you a convert to his theories'.[41] Hutton, however, was a supporter of Darwin's who went on, later in his career, to become the curator of the Otago and Canterbury museums in New Zealand.[42] The offhand comments in these sources show that conflict around new scientific ideas can be seen in the margins of communications between friends in the networks of science, allowing us to glimpse the reception of new ideas in Ireland as it happened.

Former RDS mineralogist Robert Scott provides another example of letters affording a view into scientific debate. Scott had relocated to London in 1867 to serve as head of the Meteorological Office, and he maintained a correspondence with Carte that signals a close friendship.[43] He described a meeting of the London Geological Society where a paper on fossil bears was presented, after which there was a discussion on anatomy. It was a subject Carte had written on, based on collections of cave fossils in the Natural History Museum. Scott related the proceedings:

> I was last night at the Geol Soc, where Busk read a paper on bears, especially their teeth. He said casually that one of the Leeds skulls was *U Poniscus* ... Then Dawkins got up and said that there were some bones in Dublin said to be *Mariticus* which were *Opeldus.* I got up and asked him to state the grounds of his disputing your determination, and gave him a bit of my mind. ... If I were you I would take up the cudgels and knock Dawkins down, he is only an Englishman. I also told Busk that I was sure that the Leeds skulls were really Irish as Glennon had had them. I hope you approve of my having stuck up for you.[44]

George Busk was a well-known and highly regarded zoologist, and a fixture in the networks of London science.[45] Scott used his local knowledge of Irish scientific exchanges to assert that the specimen Busk was exhibiting originated from taxidermist Richard Glennon's shop in Dublin, and therefore had likely been discovered in Ireland, and to defend Carte's determinations based on his publications on prehistoric megafauna, one proposing that polar bears had once ranged in Ireland.[46] Though most letters are not as entertaining as Scott's, the body of correspondence addressed to Carte contains names, dates and connections that illuminate the relationships through which scientific information was slowly built and solidified, and the ways that debate and discourse shaped the classification of newly discovered species, assembling the map of their distribution around the globe.

Carte's letters also show how specimens and information moved through the networks of natural science in the learned societies. Donation records show what came in to the museum, from whom and when, but letters indicate how donors within the scientific networks went about communicating ideas and evidence among themselves. Historian R.V. Comerford has declared that the Victorian network of 'railways multiplied traffic not only in persons and goods but in what are often rather grandly referred to as "ideas" – the bulk of its communication of a pedestrian type and not at all calculated to turn the world upside down'.[47] While the volumes of material moved by rail, including correspondence, may have been largely mundane, the rail system was essential to swift exchanges between scientific specialists. The relatively new innovation of the penny post in the 1840s, making letters affordable, was also vital in these efforts. The ability to ship a specimen, accompanied by notes, to a fellow man of science and receive a reply in short order facilitated the rapid development of new scientific knowledge. For instance, the fossil bear skulls that had migrated from Dublin to London, or the rare dove that arrived in Dublin on the train, had the potential to generate new scientific information. The latest information on the naming and classification of species, or developments in geology, could be distributed quickly and accurately as transportation and technology facilitated the spread of ideas.

For Carte's close contacts, speedy correspondence was a way to work out specific information or test ideas on a respected colleague. Andrew Leith Adams, an army surgeon and naturalist who later became a professor of natural history at TCD and Queen's College Cork, wrote to Carte from India, Malta, Canada and Dublin.[48] His letters are filled with information and debates on scientific identifications and discussion around the establishment of species, as well as friendly chat about mutual connections.[49] When stationed in Malta in the early 1860s, he identified and described a new fossil rodent, a giant Pleistocene dormouse. An 1862 letter to Carte discussed the find, thanking him for sending drawings of another species for comparison, and discussing the references he was consulting in preparation for establishing a new species.[50] Leith's find became accepted as *Leithia melitensis* and a variant of the species from Sicily was established as *Leithia cartei*, recording their mutual effort. An undated letter about proofs of a paper to which they were both making corrections says 'I know how hard you are worked – it is pleasant labour unless too hard'.[51] A number of the letters from his peers and fellow men of science note Carte's workload, and the sheer number of requests made of him in the correspondence files, in addition to his regular duties at the museum, indicate that he was kept busy indeed.

Carte's correspondence also shows his own active participation in the networks of natural history in London, illuminating his role as a participant in building scientific knowledge in addition to being a conduit for others. He exchanged letters with experts at the British Museum, including Richard Owen, head of the natural history department, and George Waterhouse of the geological department. A series of letters exchanged with Philip Sclater at the Zoological Society of London and well-known ornithological illustrator William Gould resulted in the identification of a new species of bird.[52] William Flower of the Royal College of Surgeons, England, helped Carte arrange the manuscript and illustrations for the reading and publication of a paper at the prestigious Royal Society, an anatomical description of a piked whale (now known as the lesser fin) that had become tangled in a fisherman's net north of Dublin, and then transported to the museum where Carte and anatomist Alexander Macalister conducted and recorded its dissection.[53] Flower read the paper at a meeting of the Royal Society on Carte's behalf, and the accompanying illustrations were made by William Baily of the Geological Survey. Carte and his Irish colleagues used instances like these to highlight the work being done on natural history in Ireland, inserting it into the regional and global networks that converged in London, an important centre for natural science.

Specimen dealers

Carte also maintained a series of relationships with dealers in natural history materials, who were often skilled naturalists in their own right. They were an important resource, motivated to find what might be of use to a museum, and they frequently sent lists of their offerings, and sometimes a box of specimens for examination, usually including instructions about where to send it next and how to submit payment for anything retained.[54] Reliable specimen dealers developed a systematic approach to keeping clients abreast of their offerings, and consequently were favoured with long-term relationships that could be lucrative. Parisian dealer Maison Verreaux sent lists of its current offerings for Carte's information; Carte's register of purchases records two substantial acquisitions of birds, fish and glass eyes from Verreaux in 1867, though correspondence suggests that their association continued beyond those instances.[55]

Dealers were sometimes used as intersections in the networks of natural history; for example, their premises were used as common points for the shipping and collection of specimens between geographically distant collectors, or as meeting places. The first meeting of the Natural History Society, in 1838, had been held in Glennon's Suffolk Street premises.[56] Robert Warren wrote to Carte in 1867 that he had sent a red-throated diver to Dublin, and that 'you will have to send to Glennon's … for it, as I sent it in the same box along with another for Dr Harvey'.[57] In addition, the offerings of a dealer could become common knowledge within the natural history network, especially if the specimens were unusual or of high quality. When Scott stood up to defend Carte at the meeting of the Geological Society, he felt certain in asserting that the bear skulls being examined were Irish in origin, 'as Glennon had had them'.[58]

Carte's register of purchases shows that he maintained contact with a number of dealers, and he also purchased from men of science within his network. He dealt with the Williams Brothers of Dame Street, whose shop next to Dublin Castle later became Dublin's premier taxidermy establishment.[59] Bryce Wright, a London dealer of minerals, geology and shells, corresponded regularly with Carte, and his name also appears in William Andrews' letters.[60] James Marder, fossil dealer from Lyme Regis, was also a regular source. The correspondence files contain fourteen letters from him, and there is a file of purchases made from him in the general records.[61] Carte also purchased from people within his immediate network; William Baily, Robert Scott and William Andrews also appear in the register of purchases.[62] William Willoughby Cole, the earl of Enniskillen, was an expert in fossil fish, who had his own museum and regularly bought and sold marine fossils. He was a prolific correspondent who offered material for sale, but also made numerous requests for favours and information. After the death of a well-known naturalist, for instance, Enniskillen asked Carte to 'find out whether the auction of Admiral Jones's effects has taken place' as he wanted to purchase the late admiral's lapidary polishing wheel.[63] He also requested that Carte find the purchaser if it had already been sold, and try to buy it back, ending his letter with 'I am afraid you will think me very troublesome in thus commissioning you'.[64] However, letters record that Enniskillen returned favours. When Richard Owen of the British Museum was visiting him, he wrote to Carte to say that he had 'little doubt that as [Owen] returns he will pay you a visit'.[65] As a dealer in natural materials, Enniskillen understood his role in the circuit of exchange, sharing his important visitors, passing on information and making occasional donations to the collections.

One of most intriguing dealers in Carte's network was a man named William Hinchy from Limerick. Little is known about Hinchy; his letters indicate that he was not well educated, and they describe straitened personal circumstances.[66] He came into the orbit of Dublin naturalists because he had a talent for finding high-quality fossils of the giant Irish deer, *Cervus megaceros*. Skulls with antlers and full fossil skeletons of giant Irish deer were sought after by museums and private collectors, as the size of the animal and the spread of its antlers make a dramatic centrepiece. The letters between Carte and Hinchy, about thirty-three of them, extended from 1862–69. Hinchy also figured in the correspondence of others; Carte had recommended him to Lord Powerscourt, who wrote in 1864 that 'Hinchy has been here, and I have given him £5 on account … I am so much obliged to you for your letter about the skeleton, I will have it set up some day when you are here and we will arrange where it is to go'.[67] A later letter asks Carte to convey to Hinchy a cheque of £50 for the balance of the skeleton's cost.

Powerscourt's skeleton was likely to have been the subject of an earlier exchange between Hinchy and Carte. A letter from Hinchy detailed his plans to repair a specimen in which Carte was interested, saying that 'I wish to show you in a more plainer manner that I can make all the breaks very strong and I would presume to say it would be very near what you want', including a drawing of the skull and antlers to show his plan[68] (Fig. 5.1). Hinchy's

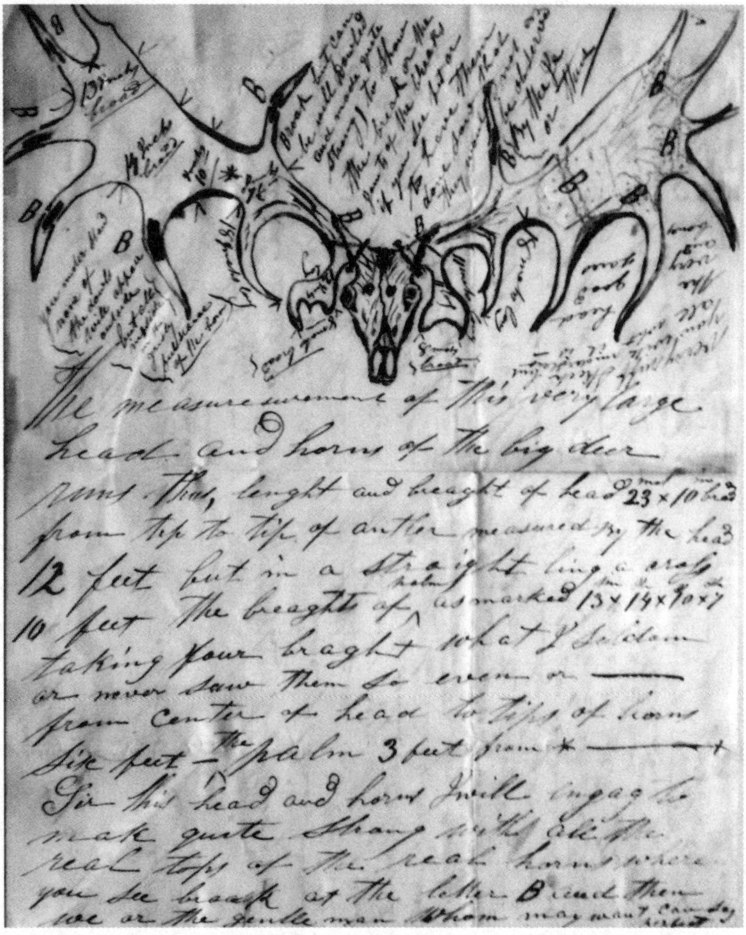
The measurement of this very large
head and horns of the big deer
runs thus, lenght and height of head 23 x 10
from tip to tip of antler measured by the head
12 feet but in a straight line a cross
10 feet The heights of palms as marked 13 x 14 x 10 x 7
taking your height what I seldom
or never saw them so even or —
from center of head to tips of horns
six feet — the palm 3 feet from * —— +
Sir this head and horns I will engage to
make quite strong with all the
real tops of the real horns where
you see breaks at the letter B and then
we or the gentle man whom may want

Fig. 5.1 Letter to Carte from William Hinchy, showing the way that he planned to repair the skull and antlers of a giant fossil deer for potential sale to a wealthy patron. COURTESY OF THE NATIONAL MUSEUM OF IRELAND, NATURAL HISTORY

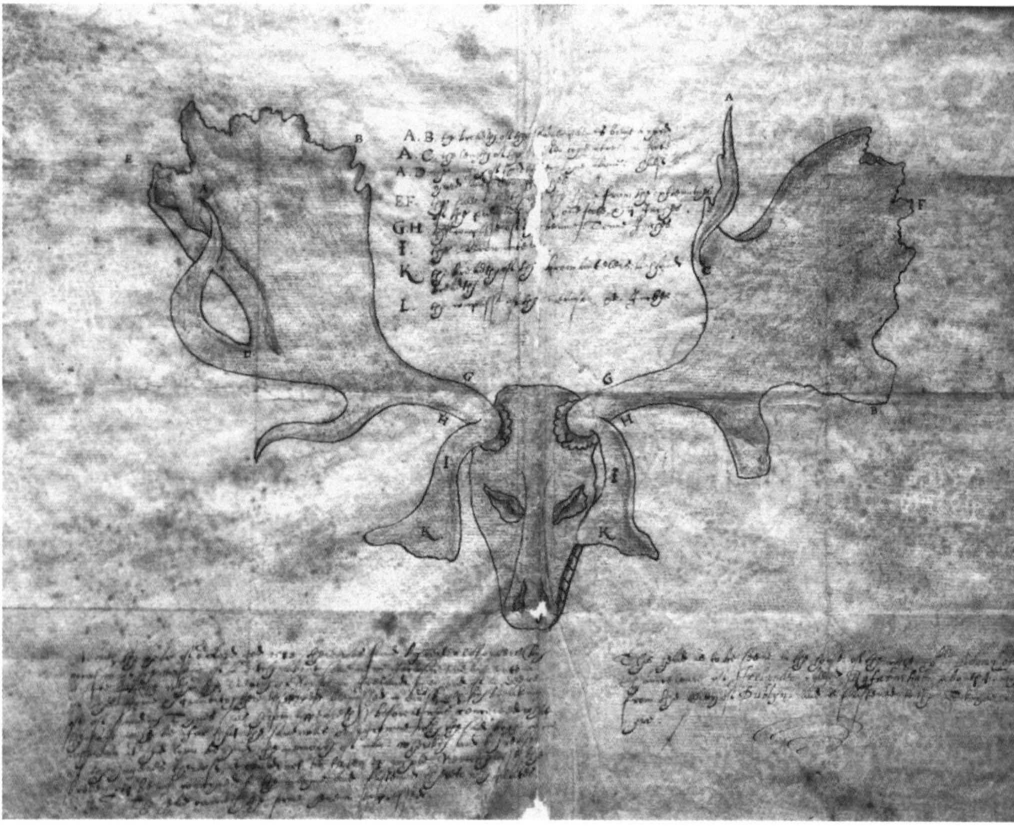

Fig. 5.2 Drawing by Thomas Loftus of the first recorded find of a giant Irish deer in 1588. COURTESY OF THE NATIONAL MUSEUM OF IRELAND, NATURAL HISTORY, NOW HELD IN THE NATIONAL GALLERY OF IRELAND

drawing is schematic, but takes its form from a set of visual conventions for depicting the species which had already been established. In 1588, Adam Loftus, judge-martial (later viscount) and archdeacon of Glendalough, had made the first known drawing of the Irish 'elk' based on an example sent to him from England.[69] (Fig. 5.2). An account of the first example found in Ireland was published by Thomas Molyneaux in 1695, with accompanying images showing the structures of the animal's skull and antlers[70] Hinchy's drawing follows the same conventions, suggesting that this form of schematic drawing had become a conventional means for depicting this species, and showing that Hinchy was familiar with it, perhaps due to his contact with Carte. Hinchy's letter continues, 'sir I would be very oblight [sic] to you if you will let me know about the skeleton or who is the gentleman' and offered alternative specimens as well.[71] He concludes with 'sir in hopes that the paper you gave about the bear bones will be a very good help to sell all'.[72] Carte's paper on bones of cave bear found at Lough Gur, County Limerick in 1864 had cited Hinchy as 'the chief agent in procuring the bones'.[73] In a later paper on *Cervus megaceros* bones, Carte again named Hinchy as the source of his specimens.[74]

Carte's relationship with Hinchy demonstrates a circuit of exchange across social groupings, from the landed gentry to a working-class fossil dealer, a type of interaction in which Carte commonly acted as intermediary. Carte's long-term association with Hinchy extended to an interest in the dealer's welfare and circumstances, leading him to recommend Hinchy to others. It is possible to speculate that their common connection to Limerick meant that they had known one another for some time, though it has not been possible to confirm. Letters to the British Museum from both Carte and Baily offered *Cervus megaceros* skeletons to George Waterhouse, Carte's from 'a person in the country' and Baily's from 'a person in Limerick'.[75] The quality of Hinchy's specimens allowed them to be confident in offering desirable items for the British Museum collections, bolstering their own reputations for reliability while at the same time strengthening their relationship with an important source of materials.

Circuits of exchange among museums of natural history

Museum curators and professionals relied upon one another for information, support and to fill gaps in collections through exchanges of various types of material. The combined records of donation, membership and correspondence show that Carte had regular interaction and exchange with a variety of other museums, both benefiting from their largesse and being generous in his turn. Carte actively sought to create a museum that would take its place among its peers in Europe, and he measured its progress against them. That he was sent on several trips to gather information about how other museums in Great Britain and on the continent were structured indicates that the council and the Natural History Committee at the Royal Dublin Society understood that museums were evolving entities.[76] Some museums made donations to the RDS, such as the East India Company's museum, which had donated several small but significant collections of birds and mammals.[77] The Royal Zoological Society in Dublin was a regular contributor to the RDS museum, and Carte seems to have enjoyed warm relations with its secretary Robert J. Montgomery, as indicated by a letter from him about donations he was sending, and a draft reply from Carte urging him to come to the museum so that they could go over the catalogue of the zoo's birds and be sure it was correct.[78]

The common practice of exchanging specimens and materials between museums was an economical way of growing collections by culling duplicate specimens and trading them for ones that were lacking. Exchanges might also be undertaken as a means of completion or repair, such as completing a skeleton by requesting spare bones. Exchanges served to maintain a web of international contacts among museums. The museums with which Carte undertook exchanges were varied; the Whitby Museum, for instance, was a small, local organisation in Yorkshire, run primarily by its curator Martin Simpson.[79] Likewise, the Bath Royal Literary and Scientific Institution was curated by geologist Charles Moore, founded from his personal collection. He wrote to Carte seeking an exchange, but noted that 'the cost of my museum is borne by myself and I cannot afford to send much'.[80] The Australian Museum in Sydney requested an exchange of duplicates in 1856.[81] Carte proved himself generous in aiding the cause of smaller museums with fewer resources than his own, routinely fulfilling these requests to the extent that he was able, and not always with the expectation of an equivalent return. Larger museums also provided occasions for exchanges of material. Several letters between Carte and George Waterhouse of the British Museum show an exchange of casts taken from fossil specimens. Carte had a cast of a fossil bear's skull made for Waterhouse, sending it in April 1864. Waterhouse had agreed to send him a cast of a fossil fish in return, and Carte asked 'is it too much to ask you to have the cast of *H. nobilissimus* coloured? It would add considerably to the appearance of the specimen'.[82] An 1870 letter from Waterhouse to Carte informs him that 'at last I have received the cast of the *Holoptychius nobilissimus* ... it will be sent off this evening, if possible', indicating that while exchanges may have been economical in building collections, they were not always timely.[83]

The sequence of events which initiated an exchange can sometimes be traced through correspondence, thereby showing the operation of a network in action. In July 1869, Scott wrote from London to say that:

> I met one Dr Kaup of Darmstadt with Enniskillen on Thursday. This is your friend to whom you wrote the magnificent ... letter and afterwards

> fell out with him about the price. Suffice it to say that he told me before ladies that he wanted the rump of a *megaceros*, all of it except the head. ... Can you make him out a skeleton, minus the head which he already has. He goes to Florence Court [Enniskillen's home] and probably returns through Dublin. I charged him to see you[.][84]

In his customary light-hearted tone, Scott let Carte know that Kaup had committed a social faux pas by requesting the nether parts of a fossil deer in mixed company. Nonetheless, the exchange was initiated. In August 1869 Kaup, curator of the Ducal Museum of Darmstadt, wrote to Carte to say that Enniskillen had presented a set of *Cervus megaceros* bones to his museum, and that many were duplicates. Therefore, he needed a number of additional bones to complete a full skeleton. He proposed an exchange, saying that 'you shall have from our museum nearly all the bones of *Dinornis casuarinis*', an extinct moa from New Zealand, as well as other specimens, in return.[85] He included a sketch with measurements to show what precisely he needed, as his command of English was incomplete (Fig. 5.3). Carte's register of purchases shows that he bought the requested bones from William Hinchy in order to exchange them with Kaup.[86] Kaup wrote to Carte three more times, regarding the sending of the bones and other specimens he included, mostly butterflies from Guatemala sent by one of Kaup's regular contributors there.[87]

This particular exchange involved two of Carte's regular network, Enniskillen and Scott, who met by chance in London, where one of them happened to be entertaining someone with whom Carte had previously communicated. The meeting prompted renewed contact between curators Kaup and Carte, and an exchange of material between museums in Ireland and Germany. As a result, materials were exchanged which came from Ireland, New Zealand and Guatemala. The purchased fossil bones came from Hinchy, another of Carte's regular contacts. In exhorting scholars to follow the actors, Latour makes it clear that tracing such networks is a slow process that can be frustrating.[88] He argues, however, that the method of looking at the banal interactions of actors' normal worlds allows for understanding a terrain that cannot be achieved through imposing predetermined frameworks on a body

Following spread: Fig. 5.3 Letter to Carte from curator Johann Jacob Kaup of the Darmstadt Museum, seeking skeleton pieces to complete a fossil deer skeleton, and offering valuable specimens in return. COURTESY OF THE NATIONAL MUSEUM OF IRELAND, NATURAL HISTORY

Is this specimen seted up I send you one of this; our old one or the new one.
It would be toorisKant to send the whole upseted skeleton, therefore I send it in parts with the iron frame, so that one of yours conservators can arrange the whole skeleton in fewhours. You shall have it stil before the end of this year.
I expect in few weeks a new collection from New Zealand with bones of Dinornidae and with this new addition I am able to set up different species.
We possess in restored Sceletons: Palapteryx ingens, (cast from Vienna Dinornis casuarinus and didiformis. I hope to have in the next year the greatest part of all the species in upseted skeletons.
If it is of interest for your charming collection to have the casts of all the lower jaw (old, female and young) and the fragments of the palatins of Dinotherium, you would have the Kindness to wish such things; also the complet skulls of Rhenoceros Schleurmacheri and Aceratherium incisivum.
You would do to me a great favour, when you have the Kindness, to give to me instruction in which manner you have fixed the head of the Cerv. irlandicus up his skeleton. At Strasburg the skull is fixed on the cover of the salon; which I will not imitate, because it look very bad.

e possess only the
ft posterior extremitat
mplet
l the bones which are
ned with points are
anting
l vertebres we have
ly the Atlas
l the others are of such
ecimens, which are too different
n size, that we cannot use it
ll the ribs, which I have received
our friend Lord Ennes Killen,
e only fragments. Of the sternum
e have only three bones.
n the lower jaws the incisores are
wanting.

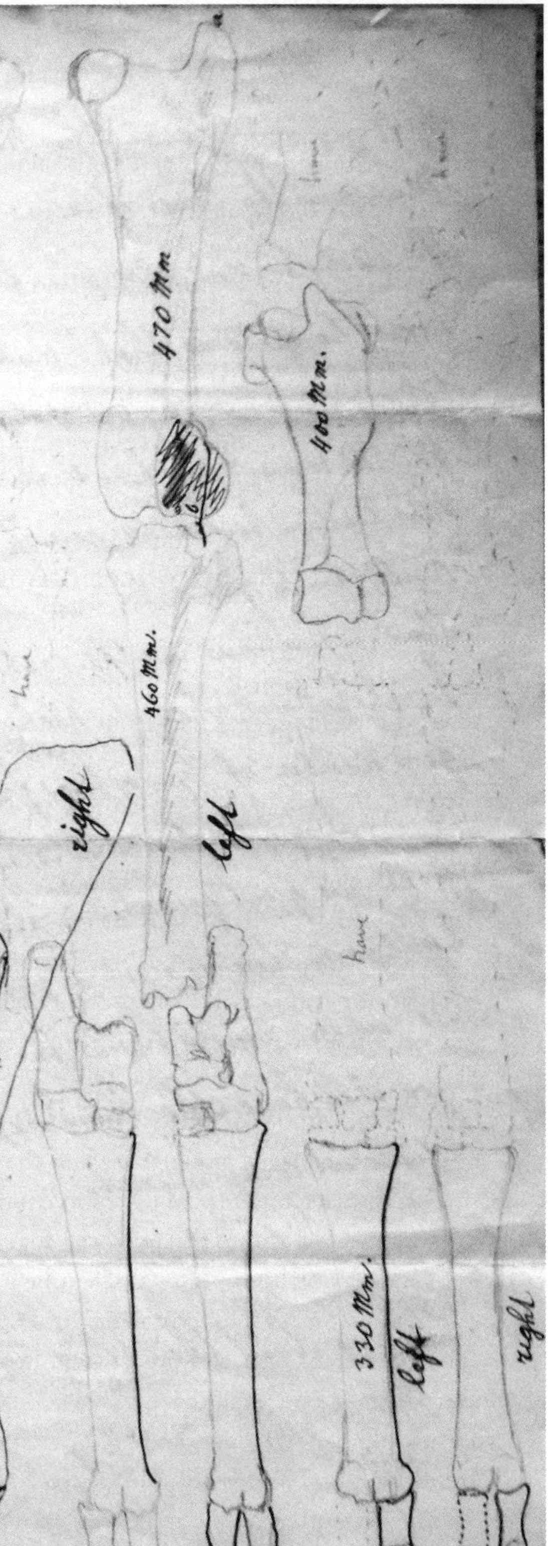

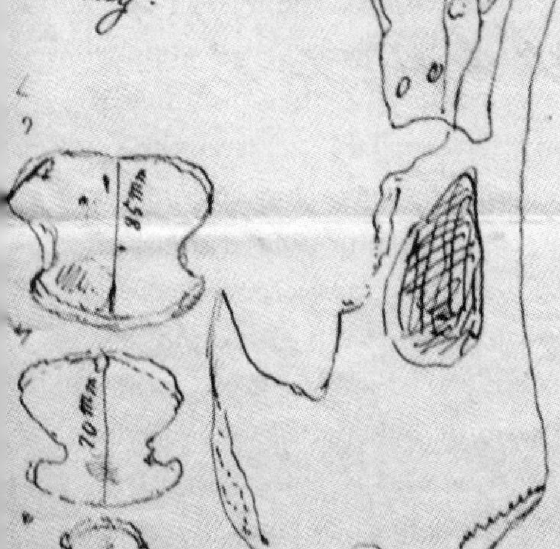

of information, or by looking at official publications. In unpacking the kinds of small events that occurred during the exchanges between Carte, Kaup and their contacts, we can arrive at a sense of what it was like to practise natural history in mid-nineteenth-century Europe, and see that it may or may not align with literature that traces the history of science through larger-than-life figures and epistemic breakthroughs. We can also see the ways that interactions between men of science and museum curators built the museum's collections over time as they continued to correspond and socialise, adding dimension to official records and proceedings.

From collections to knowledge

Though the museum was supported by the public through donations and by central government as a venue for science education, a smaller cadre of focused men of science used it in a different way. While they were certainly alert to the utility of museums in education, this group of people generally treated collections as a shared body of potential resources for formulating and disseminating scientific knowledge. The overarching priorities of institutions and government departments do not tend to appear in the correspondence between men of science, nor in their papers and writings. Rather, these sources suggest that they tended to operate according to the priorities that were set out within networks of their peers. Public talks, events such as the British Association annual meeting, and regular meetings of learned societies were places where they met, exchanged ideas, mounted critiques and formed social bonds. This is not to say that they did not evince a sense of institutional pride; Carte made his museum the best that he could, given the constraints of space and financing limiting its completion. However, Table 5.1, even though it is abbreviated, shows the potential for sharing resources and information in the pursuit of both personal scientific interest and in making institutional collections stronger through collaboration. The exchange of specimens, papers, correspondence, casts and other scientific materials between institutions and individuals shows that these people, especially museum curators, formed a network that was not limited by institutional boundaries or concerns. Unofficially and informally, this network functioned as an entity unto itself.

This is another of the important results of heeding Latour in 'following the actors'; it suggests that the history of natural history in Ireland does not readily conform to standard biographical or institutional models. Rather, it is the net result of countless individual actions that link people and things. Membership records, correspondence and donations indicate that a constant stream of exchange, communication and donation knit this group of people together across space and over a period of time, making them a community of substance that had a discernible impact on scientific ideas. The traditional arrangement of organising the history of science around influential central figures simply does not apply here. There are no larger-than-life heroic individuals making great discoveries, but instead a small group of interconnected people patiently piecing together the evidence that arrives in the post, by ship or on the train. In this way, the idea of a museum and its influence expands beyond the confines of a building and its objects into an active intellectual enterprise that is mobile and social. Through the interactions between people, the museum becomes a set of ideas in addition to being a place or thing; it becomes a centre of authority and knowledge, with attributes that can be transferred through speech, writing or specimens to other places, allowing people to participate from a distance in its growth and development.

Though the correspondence, donations and publications show that Alexander Carte was at the centre of his network in Dublin, he remains an enigmatic figure due to the dearth of information about him. There appear to be few of his letters extant in the files of other institutions, and the museum's archives have only a few draft replies attached to incoming letters.[89] The biographical material for him is scant, and he is legible as a personality primarily through his actions, and via letters from his friends, such as McClintock and Scott. A letter from John Locke, one of only a few in the files that are wholly personal, begins: 'Dear Alick, Coming home by 6 o'c. bus this evening, I spied you in Stephen's Green, looking fagged, I thought – but old age is creeping on us both, old friend.'[90] The letter continues, discussing events in Locke's family, with reference to Carte's family and friends. It suggests that the strain of working for the Natural History Museum, first for the RDS and then for the Science and Art Department, while simultaneously participating in numerous other scientific activities, perhaps took its toll on Carte's health. He was still working when he died in 1881, at the age of seventy-six. He was buried in his family's vault in Mount Jerome cemetery; a visit to the cemetery to find it yielded no results even though it is numbered and registered in the archives there.[91] It seems to have deteriorated to the extent that it can no longer be located.

What does remain, however, are his contributions to natural science in Ireland. Latour points out that social ties, simple associations between people and things, are not durable enough to sustain analysis of how 'the social' becomes a force that illuminates a given subject of study.[92] Instead, he argues that something must be added to social interaction to make social ties durable, and therefore useful in understanding a group of people. Consequently, it is not simply that Irish men of science knew one another and belonged to the same organisations, but that the added 'things' of scientific work, such as specimens, publications, exchanges, correspondence and lectures, served to make their interactions durable and meaningful. Carte's generosity in granting access to the museum's resources and connections made it possible for a small number of Irish men of science to publish their investigations in scientific journals, and to deliver their ideas as papers to scientific meetings. The results of their activity endure today, both in the collections of the museum itself and in lasting contributions to scientific knowledge. An even more focused grouping of dedicated men of science, including Carte, studied deeply in their own fields of interest, and analysed specific aspects of the museum's collections, publishing results that situated Irish science squarely within the emergence of European natural sciences. The next chapter will consider scientific papers as the meaningful and durable consequences of interactions between Irish men of science and the museum's collections.

CHAPTER 6

SPECIMENS AND NETWORKS: COLLECTIONS AND SCIENTIFIC PAPERS

Interpreting collections and distributing knowledge

THROUGHOUT THE NINETEENTH CENTURY, natural history museums played a vital role in establishing the distribution of species across time and geography. Men of science exchanged specimens, images and texts, and compared their own researches against the work of their contemporaries as they participated in the century's grand project of attempting to map the whole of the natural world. The discovery, classification and naming of new species required cooperation and the timely sharing of information. Scientific publications and museum catalogues, always important in advertising collections, became important means of disseminating new knowledge among the community of natural history. They facilitated the circulation of new data, so that important information could be scientifically noted and considered as research progressed. Publication became increasingly significant in creating scientific reputations, and natural history museums were embedded into this process as their authority was widely accepted, and they held the materials that allowed for analysis and comparison, as well as expertise that was relied upon by the scientific community.

In the process of establishing new information, specimens and collections became forms of evidence, initiating and sustaining scientific networks. Latour argues that objects as well as people may assume the role of an actor in a network because they prompt activity and change, asserting that '*any thing* that does modify a state of affairs by making a difference is an actor'.[1] He declares that physical objects may exert influence over a group of people, behaving as catalysts for the formation of a network that will usually be temporary but has substance for the length of its duration.[2] In networks of scientific knowledge in the mid-nineteenth century, natural history specimens sometimes served to draw people together, especially if they were new, rare or unusual, or had been collected in a comprehensive series. Scientific papers originating within the Natural History Museum's collections show how particular specimens gathered people together through common interest and social ties, and were then transformed into scientific knowledge by a small group of dedicated scholars who used print and images to disseminate their findings.

The development of new knowledge in natural history in nineteenth-century Ireland can be observed through published papers on specific specimens or collections that generated interaction and study among members of the learned societies and their contacts. Published papers from scientific journals show how specimens in the collections became 'actors' by drawing people together through scholarship, talks, correspondences, debates, exploration and travel, as meaning was pieced together from fragments of evidence. Though presented as additions to, or elaborations of, bodies of natural knowledge, each of the four scientific papers examined here represents a variety of activities and interactions. Each one signifies a different type of collaboration within natural history in Dublin, throughout Ireland and internationally.

The emphasis on personal relationships in nineteenth-century natural history often meant that the production and reception of new information was based on individual reputation. It was customary that scientific papers were first presented as lectures before a reputable learned society, which would then reproduce them in print. The speech of trusted experts was central to the formation of scientific knowledge, as key aspects of it were 'communicated primarily through the spoken word. Certain knowledge was intimate knowledge, grounded in private conversation, discussions at meetings, and lectures by celebrated speakers'.[3] One of the key features of the published scientific paper was that it had first been submitted for scrutiny to a body of peers, often in the form of a talk, before being committed to print. The papers in this chapter were also the result of collaboration: though they are authored by one or two people, the results within them were arrived at through consultation and consensus as the authors sought information and confirmation from within their trusted circles of expert colleagues. The scientific paper examined physical examples that were located in one place, but publications about specimens and collections made it possible to distribute them to distant places for comparison and analysis, so that the shape of natural history could be developed by an interconnected body of international scholars. The specimens referred to in this chapter belonged to the RDS museum, but the papers were published in journals and proceedings from other societies, as well as the *Journal of the Royal Dublin Society*, showing how collections were used and valued beyond their home institutions. Each paper raises issues that were germane to natural history in the period, and they show how Irish men of science contributed to wider debates at the same time as they advanced their fields at home.

Richard Griffith's fossils and the structure of Ireland

Richard Griffith, 'The Localities of the Irish Carboniferous Fossils, arranged according to the stratigraphical subdivisions of the carboniferous system adopted in the geological map of Ireland, with the Irish mining localities as appended to the synoptical table of fossils, engraved on the margin of that map, and as originally compiled for the use of the general valuation of Ireland', *Journal of the Geological Society of Dublin*, vol IX, 1860–2.

In 1860, engineer and geologist Richard Griffith published a paper collating decades of work in geology into tables of reference, with a lengthy title that summarised his working methods and synopsised his career. Comprised of extensive tables showing the appearance of fossil types within Ireland's geology, the paper shows the methods Griffith had used to propose the ages of Ireland's land masses and fossil species. It divided the information he had collected across three columns: first, the species of fossil; second, the location where it was found; and third, the type of geological layer it was found within. This last would give some idea of the time frame for the species when compared with geological maps that showed stratigraphy, or the order of the layers of rock making up land masses, each layer associated with an era in the past, and defined by the organisms found within it. Using fossil evidence, Griffith assessed the progression of life forms across the Irish landscape in the distant past, charting them for comparison with similar information from other parts of Europe.[4] Griffith's tables also showed how fossil types in Ireland corresponded to layers of geological structure, so that the appearance of particular fossils could be used to help determine a time scale for the places where they were found. He had written the paper as a defence of his 'views of the Carboniferous system as developed in Ireland' and to explain that his professional duties had thus far prevented him from publishing a fully developed work on Irish geology.[5]

Griffith had donated the first significant collection of Irish fossils to the Royal Dublin Society in 1844. He had written to the RDS in March, offering some 2,000 specimens of Irish fossils found in carboniferous limestone.[6] Records note that 'Mr. Griffith's letter was accompanied with a copy of the plates of his intended work on this subject, for presentation to this Society, and has further intimated his intention of being soon able to present another collection of fossils from the Silurian series'.[7] Griffith's letter asserted that the collection was 'very valuable, and in fact, unique', continuing, 'I look upon the Royal Dublin Society as the parent of geology in Ireland, and hence it is my wish that this collection should be enriched by the best of everything I have been able to collect'.[8] Griffith had engaged Frederick McCoy, then a young geologist, to write catalogues of the two collections, and the RDS also engaged him to 'make the selection of the best from a large number of specimens, agreeably to the wishes of Mr. Griffith' and to arrange them under Scouler's direction.[9]

Griffith's career had begun at the RDS in 1809 when the society employed him as a mining engineer, tasking him with surveying and mapping coal fields in the Leinster region. Gordon Herries-Davies points out that the survey was 'conducted in hope that there would be found a mineral wealth sufficient to stimulate an Irish Industrial Revolution comparable to the revolution which was then transforming the economy of Britain'.[10] Griffith went on to occupy numerous positions in the Irish administration, often holding several simultaneously. As he conducted the Leinster coal field survey, he was also employed by the Irish Bogs Commission, and by Dublin Castle as a road engineer from 1822–36.[11] He resigned as the society's mining engineer in 1830, having already taken up a position as director of the General Boundary Survey of Ireland in 1824, tasked with preparing accurate lines for all civic boundaries, in preparation for the work of the newly inaugurated Irish Ordnance Survey.[12] In 1830 he took on the additional post of commissioner for the general survey and valuation of rateable property, more commonly known as Griffith's Valuation, which was to devise a system for assigning value to all taxable properties in order to arrive at a rational table of taxation for Ireland.[13] Griffith was appointed commissioner of railways in 1836, and was also made deputy commissioner of the Board of Works in 1846, becoming chairman in 1850.[14] This post gave him a role in the construction of the Natural History Museum in 1856–7.[15] While occupying these interwoven positions he also remained an RDS member, sitting on committees and applying his influence and expertise to advancing the goals of the society.

During the fulfilment of his professional duties throughout his career, Griffith collected fossils. He understood that the distribution of minerals and fossils could be indicative of soil quality or the presence of valuable mineral resources; for instance, during the Leinster coal field survey, he realised that the distribution of fossil evidence might predict the presence of coal seams. His introduction to the Leinster report detailed fossil, geological and mineral features of the region, connecting them to the likelihood of finding coal. Accounting for his audience of practically minded society gentlemen, whose patience with 'pure science' was limited, he asserted that 'the first step toward the general improvement of mining must be to diffuse a knowledge of the geology of the country; and the more accurately and scientifically we commence, the more perfect and satisfactory will be our conclusion'.[16]

Griffith's interest in the relationship of fossils to geological strata was driven by an ambition to author the first comprehensive geological map of Ireland. He stated that '[t]he chief public object of my life is to complete an accurate map, geological and descriptive, of Ireland'.[17] He was aided in this goal by developments in the field at large, and was encouraged by men of science he met during his early researches, especially in pointing him towards an understanding of stratigraphy, which was used to record the layering of the Earth's visible structures by examining features in the landscape, which were then recorded and compared through maps, charts and texts, a laborious and contentious process that sometimes gave rise to spectacular controversies.[18] Fossils are formed by organisms becoming buried in sediment as layers of strata are deposited, and are then preserved in rock formations. This led geologists in the early nineteenth century to determine that layers of fossils were diagnostic of time periods, positing that those nearer the surface were closer to the present, and the deeper they were buried, the older and more unfamiliar they became.[19] The combination of stratigraphy and fossil evidence made it possible to discern the relative ages of geological layers, providing information about the overall geology of a region. Some of the period's foremost geologists and palaeontologists, including Louis Agassiz, Roderick Murchison and Adam Sedgwick, were present at the 1835 meeting of the British Association for the Advancement of Science in Dublin, where Griffith displayed an early version of his geological map. He later met with them at Enniskillen's estate, where they 'must have impressed upon Griffith the essential role of palaeontology in any future stratigraphical research in Ireland'.[20] When Griffith later came to write instructions for his staff in the General Valuation survey, he asked them to collect mineral and soil samples, to make observations on the geological features of the region they were surveying, and to collect fossils.[21] The evidence they accrued helped to provide a basis for the valuation of land based on its potential for productivity, but also provided Griffith with a comprehensive collection of fossils, and a body of data for his geological map.

The fossil collections that Griffith donated to the RDS collections had been used as evidence in determining, 'by paleontological means, the Carboniferous age of the limestones of the south of Ireland'.[22] Griffith was not a palaeontologist, and Irish palaeontology was poorly understood in the 1830s, but when he hired McCoy and began working with Scouler, they began to formulate a body of evidence derived from specimens, samples, descriptions and images.[23] The plates that Griffith had provided for the 1844 catalogue included fossils that McCoy had identified as new species, for which he drew his own illustrations.[24] The classification and cataloguing of Griffith's donation was an opportunity for McCoy to strengthen his own reputation by identifying and describing new species, providing him with a calling card for his own career ambitions; he subsequently became a professor of natural science at the University of Melbourne, and founded its National Museum of Natural History and Geology in Victoria.[25] His classifications of Griffith's collections are still regarded as 'important to present-day palaeontologists as sources of many valid fossil groups'.[26]

Griffith's donations to the museum were more than civic-minded acts of scientific generosity; they were also a way of inserting his geological ideas into an accepted scientific framework in order to publicise his findings and legitimise his geological and mapping work. McCoy's classification and catalogues made Griffith's ideas portable, and subsequent versions of the geological map, based on the new Ordnance Survey maps and hand-painted to demonstrate geological regions, put his assertions into an attractive visual form. He published the final version of his map in 1855, donating a copy to the RDS museum the following year.[27] In producing it, Griffith had also relied on his staff geologists, especially John Kelly, Patrick Knight and Patrick Ganly, whose expertise in collecting fossils and identifying geology was essential in the success of the valuation survey, but also in establishing the structures realised in the map.[28] Nineteenth-century natural history was a collaborative process, and the work of contributors was customarily acknowledged in publications, but Griffith's maps and papers took credit under his own name for work that included the collections and observations of his valuators.

Griffith's geological maps, the first to begin recording the stratigraphy, fossil and mineral attributes of the island, were made possible due to his lifelong habit of occupying multiple administrative posts simultaneously. This allowed him the autonomy and resources to collect information and specimens at an accelerated rate in the process of fulfilling his duties for the crown. The fossil specimens in the museum were part of a larger body of primary evidence that provided the basis for the tables in the 1860 paper. The fossils Griffith donated to the museum were the first to expand out from the Leskean collection by adding comprehensive Irish materials to the society's core geological holdings. They were used to help determine Ireland's geological structure and its economic value, directly contributing to the scientific understanding of Ireland as a physical entity. McCoy's catalogues and Griffith's comprehensive paper for the Geological Society distributed this information into national and international scientific networks, demonstrating the information through descriptions and drawings, allowing the structures of Ireland's geology to be compared to formations across Europe and inserted into the emerging field of geology as it challenged long-held certainties about the age and nature of the Earth.

'Economic zoology': William Andrews and Irish fisheries

William Andrews, 'Notes on the Salmon Fisheries of Ireland', *Journal of the Royal Dublin Society*, vol. IV, 1863–5.

During the Natural History Museum's inaugural event in 1857, the *Freeman's Journal* noted that the collections on display contained lobsters, shellfish, oysters and various other types of edible crustacea and molluscs, as 'instances of what might be done in the way of economic zoology'.[29] The economic potential of the species residing in Ireland's waters, especially for stabilising the food supply, was the chief concern of RDS member William Andrews. A regular member of the Natural History Committee, and deeply involved with the Natural History Society of Dublin, he was ideally positioned to influence and facilitate the amassing of clear scientific information about the breeding habits and migrations of fish. He authored numerous scientific papers, most of them on fish and fisheries.[30] Andrews was adamant about the inseparability of natural history from the practical development of natural resources, asserting that 'science and practice must go hand in hand to acquire certain and definite knowledge'.[31]

In the closing pages of the RDS-sponsored *The Industrial Resources of Ireland,* Robert Kane noted that he had not 'at all alluded to the subject, so important in itself, of fisheries' because 'their importance and their practicability are universally recognised'.[32] The society had included fisheries among its concerns as early as 1733, encouraging study and awarding prizes for the pursuit of practical advances in improving fisheries and preserving fish for sale.[33] In 1853, Carte had discussed plans to install a tank for propagating salmon on the grounds of the museum as a way of observing the species, but an 1865 letter to an acquaintance indicates that the plan was never realised.[34] In the *Journal of the Royal Dublin Society,* papers on the fisheries were a regular feature, and Carte's donations lists recorded a steady increase in fish, crustaceans and molluscs to the collections. In the first volume of the journal, Carte noted that donations of fish 'have been but few', and in the section on mollusca he called for increased donations to 'materially aid the cause of science, this section of the Museum being much frequented by our younger naturalists'.[35] Carte's 1856 records began to show the increase he had requested, with greater numbers of molluscs, crustacea and fish documented from then on.[36] The enumeration of crabs, lobsters and shrimp provided insight into the potential for the pursuit of 'economic zoology' in Irish waters, and papers on fish and fisheries by Andrews soon became a regular feature of the *JRDS.*

Andrews published a pamphlet in 1848, *On the Fisheries of the Coasts of Ireland,* lobbying for the establishment of a company for 'supplying to our own country what is now so largely imported to us by others', concentrating on fresh fish and shellfish, but also on cured fish and fish oils, and highlighting the potential for employment provided by a healthy fishing industry.[37] He had written to Secretary of the Treasury Charles Trevelyan earlier in the year, seeking government support in the testing of fishing banks to determine the scope and potential of their resources. An advocate of laissez-faire policy, the secretary disagreed with Andrews' scientifically minded approach, averring that 'what was most wanted in that quarter was not new information regarding the fishery banks, but capital and skill, and well-conducted persevering enterprise, to make use of the abundant means which were already known to be available'.[38] The Royal Irish Fisheries Company was established by patent in the same year, in which Andrews became a manager.[39] By the time he became a member of the RDS in 1848 and began presenting papers at the society's evening meetings, he was an acknowledged authority on Irish fisheries.

In 1863 Andrews read a paper at the RDS evening scientific meeting and published it in the society's journal; entitled 'Notes on the Salmon Fisheries of Ireland', it summarised his previous studies on the species, and proposed a series of considerations for its management. Andrews' paper was delivered in the context of an 1863 parliamentary bill proposing to rationalise the legal statutes around salmon fishery in Ireland with the laws in England. The salmon fishery was a particular focus of debate and discord in nineteenth-century Ireland, as it comprised a uniquely complex set of factors centring around the habits and breeding of the fish itself. There were two primary competitors for access to the profitable salmon fishery. First, the owners of inland or riverfront property that included fishery rights, who claimed that the salmon was 'as much their property as the banks of the river, or the pigeons in the dove-cot, and that the true residence of the salmon is the fresh water'.[40] Second, the owners of coastal lands and the proprietors of coastal fisheries, who took salmon when the mature fish left the ocean to return to their inland spawning grounds.[41]

Andrews' 1863 paper on the salmon fishery was a summation of work and research conducted over a number of years, which sought to communicate his view that a clear understanding of the growth cycle and stages of development in the fish was essential to its management and for rational legislation surrounding its use as a resource.[42] By understanding the movement of the salmon throughout its life cycle, any proposed legislation regulating competing claims to the valuable fish could be underpinned by scientific information, allowing stocks to be maintained at healthy levels.

The lack of clarity surrounding the proportion of the catch to which inland and coastal landowners were entitled, as well as uncertainty around how habitat affected breeding cycles and populations, led to a bitter and prolonged debate around the proposed statutes of 1863.[43] The legislation around salmon was, according to Andrews, faulty because it was based on an incomplete understanding of the breeding and development of the species through its various stages.[44] Andrews sought to dispel some of the confusion by setting out a clear summary of the salmon's developmental states, the stages at which it was resident in rivers and oceans, and the differing time frames for its appearances across Ireland's geography based on water temperature and the variations in the fish's movements according to local conditions.[45] His 1863 paper argued that any change in Irish fisheries policy must be informed by careful scientific observation, noting that the 'true habits of the salmon, in its distribution, have caused much perplexity; and nowhere do difficulties more beset the subject, than where practical knowledge cannot combine scientific inquiry, or where scientific knowledge is destitute of practical investigation'.[46]

Andrews presented his paper on salmon at the RDS evening scientific meeting, prompting a heated debate around the proposed statutes. An editorial in the *Irish Times* noted that '[t]he Parliamentary warfare respecting one of the most productive natural resources of Ireland may be said to have commenced last night at the fortnightly meeting of the Royal Dublin Society. A very able and interesting paper on the salmon, its habits, and the various modes of its capture, was read by Mr. Andrews, President of the Natural History Society'[.][47] A protracted and apparently fiery discussion ensued among those with an interest in the fish who had attended to hear his paper. The debate was reproduced along with the paper in the *JRDS*, and was described in the *Irish Times* as 'most warm and animated, and formed by no means an unpleasing exception to the usually grave and purely scientific debates of a learned society'.[48] Observing that the value of salmon annually in Ireland was £300,000, compared to £20,000 in England, the editors called for a royal commission to be appointed before the passing of any new law, citing 'the new lights thrown upon the habits of the fish' by Andrews' paper, and demanding that such a commission comprise 'not only practical fishermen, but men of science should be examined, and appointed to examine witnesses'.[49]

Andrews continually asserted that the collection of species, observation of their behaviour and publication of the results were integral to sound regulation, stating that '[a] correct knowledge of the natural history of the salmon is of essential value in an economic point of view'.[50] In gathering evidence for his assertions, Andrews also added to the collections at the same time as he was writing about the species. Carte's list of donations for 1863 recorded the contribution of a collection of salmon by Andrews; a letter from Dingle in 1864 also asked if Carte wanted 'any other young Salmonidae'.[51] As an active and highly visible member of the five learned societies discussed in the previous chapter, Andrews consistently threaded together natural history, collection, improvement and economic stability in an ongoing bid to establish Ireland's fisheries as a viable and secure national resource. The distribution of his work through scientific papers, talks at the learned societies, meetings of the British Association and within the newspapers added to the public debates about the economic value of salmon, informed by scientific observation. His involvement with the museum and the learned societies conferred him with the status of an authority, who wielded potential to influence government policy through the application of scientific principles to the development and preservation of natural resources. As with Griffith's fossil collections, his work was relevant across a range of contexts, and sought to establish a body of fundamental knowledge about important but poorly understood elements of Irish natural history with potential for economic impact. The specimens he brought to the museum operated as a body of physical evidence for scientific assessments that would determine how value should be assigned and how salmon stocks would be accessed and utilised. Andrews's concern for the preservation of natural resources through judicious management based on scientific understanding perhaps put him ahead of his time, given that conservation did not generally concern Victorian science.

Far-flung networks and scientific communication: a Jamaican petrel

Alexander Carte, 'On an Undescribed Species of Petrel from the Blue Mountains of Jamaica', *Proceedings of the Zoological Society of London*, 1866.

In 1855, Jamaican civil servant William Thomas March sent Carte a rare bird which appeared to be new to science.[52] While most of the civil servants who donated to the museum were British or Irish men in foreign postings, March, clerk of the crown of Spanish Town, St Catherine, Jamaica, was a native Jamaican. Though March was an able naturalist, he did not write about or publish his collections, preferring to make his name through donations to well-known institutions in Europe and the Americas, including the Dublin museum, Harvard and the British Museum. He was a regular correspondent of botanist William Hooker, as well as with the museums where he donated.[53] March's areas of expertise were botany and ornithology, and throughout the 1850s and '60s he sent specimens of Jamaican birds to the RDS Natural History Museum.

March referred to the rare species he sent to Dublin as a *Prion caribbaea*, or a Blue Mountain duck. In trying to classify it, Carte wrote to the celebrated bird expert John Gould in 1859, seeking any description of it that might already exist; Gould replied, 'you ask for information about the Blue Mountain Duck mentioned by Gosse in his Birds of Jamaica; but I do not find any such bird alluded to', continuing to say that 'if the bird you have be a Prion it will be of especial interest as until I described one in the Proceedings of the Zool. Soc. for 1855 no member of the genus was known to exist north of the equator'.[54] Gould had been a taxidermist and the curator of the museum of the Zoological Society in London; by the time Carte wrote to him, he had become an artist and publisher of lavishly illustrated volumes on bird species.[55] His determination that March's donation might be new or poorly understood would have carried weight within the community of natural history, and perhaps encouraged Carte to investigate it himself.

However, it was ten years before Carte followed up on creating a firm identification for the species. Writing to March in 1865, Carte discerned that the bird had been noticed and possibly named by previous naturalists, but never formally identified and described scientifically, and no scientific publication on it had been made.[56] This meant that it would be understood as a new species, and by creating its first formal published description and presenting it to scientific peers, Carte would be credited with the official identification of a new species. From previous descriptions and March's letters, it was clear that the bird was rare; Carte's specimens were only the third recorded instance of the bird in a collection.[57] In order to secure advice from experts in London, he sent the rare specimen to England with Charles H. Gatty, a wealthy natural history enthusiast who lived in Felbridge, Sussex. Carte and Gatty shared membership of the Linnaean Society and the Zoological Society of London, as well as the Geological Society.[58] Gatty wrote in December 1865 to say that he had 'arrived safely in London this morning with your bird, and have left it with Dr Sclater'[.][59] Sclater, secretary of the Zoological Society, undertook consultations to discern the bird's species. Carte had sent inquiries to Sclater in

June, receiving the reply that the bird was 'probably new' but that 'it would be better, however, to send it over to the British Museum for comparison before describing it'.[60] Sclater contacted George Robert Gray, head of ornithology at the British Museum, who examined the bird and deemed the species as undescribed.[61] Aside from being the expert on birds at the British Museum, Gray's authority stemmed from his 1849 publication of *The Genera of Birds: Comprising their generic characters, a notice of the habits of each genus, and an extensive list of species referred to their several genera.*

Gray's verdict led Sclater to tell Carte, 'I think you may safely describe the bird, and I suggest that you should call it *Pterodroma caribbaea.* … We can give you a figure in the "Proceedings" – I should like to have the paper on the pil [sic] soon, as the plate is almost ready'.[62] This indicates that Carte and Sclater were confident enough in their determinations that they had already set in motion the expensive process of preparing a paper, with a full-page colour lithograph, for scientific publication[63] (Fig. 6.1). The paper was read to the membership of the Zoological Society of London, and subsequently

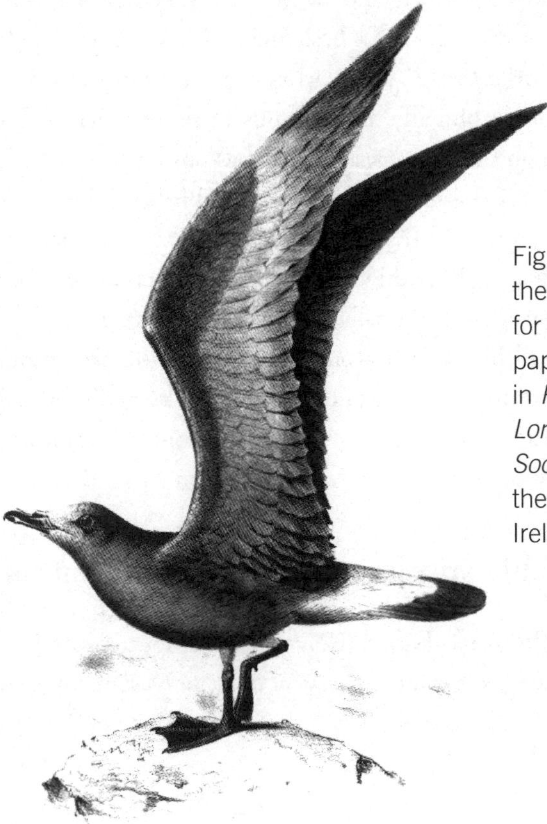

Fig. 6.1 Illustration of the Jamaican petrel for Alexander Carte's paper on the rare bird, in *Proceedings of the London Zoological Society*, 1866. (Courtesy the National Museum of Ireland, Natural History)

published. Gatty wrote to Carte in February 1866 to say that he had been at the meeting 'at which your paper was read by Mr. Sclater', adding that 'Mr. Gould was in the chair, and after the reading of the paper said "this is undoubtedly a new species"'.[64] Based upon Carte's description in the published paper, the two Dublin specimens, one mounted and one a stuffed skin for study, were designated as type specimens, the foundational examples of the species against which other possible identifications would be compared in the future.

The steps Carte took in identifying and naming this bird encapsulate the ways that international communication in scientific networks behaved as a regulating mechanism, showing how new information in natural science was often constructed by a number of people who used their mutual contacts and plied their individual expertise in determining the establishment of a species. In this case, the arrival of a rare bird from a specific local habitat in a remote location meant that extra care and consultation among trusted experts and friends was required, especially as it was uncertain at the outset whether someone else had already described and named the species. This series of events also demonstrates the ways that Irish men of science were active in London's scientific networks. Carte's publication became a contribution to the identification of new species globally, and the museum's specimens remain its primary examples. Though the *Pterodroma caribbaea* has not been collected since 1879, its status is unclear. Conservation organisation BirdLife International's factsheet on the species points out that nocturnal petrels are extremely hard to record, as they are active at night and live largely on the open ocean, therefore the bird is currently considered critically endangered or extinct rather than simply extinct.[65] In cases like this, Latour's designation of the immutable mobile takes on new significance; should the species be rediscovered, the museum's specimens and Carte's identification would come back into play as the most complete body of information for comparison.[66]

A most desirable specimen: *Plesiosaurus cramptoni*

Alexander Carte and W.H. Baily, 'Description of a New Species of *Plesiosaurus* from the Lias, near Whitby, Yorkshire', *Journal of the Royal Dublin Society*, vol. IV, 1863–5.

In the fourth volume of the *Journal of the Royal Dublin Society,* Alexander Carte and geologist William Baily co-published a paper that Baily had delivered at the 1862 British Association meeting at Cambridge. It described a prehistoric aquatic reptile fossil presented to the RDS in the early 1860s. In 1853, a large fossil *Plesiosaurus* had been loaned to the Royal Zoological Society of Ireland by Sir Philip Crampton, and was bequeathed by him in 1858. It had been a gift from his friend the marquess of Normanby, found in an alum pit at Kettleness works near Whitby in North Yorkshire in 1848.[67] A spectacular and well-preserved specimen, it measured twenty-two feet long and thirteen feet wide; the council of the Zoological Society had hoped that its display would attract an increased number of visitors during the Great Irish Industrial Exhibition of 1853.[68] Though the zoo had built a special housing for exhibiting the fossil, little had been done to place it into a scientific context. In 1861, the specimen was loaned to the Royal Dublin Society.[69] Carte noted that the council of the Zoological Society 'considered that the specimen would contribute more to the public convenience, as well as to general scientific utility by being placed in a more central locality' and therefore it had been 'deposited in the Natural History Museum of the Royal Dublin Society, where it is now conspicuously placed for inspection and study'.[70]

Carte and Baily felt that the fossil represented a new species and began gathering evidence. Carte set about gathering information from Normanby and his staff about the discovery and subsequent treatment of the plesiosaur, though it had been found fifteen years earlier. The paper published by Carte and Baily distils the information contained in a series of letters from Normanby, his agent John Kerr, a worker from Kettleness named John Taylor and Martin Simpson, curator of the Whitby Museum.[71] The letters convey recollections of finding and cleaning the fossil, with Taylor noting that it had been placed in a rock kiln for some time before it had been cleaned and assembled. He also alerted Carte to a similar specimen found nearby in 1847, in the collection of the York Museum.[72] Carte travelled to York to take measurements himself, as the fossil there was 'as yet undescribed'.[73] Carte knew of another plesiosaur in the Whitby Museum; he had written to Simpson, who replied that he was not able to send all the measurements Carte required for comparison, because 'our fossil corresponds well with your photograph, but yours is a much more perfect specimen', describing the damage to the Whitby fossil.[74] These were the examples against which Carte and Baily compared the plesiosaur in the Natural History Museum, outlining the differences between them, and identifying each as different species. The museum's specimen was determined to be a new species, which was named *Plesiosaurus cramptoni,* after its donor. Part of that designation holds today, though modern re-assessment has assigned it as a rhomelosaur, so it is now known as *Rhomelosaurus cramptoni.*[75]

In its discovery and description, the plesiosaur behaved as an actor, in Latour's sense, as it generated an interested and interconnected network. It assembled quarrymen, men of title, men of science and museum curators into a configuration which sought to establish the unique qualities of the specimen and secure it as new to science. Baily's reading of a preliminary version of the joint paper at the British Association brought the importance of their observations to the attention of the wider scientific community; as a result, they received confirmation from the British Museum's Richard Owen, an expert in saurian fossils, that their identification was correct.[76] Carte and Baily's published paper condensed the information provided by this network into a paper format, an immutable mobile, which could be distributed to the wider sphere of natural science by reducing the massive specimen in its slab of rock to descriptions, measurements and images on paper. The variety of representations provided as complete a body of information as possible. Carte's descriptions and measurements laid out objective data for comparison against known examples and for use against future finds. The tables which provided measurements of already named specimens in specific collections added to the corpus of emerging information about fossil species; all three were found in the same region, which helped to create a clearer picture of the distribution of prehistoric life. Normanby's agent Kerr had drawn a diagram of the fossil's location in the quarry, which Carte reproduced in print in his paper. Baily's illustrations of the fossil became part of the proof in that they showed the shape and proportions of the full fossil, and they also showed the individual points of comparison upon which Carte had focused in his identification of a new species (Fig. 6.2). In addition, Baily's images showed a rare and dramatic specimen in an excellent state of preservation, which was certain to gain the attention of the natural history community. In fact, Carte and Baily's description established this example as a type specimen, the reference against which all future designations of the species would be made. Their paper remained the primary work describing this species until 2007, when palaeontologist Adam Stuart Smith re-examined the fossil, still in the museum's collections.[77]

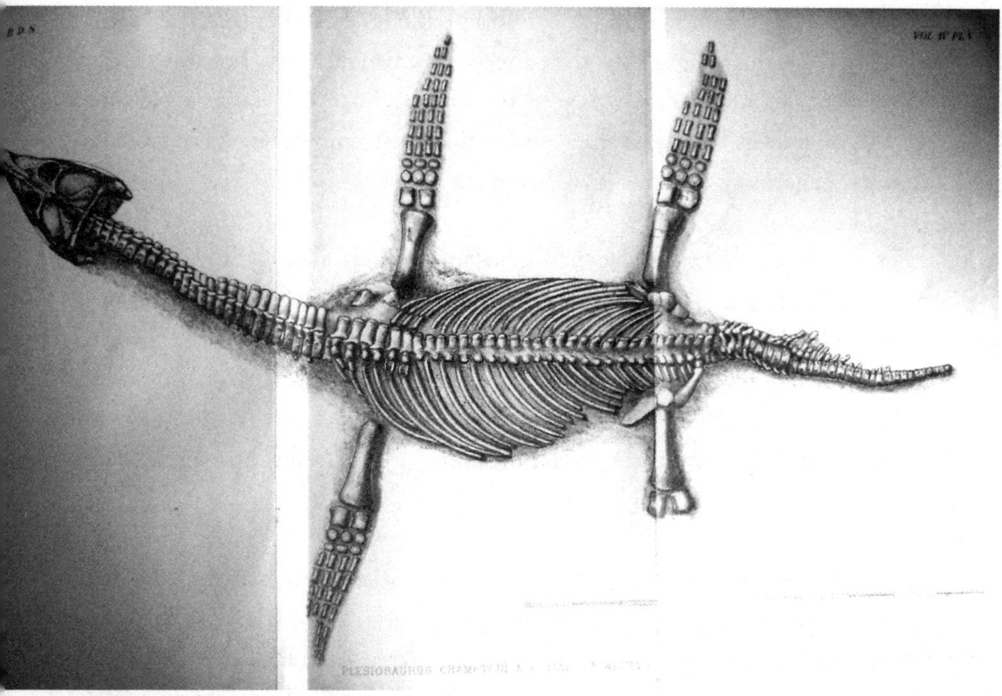

Fig. 6.2 Image from Carte and Baily's 1864 paper in the *Journal of the Royal Dublin Society* on the spectacular specimen *Plesiosaurus cramptoni*, which prompted a flurry of requests for casts from museums around the world. (Courtesy of the National Museum of Ireland, Natural History)

An unexpected result of the presentation of the paper to the British Association and its subsequent publication was the ensuing stream of requests for casts of the plesiosaur from museum curators. The specimen became an object of desire due to its newness, its state of preservation and its dramatic size. Letters to Carte requesting casts consistently refer to it as the finest example of a plesiosaur then in existence. High-quality plaster casts of extraordinary specimens allowed museums to expand their holdings and to have access to facsimiles for scientific research, and their sale or exchange was common practice. When requesting a cast from another institution, custom among museum curators dictated that objects or casts from their own collections be offered in exchange. Thomas J. Moore, curator of the Liverpool Museum of Natural History, wrote to Carte that he was 'anxious to secure a cast of your Plesiosaurus', offering a cast of a large fossil Indian tortoise from his own collections in exchange, but confessing that he was 'somewhat at a loss to know what to offer in kind by way of return'.[78]

A note in Carte's handwriting at the top of the letter shows that the Natural History Committee agreed to the proposed exchange. A draft reply in Carte's handwriting is attached, which provides an insight into Carte's management of his collections, and the value he placed on fostering networks of exchange through generosity with his own resources:

> You will bear in mind that the Plesiosaur is a very striking object not alone for its size, but also for its perfect state of preservation, and therefore of considerable value. At the same time I am of [the] opinion that in institutions like ours, the great object to be kept in view, is not so much the absolute equality of the specimen to be exchanged, as the advantages the public will gain by the transaction and the kindly feeling which is thus promoted by such an initiative.[79]

Similar requests were received from curator Charles Moore at the Bath Royal Literary and Scientific Institution, Joseph Bennett, curator of the Australian Museum in Sydney, and Constant Guillou, a barrister in Philadelphia seeking a cast for his city's Academy of Natural Sciences.[80] There is also a short draft reply in Carte's handwriting penned directly onto Charles Moore's letter, indicating Carte's favourable response to the request, and suggesting a series of duplicate fossils as an appropriate exchange.[81] Though the number of draft replies from Carte in the correspondence files is small, they suggest that he was favourably inclined to sharing the extraordinary specimen in his collection, especially with smaller institutions that had fewer resources than the RDS, and that he behaved generously with his scientific peers; his responses were cordial and encouraging.

The most persistent requests for a copy of the plesiosaur came from an unusual source. Henry Ward may best be described as a scientific entrepreneur; science historian Mary P. Winsor refers to him as the 'king of the museum supply business'.[82] He was a dealer in fossil casts who specialised in selling complete collections to museums and educational institutions. His company, Ward's Natural Science Establishment of Rochester, New York, obtained casts of well-known specimens from museums and private collections around the world, and then reproduced them for commercial sale, advertising his offerings through illustrated catalogues.[83] He assembled packages of casts that were, in effect, instant fossil collections that could be purchased by institutions. His College Series, offering 330 specimens, contained casts of 'four of the largest fossils known to science' including 'the *Megatherium*; the *Elephas Ganesa* [sic] ...; the *Colossochelys* ...; and the great *Plesiosaurus cramptoni*, the latter *twenty-two feet long!*'.[84] Ward's 1866 catalogue also offered a cast of a large set of antlers of the *Megaceros hibernicus* from his private collection, obtained 'from the deposits of shell-marl that underlie the peat-bogs in the neighbourhood of Limerick, Ireland'.[85] While he is not named, it is hard to imagine that his specimen originated from anyone other than William Hinchy.

The earliest letter from Ward in the correspondence files was written on 11 November 1863, stating that he had been home for two months. Ward had met Carte in Ireland, and had obviously seen the plesiosaur and discussed having it cast. His letter asks, 'have you been able to send the *Plesiosaurus* yet? I have not heard from it and commence to be a good deal anxious lest it shall in some way be lost en route'.[86] He was to be disappointed. His letters from 1863–5 all ask a variation on the same question: when will the plesiosaur arrive? An 1864 letter deemed the specimen 'magnificent', and Ward stated that 'I must have a cast of it', proceeding to detail the costs involved in making and shipping casts as a means of working out an equitable exchange from his offerings.[87] An 1865 letter asked about the arrival of some casts sent to Dublin, inquiring 'have you yet sent the *Plesiosaurus*?', continuing to say that 'I am very anxious to have this cast to mount at Rochester before New Years' and that 'it will make material difficulty in my plans if I am disappointed'.[88] As the specimen was advertised in Ward's 1866 and 1870 catalogues, it is clear that Carte eventually sent the specimen, but less clear is the reason for his hesitation. However, all his activities in Dublin's networks of science, as well as his expressed views that scientific exchanges should be mutually beneficial and for the benefit of the public, may indicate that he was reluctant to treat extraordinary specimens as opportunities for private profit.

Throughout the course of its progress through the museum, this specimen behaved as an actor that united two separate groups of interested people. First, Carte, Baily, Crampton, Normanby and the people who found and preserved it for Normanby. By coming to rest in the Natural History Museum, the plesiosaur attracted the attention of the people who established it as a discrete species, defining it permanently for the future. In so doing, they enlisted experts and previous descriptions which aided them in creating taxonomies of extinct animals which again added to the corpus of information about the distribution of what were then largely unknown species. In the creation of text, charts, speech and images which could broadcast the specimen to others,

Carte and Baily assembled a second network around this specimen, comprised of museum curators like themselves, who wanted to share in the dramatic find by having a copy of it in their collections. This was further extended through Ward, who perhaps was able to supply more curators than Carte would have been able to through the available resources at the RDS. The two groups of people that assembled around this specimen ranged from anonymous quarry workers to Richard Owen, one of the most famous men of science of his day, again demonstrating that the manufacture of natural knowledge in mid-century Ireland was undertaken by a range of people, and took place well outside the Ascendancy frameworks to which scientific activity in nineteenth-century Ireland is so frequently relegated.

The Natural History Museum's contributions to scientific culture

The scientific papers discussed above demonstrate a variety of possibilities for the ways that museum objects come to represent nature, as well as the ways in which they are used to create bodies of information that have cultural impact. Griffith's fossils, the petrified remains of long-dead plants and animals, became significant factors in understanding the layering of the rocks which form the land mass of Ireland, indicating its age and composition. While this information was used to predict the value of land, it was also used to form one of the first complete pictures of Ireland's physical structure, and helped determine how it might be related to European land masses. The arrangement of Irish fossils in drawers in the museum allowed that structure to be visible to anyone who wished to study them, and to be compared against European specimens in the Leskean fossils. William Andrews' paper signifies a growing awareness that scientific methods were vital in formulating practices and policies that would allow natural resources to be fully understood and utilised, and that museum collections contained physical evidence that could play a role in shaping the economic potential and legislative directives that governed their use of resources. Carte's papers show how specimens moved through the networks of scientific study in order to establish sound evidence that would withstand scrutiny by peers, and the ways that differing types of people contributed to the publication of new scientific information. They also show how the interconnected social and professional relationships of men of science served as a self-regulating structure, bound to institutional priorities but also operating as an interconnected and interdependent body with common goals.

These examples demonstrate that the Natural History Museum was active in creating new knowledge in an international context, rather than simply behaving as a static repository for physical materials. While Carte organised the collections to show the structures of scientific knowledge to museum-goers, he was also involved in adding to the corpus of natural history in ways which have largely been ignored in the history of Irish science. Some of his identifications of species stand today, and he was instrumental in bringing together people and information, both locally and internationally, in ways that generated material improvements in scientific knowledge and in the museum collections which supported its construction. His scientific papers are stable explanations of ideas that allowed people to argue and discuss across distances, the immutable mobiles of natural science, created through the scientific network in which Carte immersed himself. The work seen in these papers has today become largely invisible to the average museum-goer, and yet they represent one of the primary functions of the museum in its period context – the creation of knowledge. For scientists and historians of science, these historical researches maintain their significance, and the museum's collections, correspondence, manuscript lists and publications remain active scientific sources.

CONCLUSION

The Natural History Museum as a Cultural Formation

In 1877, the Dublin Science and Art Museum Act began to consolidate the most important collections in Ireland into a national museum and library complex, administered through the Science and Art Department. This occasioned a new era of museums in Ireland, removing collections from the learned societies and instituting a fully professional museum structure loosely adhering to the South Kensington model. The Royal Dublin Society retained its Leinster House headquarters, but ceded the 'new museum' building to the state. The National Museum and the National Library on Kildare Street were opened in 1890, and the Natural History Museum and National Gallery were updated. As the new museum structure developed into an organised complex, operations became regularised, educational functions consolidated, and collections continued apace. A new publication programme commenced, producing guides, catalogues, and in 1911 the first issue of the *Museum Bulletin*, from the National Museum of Science and Art, Dublin.

In 1922, the newly formed Irish Free State selected Leinster House as the most attractive building for seating the government, in part due to its excellent lecture theatre. When the building was finally purchased in 1924, the Royal Dublin Society relocated to its suburban property in Ballsbridge. Ireland's new administration assumed responsibility for cultural institutions from the British parliament and set about restructuring them to reflect a distinct Irish identity. Seeking international advice, Minister for Education Eoin MacNeill commissioned a report. The resulting Lithberg Report (1927), authored by Professor Nils Lithberg, director of the Northern Museum, Stockholm, shaped the future direction of Ireland's national museums. One of its primary recommendations was that the newly formed state focus its efforts and funding on Irish antiquities and archaeology as a means of constructing a clear sense of national identity.[1]

Lithberg's findings were validated by the Carnegie Report (1928), which seconded a focus on 'national character', urging attention to Ireland's ethnology, folklore and history.[2] The new government heeded these findings, but the choice to focus attention and funding primarily on Irish antiquities and ethnography, coupled with severe budgetary limitations, left the rest of the collections in a precarious state, and set the Natural History Museum onto a path of creeping neglect. Lithberg had also recommended that the staff and funding for the Natural History Museum be increased, but Dáil Éireann chose to ignore his suggestion. Explanations for the subsequent neglect of the Natural History Museum throughout most of the twentieth century have ranged from an assumption that the Free State was biased against the Anglo-Irish influence in Irish science, to the perception of an anti-modern tendency in the heart of romantic nationalism. However, Nicholas Whyte proposes that for the new government 'the common thread [was] not the down-grading of science, but the cutting of government expenditure ... The new Free State was not hostile to modernity. It was simply hostile to spending money'.[3]

The long-term aftermath of those early choices was that the study of natural science as an essential element in the understanding of Ireland's character as a nation was abandoned in favour of a focus on antiquities that could be usefully bound to a nationalist political vision.[4] The Natural History Museum became the subject of regular protests in Dáil Éireann as it slowly fell into disrepair and disorganisation due to consistent understaffing and underfunding. In 1929, Ernest Alton, TD asserted that the collections of fine art and natural history were 'almost derelict' due to lack of financial support. Other TDs supported Alton in demanding adequate provision for all collections, citing their educational value.[5] A Seanad debate in 1957 indicated that thirty years later little had changed. Senator William Bedell Stanford outlined the poor condition of the museums, stating that the 'Archaeological Museum and the Natural History Museum are not worthy of our capital city', noting that the Natural History Museum in particular had deteriorated significantly over the previous forty years.[6] Stanford added that 'we had a very large conference in this city last September, that of the British Association; and it was very sad for many of our scientists in Dublin that when members of that great and influential association went to see our Natural History Museum, they were bound to be gravely disappointed'.[7] Ironically, that meeting took place just shy of one hundred years after the British Association gathering that had launched the new museum at the RDS. From the inception of the Free State, the programme of active science at Dublin's Natural History Museum slowed dramatically, remaining sluggish even throughout the 1980s, a period when European and American museums generally, and science museums in particular, saw seismic shifts in their approaches to exhibition, and in their engagement with museum audiences.[8]

In 1988, funding became available to rewire and redecorate the Natural History Museum.[9] The works were a restoration rather than a modernisation; repairs, cleaning and repainting returned it to something approximating its late Victorian condition. Dublin possessed, through accident engendered by neglect, an intact example of the Victorian cabinet museum, untouched by twentieth-century museum theory. The restoration caught the attention of evolutionary biologist and popular science author Stephen Jay Gould, who marked the occasion with a paean entitled 'Cabinet museums revisited', extolling the virtues of Dublin's Victorian-style museum. Gould had made a research visit in 1971, and described his experience of working in a dark, disorganised and dusty collection.[10] On revisiting in 1993, he discovered that the exhibitions had remained exactly the same, but had been restored to an approximation of their original state.[11] Gould argued for the benefits of maintaining Victorian museums as a historicising counterpoint to the modernising trends of fewer specimens and increased interactivity; he praised the Dublin curators for restoring 'their original housing to one of the world's finest and fullest exhibits in the old and still-stunning cabinet style – not just a room to showcase the past, but an entire building in its full integrity'.[12] Long-term neglect had shifted the Natural History Museum's purpose to what is now most often described as a 'museum of a museum', itself an object of display that preserves the material history of the museum's past.

However, if, as Roland Barthes asserts, objects are never just 'themselves, but are a form of communication, a type of social usage which is added to pure matter', then the physical qualities of this museum, its 'matter', are keys to a series of period social usages that were largely erased while the museum languished in civic limbo.[13] In order to restore the museum to its correct place in Irish cultural and scientific history, it is necessary to move beyond the comfortable mythologies that have come to surround it. For it to truly be a 'museum of a museum', its past uses and purposes must be visible so that visitors can see how its organisation and styles of display demonstrate a way of thinking about nature, and how they were a stepping stone that helped bring us to our present understanding. The museum encapsulates the Victorian method for attempting to create order from the apparent chaos of the natural world, a form of data collection that now appears problematic, but which made sense in the logic of the day. Its ability to transport visitors to the past is not only an exercise in nostalgia, but challenges us to consider the conditions of the past and use them to think about the present. The collections also carry stories and histories that have been buried in archives and storage as the focus on cultural nationalism in museum collections dictated that this building full of taxidermy and glass jars was not essential to Irish history or identity.

The trope 'museum of a museum' has given rise to a widespread public perception that the Natural History Museum is an unaltered example of a nineteenth-century science museum.[14] This mythology was in full force in April 2010, when the museum reopened after another period of closure, repair and refurbishment, undertaken in the aftermath of the collapse of a stone staircase in 2007. During the week it re-opened, press and broadcast accounts were filled with nostalgic reminiscences of childhood hours spent among the specimens, and declarations of affection for the 'Dead Zoo'. Consistently repeated was the notion that the museum had 'remained virtually unchanged since it was opened in 1857'.[15] Archival records tell a different story, showing a cultural institution that took time to develop and reach its full potential, struggling to achieve its own goals and to meet the expectations being heaped upon it from numerous quarters. Archives bring simple facts to light, such as evidence that the museum in 1857 was an unfinished shell, and that change was constant for the ensuing twenty years. Unearthing the museum's history and its importance in nineteenth-century intellectual culture shows that the kind of stasis assumed by such sweeping statements really began in the early twentieth century, and that nostalgia has obscured the importance of this museum in the history of Irish science and education. Under Carte's guidance, the museum was far from a 'dead zoo', but was an active and ambitious institution.

Situating the Natural History Museum within aspects of the intellectual and cultural environments of Dublin in the mid-nineteenth century reveals that its character and activities were far from the mythology of polite and genteel stasis through which it is viewed today, and uncovers its contributions to the emergence of scientific knowledge within an increasingly professionalised field of inquiry. It also reveals that, though the science undertaken in Dublin may be considered within the context of science in Great Britain due to the complexity of Ireland's political status in the nineteenth century, it also evinces a series of distinctive characteristics revolving around the social, intellectual and economic conditions of Ireland in the same period. The museum's development, as well as how it was used and understood as an institution, challenges Oliver MacDonagh's assertion that the period 1845–70 was 'among the most barren culturally in modern Irish history'.[16] Considering science and museums as cultural configurations in the nineteenth century foregrounds the importance of natural history museums in Ireland as they bore the weight of expectation from a number of constituencies. The RDS saw the museum as central to its control of the discourse around science and improvement in Ireland, and as a source of approval from parliament, where it was otherwise so often at odds. Central government relied upon the museum for the growth and establishment of formal scientific and technical education in Ireland. Irish men of science used it as a source of institutional legitimacy that allowed them to participate in the development of natural science on an international level. It was used by Irish men on active duty within British military structures, primarily in exploration, surveys and military and colonial service, as a means of adding significance to their positions by contributing to the collections as an act of public service. Members of the public contributed to the collections in varying ways that reveal engagement with natural history as an amateur pursuit in Ireland.

The Royal Dublin Society's Natural History Museum was conceptually and materially bound to the growth and development of museums in Europe at large. The activities of the learned societies demonstrate that the assumption of 'cultural desuetude' in mid-century Ireland, as identified by Murphy, must be reconsidered.[17] Comerford's assertion that 'this era has had its distinctiveness ignored or distorted by the preoccupation of popular historiography with the mythic march of the nation' touches on aspects of the period which have been given little attention in published histories, including the histories of museums.[18] The popularity of the museum on its public open days, the success of the 1857 British Association meeting, the wealth of lectures on science and technology, the level of reportage on broadly scientific topics, the plethora of scientific publications and the insistence of central government on the value of museums as educational formations, all point to the migration of aspects of cultural activity into the arena of scientific culture. In addition, the exhibitions and shows that formed part of popular entertainment culture were frequently scientific in tone and content; events covered in the newspapers, such as a private lecture on mesmerism and phrenology by Robert McDonnell, MD, or a temporary exhibition of wax anatomical models from the Museum of Anatomy, Arts and Science of Berlin, underscore engagement with science as a cultural activity in the mid-century.[19] While, as Murphy points out, developments in exhibitions and science became an opportunity for political expression, their influence was wider and deeper than their uses as venues for political ideology. They remain 'blind spots' in our rear-view mirror vision of Irish history, and re-examining the Natural History Museum opens a space for the reconsideration of mid-nineteenth-century intellectual culture.

Science historian John Pickstone, in assessing the overarching constructs of nineteenth-century British science, raises the questions 'what was nineteenth century about it', and 'what was British about it?'[20] By extension, one of the questions raised by examining the history and structures of the Natural History Museum is that, if there is a historical formation that carries the designation 'Irish science', then what makes it Irish? While there is no definitive answer to that question, the issues it suggests are worth considering. While it has been framed as an Irish institution since its beginnings in the eighteenth century, its connections to other structures and institutions place the Natural History Museum in an ambivalent position. Its original collections, such as the Leskean, were comprised largely of materials from other places. Even into Scouler's era, the holdings of local materials representing Ireland's natural history were small. Though this gradually changed, there remained a focus on specimens from across the globe as men in military and colonial services sent materials for the collections. In addition, the men of science in the networks of knowledge in Irish natural history were closely entwined with their counterparts in Great Britain and the rest of Europe. The consistent impulse to measure Irish natural history in relation to the British Museum and through the apparatus of the British Association for the Advancement of Science, for example, demonstrates the importance of Great Britain in the making of scientific reputations, and in the development of Irish natural history. This was exacerbated with the intervention of the Science and Art Department, and its efforts to rationalise Irish scientific and educational institutions with those in England, Scotland and Wales. In addition, Carte kept abreast of developments on the continent, and also communicated with men of science in Australia, Jamaica and Singapore, as well as Irish men posted abroad who gave him information about museums and natural history in other places. These connections allowed Carte to insert specimens of Irish natural history into the emerging bodies of information shaping the understanding of the global distribution of species, locating Ireland within a wider and growing body of information. These examples suggest that, at least for natural history, Irish science was also international science.

That distinction becomes even more important in the present, as Dublin's Natural History Museum, as is the case with many museums that hold historical collections, is still an active scientific venue. The data collected in the past, in the form of specimens, fossils and geology, now provide raw material for scientists who are asking questions about changes to species based on human interventions, and around climate change. Historical collections provide vital information about changes to species over time, and as many of the specimens in the collections originated from around the globe, international scholars come to study in the museum's archives and storage collections. Museum staff are actively involved in scientific research and publication, and are members of international organisations such as the Natural Sciences Collections Association, which addresses the issues in the maintenance and relevance of historical collections of natural materials. The museum also stores sample materials for contemporary organisations, such as the Irish Whale and Dolphin Group, so that trends in species over time may be analysed and compared. Members of the public are still engaged with the museum, and regularly send queries to the staff and to the keeper, Dr Nigel Monaghan. The museum is still heavily used in arts and education, with visiting groups from schools and colleges studying, drawing and researching in the collections. The number of visitors to this museum continues to grow year upon year, so that, ironically, the Natural History Museum still faces a version of the issues of crowding, refurbishment and space that were foregrounded in the 1836 parliamentary report.

The building itself was assessed in 2007 after the staircase collapse, revealing the need for significant investment in remedial works, and its re-opening in 2010 was partial; two upper balconies remain closed to the public at the time of publication due to health and safety concerns. In February 2018, Ireland's National Planning Framework announced a sweeping development plan entitled *Ireland 2040*, which included 725 million for culture and heritage, with the National Museum, including the Natural History Museum, in line for renovation and repair. The National Museum's *Master Vision Statement 2018–2032* has identified a plan to address and ameliorate the ongoing structural issues in the Natural History Museum, and to bring its visitor facilities up to a modern standard. During the final editing of this book, the museum staff was engaged in moving and securing specimens on the first floor, in order to dismantle two whale skeletons suspended from the ceiling, so that the glass roof that the Natural History Committee complained about in 1858 could finally be completely repaired.

From its inception in the late eighteenth century, the Natural History Museum was understood as a valuable public resource, and it was central to government plans and civic life until its relegation to secondary status in the 1920s. It was home to collections, but also to the people who furthered Irish natural science by making sense of them, and its obscurity in the public records has also obscured some of those people who made important contributions to Ireland's intellectual culture. Examining its complexity as a nineteenth-century institution holds potential for recovering aspects of Irish history that have been eclipsed, and for reconsidering Ireland's place in the history of European scientific culture. As plans for the museum's refurbishment progress, it may be hoped that 'the first national museum that was erected in our island' will be preserved in all its integrity, and that future studies will consider the importance of this historic scientific resource and beloved Dublin institution.[21]

NOTES

Author's Note

1. Ruth Barton, 'Men of Science: Language, identity and professionalization in the mid-Victorian scientific community', *History of Science*, vol. 41, no. 1, 2003, pp. 73–119.

Introduction

1. Henry F. Berry, *A History of the Royal Dublin Society* (London: Longman's, Green & Co., 1915), p. 22.

2. Barbara T. Gates, 'Ordering Nature: Revisioning Victorian science culture', in Bernard Lightman (ed.), *Victorian Science in Context* (Chicago: University of Chicago Press, 1997), p. 179.

3. Ibid., pp. 179–86.

4. Samuel Alberti, 'Constructing Nature Behind Glass', *Museum and Society*, vol. 6, no. 2, 2008, p. 73. Emphasis in the original.

5. https://www.museum.ie/en-IE/Museums/Natural-History

6. David Fitzpatrick, 'Ireland and the Empire', in Andrew Porter (ed.), *The Oxford History of the British Empire. Vol III: The nineteenth century* (Oxford: Oxford University Press, 1999), p. 509.

7. Juliana Adelman, *Communities of Science in Nineteenth-Century Ireland* (London: Routledge, 2009), p. 11.

8. Robert Kane, *The Industrial Resources of Ireland*, 2nd ed. (Dublin: Hodges & Smith, 1845), p. 406.

9. H.B. White, 'The History of the Science and Art Institutions of Dublin', *Museum Bulletin* (National Museum of Science and Art), vol. 1, 1911, p. 7.

10. Jonah Siegel, *The Emergence of the Modern Museum* (Oxford: Oxford University Press, 2008), p. 4.

11. Ibid.

12. See *Proceedings of the Natural History Society of Dublin*, vols. I–V; *Journal of the Geological Society of Dublin; Proceedings of the Dublin University Zoological and Botanical Association*, vols. I–II.

13. *Address of the President of the Belfast Natural History Society on the Opening of the Belfast Museum* (Belfast: John Hodgson, 1831).

14. Clara Cullen, 'The Museum of Irish Industry, Robert Kane and Education for All in the Dublin of the 1850s and 1860s', *History of Education*, vol. 38, no. 1, 2009, pp. 99–113.

15. See *Journal of the Geological Society of Dublin; Proceedings of the Dublin University Zoological and Botanical Association; Transactions of the Kilkenny Archaeological Society.*

16. Oliver MacDonagh, 'Ireland and the Union, 1801–70', in W.E. Vaughan (ed.), *A New History of Ireland. Vol. 5: Ireland under the Union, 1801–70* (Oxford: Oxford University Press, 1989), p. lix.

17. James H. Murphy, *Abject Loyalty: Nationalism and monarchy in Ireland during the reign of Queen Victoria* (Cork: Cork University Press, 2001), p. 110.

18. C.P. Snow, *The Two Cultures and the Scientific Revolution* (New York: Cambridge University Press, 1961).

19. R.V. Comerford, 'Ireland, 1850–70: Post-Famine and mid-Victorian', in W.E. Vaughan (ed.), *A New history of Ireland. Vol V: Ireland under the Union, 1801–70* (Oxford: Oxford University Press, 1989), p. 372.

20. John Wilson Foster, *Recoveries: Neglected episodes in Irish cultural history, 1860–1912* (Dublin: UCD Press, 2003), pp. 1–5. Foster's own significant contribution to that end is John Wilson Foster and Helena C.G. Chesney (eds), *Nature in Ireland: A scientific and cultural history* (Dublin: Lilliput Press, 1997), though even this volume contains very little reference to the Natural History Museum, Dublin.

Chapter 1

1. Francis Bacon, *Novum Organum. Book 2: Aphorism 10,* translated by Johnathan Bennett (2005), https://www.earlymoderntexts.com/assets/pdfs/bacon1620.pdf

2. Lisbet Koener, 'Carl Linnaeus in His Time and Place', in N. Jardine, J.A. Secord and E.C. Spary (eds), *Cultures of Natural History* (Cambridge: Cambridge University Press, 1996), pp. 146–9.

3. When reorganising the Royal Irish Academy's collections of natural objects and antiquities in 1856–7, William Wilde used a Linnaean-style system to make sense of the collections.

4. James Meenan and Desmond Clarke (eds), *The Royal Dublin Society, 1731–1981* (Dublin: Royal Dublin Society, 1981), pp. 1–4.

5. Berry, *A History of the Royal Dublin Society*, p. 17.

6. *The Dublin Society's Weekly Observations* (Dublin: R. Reilly, 1739).

7. *A Copy of His Majesty's Royal Charter for Incorporating the Dublin Society* (Dublin, 1750), p. 4.

8. Meenan and Clarke, *The Royal Dublin Society*, pp. 8–10.

9. Michael Brown, *The Irish Enlightenment* (Cambridge: Harvard University Press, 2016), p. 161.

10. Meenan and Clarke, *The Royal Dublin Society*, pp. 11–14.

11. *Gentleman's Magazine*, vol. 59 (London, 1786), pp. 217–18.

12. Berry, *A History of the Royal Dublin Society*, pp. 91–3.

13. G.F. Mitchell, 'Mineralogy and Geology', in Meenan and Clarke, *The Royal Dublin Society*, pp. 154–6. Stewart's activities appear to have been modest, and not particularly effective.

14. Patrick Wyse-Jackson, 'Fluctuations in Fortune: Three hundred years of Irish geology', in Foster and Chesney (eds), *Nature in Ireland*, pp. 94–5.

15. According to the National Archives converter for historical currency, £1,350 in 1792 would be roughly equivalent to £103,627 in 2017. http://www.nationalarchives.gov.uk/currency–converter/

16. C.E. O'Riordan, *The Natural History Museum, Dublin* (Dublin: National Museum of Ireland, 1983), pp. 7–8.

17. Mitchell, 'Mineralogy and Geology', pp. 154–6.

18. Ibid., p. 154.

19. Werner specifically stated that the body of water he proposed was not the biblical deluge, but a previous event.

20. Dennis R. Dean, *James Hutton and the History of Geology* (Ithaca: Cornell University Press, 1992), pp. 92–101.

21. Hutton's theories soon displaced Werner's and became the foundation for modern geological thought.

22. Martin Guntau, 'The Natural History of the Earth', in Jardine et al. (eds), *Cultures of Natural History*, pp. 212–14.

23. Ibid., pp. 213–14.

24. Susan Pearce, *Museums, Objects and Collections: A cultural study* (Leicester: Leicester University Press, 1992), p. 2.

25. Meenan and Clarke, *The Royal Dublin Society*, p. 30.

26. Kevin Bright, *The Royal Dublin Society, 1815–45* (Dublin: Four Courts Press, 2004), p. 46.

27. E.C. Spary, *Utopia's Garden: French natural history from old regime to revolution* (Chicago: University of Chicago Press, 2000), pp. 1– 8.

28. Carla Yanni, *Nature's Museums: Victorian science and the architecture of display* (London: The Athlone Press, 1999), p. 34.

29. Peter J. Bowler, *Evolution: The history of an idea* (Berkeley: University of California Press, 1983), pp. 112–18.

30. Martin J.S. Rudwick, *Bursting the Limits of Time: The reconstruction of geohistory in an age of revolution* (Chicago: University of Chicago Press, 2005), pp. 361–2.

31. Adelman, *Communities of Science*, pp. 23–4.

32. John Hart, *A description of the skeleton of the fossil deer of Ireland, Cervus megaceros, drawn up at the instance of the Committee of Natural Philosophy of the Royal Dublin Society* (Dublin: R. Graisberry, 1825). Hart's reconstructed skeleton still stands at the front of the museum today.

33. Edward Miller, *That Noble Cabinet: A history of the British Museum* (Athens: Ohio University Press, 1973), pp. 44–6.

34. Ibid., pp. 67–90.

35. None that this author has been able to locate.

36. A. Whittaker, 'Sir Charles Lewis Giesecke, 1761–1833', in Patrick Wyse-Jackson, *Four Centuries of Geological Travel: The search for knowledge on foot, bicycle, sledge, and camel* (London: Geological Society of London, 2007), p. 157.

37. Ibid., pp. 149–158

38. Patrick Wyse-Jackson, 'Sir Charles Lewis Giesecke (1761–1833) and Greenland: A recently discovered mineral collection in Trinity College Dublin', *Irish Journal of Earth Sciences*, vol. 15, 1996, p. 163.

39. John James McGregor, *New Picture of Dublin: Comprehending a history of the city, an accurate account of its various establishments and institutions, and a correct description of all the public edifices connected with them* (Dublin: Johnston & Deas, 1821), pp. 216–22.

40. Ibid., p. 218.

41. Ibid., pp. 218–19.

42. Ibid., p. 222.

43. *Dublin Penny Journal*, 11 August 1832.

44. Constance Classen, 'Museum Manners: The sensory life of the early museum', *Journal of Social History*, vol. XL, no. 4, Summer 2007, pp. 895–914.

45. Ibid., pp. 897–8.

46. James Secord, 'How Scientific Conversation Became Shop Talk', in Aileen Fyfe and Bernard Lightman (eds), *Science in the Marketplace: Nineteenth-century sites and experiences* (Chicago: University of Chicago Press, 2007), p. 30.

47. For instance, Giesecke's publications included 'On the Mineralogy of Disko Island', in *Transactions of the Royal Society of Edinburgh*, vol. IX (Edinburgh, 1823), pp. 263–72, and *Account of a Mineralogical Excursion to the County of Donegal* (Dublin, 1826).

48. Bernard O'Reilly, *Catalogue of the subjects of natural history in the museum of the right hon. and hon. Dublin Society, systematically arranged, and also of antiquities &c.* (Dublin: Graisberry & Campbell, 1813).

49. Ibid. For more information about the authorship of this catalogue, see J.P. O'Connor, 'Bernard O'Reilly: Genius or rogue?', *The Irish Naturalists' Journal*, vol. 21, no. 9, 1985, pp. 379–84.

50. Sir Charles Lewis Giesecke, *Descriptive catalogue of a new collection of minerals in the museum of the Royal Dublin Society, to which is added an Irish mineralogy* (Dublin: R. Graisberry, 1832).

51. E. Charles Nelson, *John Scouler (c. 1804–1871), Scottish Naturalist: A life, with two voyages* (Glasgow: Glasgow Natural History Society, 2014), pp. 7–8.

52. Malcolm Nicolson, 'John Scouler', *Dictionary of Irish Biography* (Cambridge: Cambridge University Press, 2009). Hooker was influential in ensuring that all government missions of exploration and trade were supplied with botanists, thus launching the careers of numerous natural scientists.

53. Nelson, *John Scouler*, p. 10.

54. Nelson, *John Scouler*, pp. 45–50; Nicolson, 'John Scouler'.

55. *Dublin Penny Journal*, 31 October 1835. The dimensions of the rooms are taken from architectural drawings in *Catalogue of articles of manufactures, produce and invention exhibited at the Royal Dublin Society's house, July 8, 1850 and following days* (Dublin, 1850).

56. *Dublin Penny Journal*, 31 October 1835.

57. Ibid.

58. John McLeod, *The Voyage of His Majesty's Ship the Alceste, along the Coast of Corea to the Island of Lewchew* (London: John Murray, 1818). McLeod offers a long and detailed description of the snake and its habits during its transport in captivity to England on pages 288–98.

59. *Dublin Penny Journal*, 31 October 1835.

60. Ibid.

61. Ibid.

62. Ibid.

63. Ibid.

64. Pearce, *Museums, Objects and Collections*, p. 89.

65. *Report from the Select Committee on the Royal Dublin Society, HCPP 1836, XXII (445)*, p. 370. These headline figures did not always include special funding for particular purposes, such as the monies eventually granted to build the museum.

66. Bright, *The Royal Dublin Society*, pp. 125–39; the second half of Chapter 5 elaborates on the intricate political and internal structures of the RDS.

67. *Select Committee on the Royal Dublin Society*, 1836, p. ii.

68. Bright, *The Royal Dublin Society*, pp. 111–14.

69. Ibid., pp. 142–5.

70. *Select Committee on the Royal Dublin Society*, 1836, pp. iii–xviii, 41.

71. Ibid., pp. iii–xviii, 42.

72. Jim Cook, 'The Dublin Mechanics' Institute, 1824–1919', *Dublin Historical Record*, vol. 52, no. 1, Spring, 1999, pp. 15–31.

73. *Select Committee on the RDS*, 1836, pp. 128–9.

74. Ibid.

75. Ibid., p. xix.

76. *Report from the Select Committee on the British Museum*, 1836, HCPP 440 (1836).

77. *Select Committee on the British Museum*, 1836, p. 133.

78. Ibid., p. 147.

79. Ibid., p. xi.

80. Nils Lithberg, *Report of the Committee of Enquiry into the National Museum of Ireland and Report on the Same* (1927), Irish Free State Parliamentary Papers.

Chapter 2

1. *Select Committee on the RDS*, 1836, p. xviii.

2. Ibid., p. xvii.

3. *Proceedings of the Royal Dublin Society*, 5 November 1840 to 24 June 1841 (Dublin, 1841).

4. Berry, *A History of the Royal Dublin Society*, pp. 272–4.

5. *The Nation*, 26 November 1842, reprinted from the *Morning Register*.

6. Thomas Osborne Davis, 'Institutions of Dublin', in D.J. O'Donoghue (ed.), *Essays, Literary and Historical by Thomas Davis. Centenary edition, including several pieces never before collected* (Dundalk: Dundalgan Press, 1914), pp. 329–39.

7. *Freeman's Journal*, 15 March 1841.

8. Berry, *A History of the Royal Dublin Society*, pp. 274–6.

9. John Coolahan, *Irish Education: History and structure* (Dublin: Institute of Public Administration, 1981), p. 3.

10. Ibid., p. 4.

11. Ibid., p. 52.

12. *Proceedings RDS November 5, 1840 to June 24, 1841*, p. 45.

13. Berry, *A History of the Royal Dublin Society*, pp. 160–1.

14. Ibid.

15. Brian B. Kelham and Douglas McMillan, 'Experimental Science in Ireland and the Scientific Societies', in Norman McMillan (ed.), *Prometheus's Fire: A history of scientific and technical education in Ireland* (Kilkenny: Tyndall Publications, 2000), p. 111.

16. Berry, *A History of the Royal Dublin Society*, pp. 160–1.

17. *The Veterinarian: A monthly journal of veterinary science for 1837* (London, 1837) vol. X, no. 117, 1837, appendix, p. 15; *Proceedings RDS July 4, 1830 to August 20, 1840* (Dublin, 1840), p. 24.

18. RDS Natural History Committee Minutes, 1831–54, 26 November 1839.

19. *Proceedings RDS July 4, 1839 to August 20, 1840*, p. 34.

20. Linde Lunney, 'Ferguson, Hugh', in *Dictionary of Irish Biography*. Ferguson was also instrumental at the RDS as the chief veterinarian at its newly established Dublin Horse Show in 1868, helping to fashion standards for the judging of horses in early competitions.

21. Records of the lecturers can be found throughout the *Proceedings of the Royal Dublin Society*.

22. RDS Natural History Committee, 1831–54, 22 February 1848.

23. Ibid., 29 February 1848.

24. Ibid., 18 February 1840.

25. *Proceedings RDS November 4, 1852 to September 8, 1853*, pp. xxiii–iv. The RDS was inconsistent in recording attendance for its lectures, and figures for earlier years appear to be non-existent, though lectures had been conducted since 1838.

26. For discussion of the use of visual aids in scientific lectures, see Enda Leaney, 'Missionaries of Science: Provincial lectures in nineteenth-century Ireland', *Irish Historical Studies*, vol. XXIV, no. 135, May 2005, pp. 271–3; and Bernard Lightman, 'The Showmen of Science: Wood, pepper and visual spectacle', in *Victorian Popularizers of Science: Designing nature for new audiences* (Chicago: University of Chicago Press, 2007), pp. 167–218.

27. RDS Natural History Committee, 1831–54, 2 January 1849.

28. This changed after the mid-century, as an 1853 poster advertising a series of natural history lectures by Scouler shows the starting time as 8 p.m.

29. *Select Committee on the RDS*, 1836, p. viii.

30. Ibid., p. viii. Though the expanded grant made the series possible, it did not cover all costs, and local societies also paid a fee of £10, as well as travel and accommodation for the lecturer. See Leaney, 'Missionaries of Science', pp. 270–1.

31. Leaney, 'Missionaries of Science', p. 271.

32. *Nenagh Guardian*, 5 May 1851.

33. William Lane Joynt, as cited in Leaney, 'Missionaries of Science', p. 270.

34. *Proceedings RDS July 11, 1850 to July 19, 1851*, p. 20. Scientific papers were also sometimes summarised in the press.

35. Royal Dublin Society, *Reports of the Proceedings of the Meetings for the Discussion of Subjects Connected with Practical Science and Art, 1848–1855* (Dublin: M.H. Gill, 1855), pp. 114, 248.

36. John Robert Kinahan, 'Remarks on the habits and distribution of marine crustacea on the eastern shores of Port Phillip, Victoria, Australia; with descriptions of unidentified species and genera', *JRDS*, vol. I, 1856–7.

37. Royal Dublin Society, *Reports of the Proceedings, 1848–1855*, p. 115.

38. *Select Committee on the RDS*, 1836, p. xxi.

39. MS letter, 'Report from Dr. Scouler' (January 1840), bound into RDS Natural History Committee Minutes, 1831–54.

40. RDS Natural History Committee, 1831–54, 24 January 1840; also Natural History Museum Register, 1834–51 (compiled by John Scouler; held in the Natural History Museum Archives: Natural History).

41. *Proceedings RDS, July 4, 1839 to August 20, 1840*, p. 92.

42. RDS Natural History Committee, 1831–54. Committee minutes show that William Dowling was paid £5 for this task in May 1840.

43. Natural History Museum Register, 1834–51 (compiled by John Scouler), National Museum of Ireland Archives.

44. RDS Natural History Committee, 1831–54, 4 March 1840.

45. Ibid., 1 December 1840.

46. Ibid., 7 December 1841.

47. Ibid., 14 February 1842.

48. Ibid., 14 February 1842.

49. Nelson, *John Scouler*, p. 59.

50. Ibid., p. 62.

51. David E. Allen, 'Amateurs and Professionals', in Peter Bowler and John V. Pickstone, *Cambridge History of Science. Volume 6: modern biological and earth sciences* (Cambridge: Cambridge University Press, 2009), p. 15.

52. Ibid., p. 16.

53. Nelson, *John Scouler*, pp. 6–8.

54. *First Annual Report of the Dublin Natural History Society* (Dublin, 1839); Minute Book: Dublin Natural History Society, 1838 (held at the Royal Irish Academy, MS 12 P 2).

55. Clara Cullen, 'The Museum of Irish Industry (1845–1867): Research environment, popular museum and community of learning in mid-Victorian Ireland', PhD thesis, University College Dublin, 2008, pp. 99–113.

56. O.J.R. Howarth, *The British Association for the Advancement of Science: A retrospect* (London: The British Association for the Advancement of Science, 1922), p. 19.

57. Barton, 'Men of Science', p. 74.

58. Robert Patterson, 'Memoir of the Late Robert Ball', in *Proceedings of the Dublin University Zoological and Botanical Association*, vol. I (Dublin, 1858).

59. John Hart, Royal Dublin Society Past Members Database: http://entrants.rds.ie/pastmembers/index.php?r=1980

60. Patricia M. Byrne, 'Carte, Alexander', *Dictionary of Irish Biography*.

61. For instance, William Henry Harvey, *The Genera of South African Plants: Arranged according to the natural system* (Cape Town, 1838), and *A Manual of the British Algae: Containing generic and specific descriptions of all the known British species of sea-weeds, and of conferae, both marine and fresh-water* (London, 1841); John Hart, *A description of the skeleton of the fossil deer of Ireland, Cervus megaceros, drawn up at the instance of the Committee of Natural Philosophy of the Royal Dublin Society* (Dublin, 1825).

62. Royal Dublin Society Minutes, vol. 18, 1844–6 (contains entries to 1848), 28 March 1844.

63. RDS Natural History Committee, 1831–54, 1 February 1845.

64. Harriet Ritvo, 'Zoological Nomenclature and the Empire of Victorian Science', in Lightman (ed.), *Victorian Science in Context*, p. 336.

65. 'Proposed plan for rendering the nomenclature of zoology uniform and permanent, being the report of a committee for the consideration of the subject appointed by the British Association for the Advancement of Science', in *The Annals and Magazine of Natural History, including Zoology, Botany and Geology*, vol XI (London, 1843).

66. RDS Natural History Committee, 1831–54, 7 June 1845.

67. Ibid.

68. See John Turpin, 'The School of Design in Victorian Ireland', *Journal of Design History*, vol. 2, no. 4, 1989, pp. 243–56.

69. *Report upon the Royal Dublin Society, the Museum of Irish Industry and on the System of Scientific Instruction in Ireland*, HCPP 1863 (3180), p. 50.

70. Turpin, 'The School of Design in Victorian Ireland', pp. 243–56.

71. 'Ninth public distribution of prizes awarded to the successful students of the annual competition for prizes in drawing and modelling being the first ever superintendence of the Government School of Design (Appendix IX)', in *Proceedings of the Royal Dublin Society*, 7 November 1850 to 26 June 1851 (Dublin, 1851), p. cxiii. It should be noted that comparative anatomy roughly corresponded to zoology, with the terms sometimes used interchangeably.

72. Robert Hewison, *John Ruskin* (Oxford: Oxford University Press, 2007), p. 20.

73. John Ruskin, *Modern Painters. Volume One: Of general principles, and of truth*, 2nd ed. (London: George Allen, 1898), p. xxxviii.

74. George J. Allman, *The Importance of Natural History Studies to the Artist: A lecture delivered at the seventh public distribution of prizes to the pupils of the Royal Dublin Society Drawing School, 1849*, p. 3. Held as a pamphlet in the collection of the National Library of Ireland, P1177(9).

75. Ibid.

76. John Turpin, 'Exhibitions of Art and Industries in Victorian Ireland, part I', *Dublin Historical Record*, vol. 35, no. 1, 1981, p. 250.

77. McManus at the eighth awarding of prizes, as quoted in ibid.

78. W.H. Harvey, *Botany Considered in Reference to the Arts of Design: An introductory address delivered in the theatre of the Royal Dublin Society, 1849*. Held as a pamphlet in the collection of the National Library of Ireland P206(12). Emphasis in the original.

79. *RDS Proceedings*, 4 November 1852 to 8 September 1853 (Dublin, 1853), p. cxiv. The men who supplied the prizes were variously occupied in the textile industry.

80. RDS Natural History Committee, 1831–54, 19 March 1850.

81. Ibid., 25 February 1851.

82. Ibid., 7 March 1851.

83. Ibid., 7 March 1851.

84. Ibid., 19 March 1851.

85. Ibid., 19 March 1851.

86. Ibid., 19 March 1851.

87. Ibid., 19 March 1851. Several sources (White, Bourke) credit the suggestion of hiring a new curator to Scouler based on reference to the *Proceedings of the Royal Dublin Society*; Committee minutes indicate that it was the committee's initiative, though Scouler had observed that most European natural history museums had dedicated curators.

88. Samuel J.M.M. Alberti, 'The Status of Museums: Authority, identity and material culture', in David N. Livingstone and Charles Withers (eds), *Geographies of Nineteenth-Century Science* (Chicago: University of Chicago Press, 2011), p. 51.

89. RDS Natural History Committee, 1831–54; entries from April to June deal with creating the new role of curator, the search for candidates, and the election of Carte.

90. Byrne, 'Carte, Alexander', *Dictionary of Irish Biography*. His title was amended to director on 24 June.

91. RDS Natural History Committee, 1831–54, 27 May 1851.

92. Ibid., 11 June 1851.

93. Byrne, 'Carte, Alexander', *Dictionary of Irish Biography*.

94. RDS Natural History Committee, 1831–54, 11 June 1851.

95. Byrne, 'Carte, Alexander', *Dictionary of Irish Biography*.

96. RDS Natural History Committee, 1831–54, 25 June 1851.

97. RDS Natural History Committee, 1831–54: Entries for 1851 track the progress of the discussions.

Chapter 3

1. RDS Natural History Committee, 1831–54, 5 May 1852.

2. Ibid.

3. Ibid., 2 June 1852. Gideon Mantell died in late 1852.

4. *RDS Proceedings*, 4 November 1852 to 8 December 1853 (Dublin, 1853), pp. 20–1.

5. Jeffrey A. Auerbach, *The Great Exhibition of 1851: A nation on display* (New Haven: Yale University Press, 1999), pp. 14–30.

6. Ibid.

7. Ibid.

8. Michael Leapman, *The World for a Shilling: How the Great Exhibition of 1851 shaped a nation* (London: Faber & Faber, 2001), pp. 55–7.

9. Richard Bellon, 'Science at the Crystal Heart of the World', in Fyfe and Lightman (eds), *Science in the Marketplace*, p. 302.

10. Kylie Message and Ewan Johnston, 'The World within the City: The Great Exhibition, race, class and social reform', in Jeffrey A. Auerbach and Peter H. Hoffenberg (eds), *Britain, the Empire and the World at the Great Exhibition of 1851* (London: Routledge, 2008), pp. 38–40.

11. *Appletons' Annual Cyclopaedia and Register of Important Events of the Year: 1862* (New York: D. Appleton & Company, 1863), p. 412.

12. *Freeman's Journal*, 21 October 1852.

13. Auerbach, *The Great Exhibition*, pp. 21–7.

14. Murphy, *Abject Loyalty*, p. 94.

15. Ibid., p. 110.

16. John Sproule (ed.), *The Irish Industrial Exhibition of 1853: A detailed catalogue of its contents* (Dublin, 1854), p. 1.

17. Ibid., p. iv.

18. Ibid.

19. RDS Natural History Committee, 1831–54, 4 May 1853.

20. RDS, *Proceedings*, 1 July 1853 to 30 June 1854, p. lxix; RDS, *Proceedings*, 4 November 1852 to 8 September 1853, p. xxv.

21. RDS Natural History Committee, 1831–54, 6 July 1853; also 'Museum of Natural History: Ceremony of laying the foundation stone', in *JRDS*, vol. I, 1856–7 (Dublin, 1858), p. 53.

22. Henry Cole, *The Functions of the Department of Science and Art* (London, 1857), pp. 3–4.

23. Richard A. Jarrell, 'The Department of Science and Art and the Control of Irish Science, 1853–1905', *Irish Historical Studies*, vol. 23, no. 92, 1983, pp. 330–1.

24. Marie Bourke, *The Story of Irish Museums, 1790–2000* (Cork: Cork University Press, 2011), p. 186; O'Riordan, *The Natural History Museum, Dublin*, p. 17. A copy of the original contract rests in the RDS archives.

25. 'Museum of Natural History: Ceremony of laying the foundation stone', *JRDS*, vol. I, 1856–7, pp. 51–6. The event was also reported in the *Illustrated London News*.

26. *Illustrated London News*, 15 March 1856.

27. *RDS Proceedings*, 1 July 1856 to 16 July 1857 (Dublin, 1857), pp. 11–12.

28. R.B. McDowell, 'The Main Narrative', in T. Ó Raifeartaigh (ed.), *The Royal Irish Academy: A bicentennial history, 1785–1985* (Dublin: Royal Irish Academy, 1985), pp. 39–40.

29. The first volume was *A descriptive catalogue of the antiquities of stone, earthen and vegetable matter in the museum of the Royal Irish Academy* (Dublin, 1857).

30. Patrick Wyse-Jackson, 'The Geological Collections of Trinity College Dublin', *The Geological Curator*, vol. 5, no. 7, 1992, pp. 265–6.

31. Cullen, 'The Museum of Irish Industry (1845–1867)'.

32. *Proceedings of the Natural History Society of Dublin*, vol. II (Dublin, 1860), p. 69.

33. *RDS Proceedings*, 1 July 1856 to 16 July 1857 (Dublin, 1857), p. 45.

34. See Samuel J.M.M. Alberti, 'Conversaziones and the Experience of Science in Victorian England', *Journal of Victorian Culture*, vol. 8, no. 2, 2003, pp. 208–30; Susan David Bernstein, 'Supposed Differences: Lydia Becker and Victorian women's participation in the BAAS', in D. Clifford, E. Wadge, A. Warwick and M. Willis, *Repositioning Victorian Sciences: Shifting centres in nineteenth-century thinking* (London: Anthem Press, 2006), pp. 85–94.

35. Secord, 'How Scientific Talk Became Shop Talk', pp. 44–5.

36. Ibid., p. 25.

37. *RDS Proceedings*, 1 July 1856 to 16 July 1857, p. 45.

38. *Freeman's Journal*, 27 August 1857; also printed verbatim in the *Evening Freeman* and *The Nation*.

39. Newspapers, particularly the *Freeman's Journal*, *Evening Freeman* and *Dublin Evening Mail*, provided extensive coverage of all events. See also C. Withers, R. Higgit and D. Finnegan, 'Historical Geographies of Provincial Science: Themes in the setting and reception of the British Association for the Advancement of Science in Britain and Ireland, 1831–*c.* 1939', *British Journal for the History of Science*, vol. 41, no. 3, 2008, pp. 385–415.

40. 'Extraordinary Meeting of the Dublin Provisional Committee of the British Association', *The Nation*, 29 August 1857, p. 841.

41. *Dublin University Magazine*, September 1857, vol. 50, p. 271.

42. Sherra Murphy, 'The Learned Gentlemen Are in Town: The British Association meeting of 1857 in Dublin's popular press', in Juliana Adelman and Eadaoin Agnew (eds), *Science and Technology in Nineteenth-Century Ireland* (Dublin: Four Courts Press, 2011), p. 167. Also see *Report of the Twenty-Seventh Meeting of the British Association for the Advancement of Science, Held at Dublin in August and September, 1857* (London, 1858), for papers by Irish men of science, such as W.K. Sullivan, W.H. Baily, Richard Griffith, Samuel Haughton, J.R. Kinahan, William Andrews and E. Perceval Wright.

43. *Freeman's Journal*, 28 August 1857.

44. Ibid.

45. Ibid.

46. Ibid.

47. Ibid.

48. 'Annual Report of the Royal Dublin Society for the Year 1857', appended to *RDS Proceedings*, 1 July 1856 to 16 July 1857.

49. Ibid.

50. Natural History Committee Minutes, 1854–77, 4 January 1860.

51. Ibid.

52. 'Annual Report of the Royal Dublin Society', in *Ninth Report of the Science and Art Department of the Committee of Council on Education* (London, 1862), p. 160.

53. Ibid.

54. *Irish Times*, 24 September 1862.

55. *RDS Proceedings*, 3 July 1862 to 23 June 1863, p. ix; 'Annual report of the Royal Dublin Society for the year 1864' p. 4, appended to *RDS Proceedings*, 31 July 1864 to 29 June 1865.

56. 'Account of the Commissioners of Audit', p. cxcvi, appended to *RDS Proceedings*, 6 November 1851 to 24 June 1852; 'Abstract of Income and Expenditure', p. xlv, appended to *RDS Proceedings*, 4 July 1858 to 30 June 1859.

57. Nelson, *John Scouler*, p. 71.

58. 'Annual Report of the Royal Dublin Society for the Year 1863', p. 8, appended to *RDS Proceedings*, 17 July 1863 to 30 June 1864.

59. *Report upon the Royal Dublin Society, the Museum of Irish Industry and the System of Scientific Instruction in Ireland, 1862*, HCPP 1863 (3180), p. 15.

60. Ibid., pp. 18–19; Cullen, 'The Museum of Irish Industry', pp. 106–7.

61. *Report upon the Royal Dublin Society, 1862*, p. 15.

62. *Copy of Minute of the Lords' Committee of Privy Council for Trade, dated 11 April, in Reference to the Estimates for the Royal Dublin Society, and Report of the Council of the Society in Reference Thereto*, HCPP 1854 (330), pp. 6–8.

63. *Report upon the Royal Dublin Society, 1862*, pp. 26–7.

64. Ibid., p. 26.

65. Ibid., p. 55.

66. Ibid., p. 90.

67. Ibid., p. 4.

68. *Report from the Select Committee on Scientific Institutions (Dublin)*, HCPP 1864 (495), p. xii.

69. Ibid., p. xiii.

70. Ibid., p. xxiii.

71. *RDS Proceedings*, 6 July 1865 to 27 June 1866, pp. 96–7.

72. *RDS Proceedings*, 11 July 1867 to 25 June 1868, p. 82.

73. *Sixteenth Report of the Science and Art Department of the Committee of Council on Education* (London, 1869), pp. 436–7.

74. *JRDS*, vol. V, pp. 260–2.

75. *Seventeenth Report of the Science and Art Department of the Committee of Council on Education* (London, 1870), p. 504.

76. O'Riordan, *The Natural History Museum, Dublin*, p. 23.

77. *Scientific Institutions and Instruction in Dublin. Copy of minute of Committee of Council on Education relative to scientific institutions and instruction in Dublin*, HCPP 1866 (42).

78. *Dublin Science and Art Museum Act of 1877* (40 & 41 Vict., ch. ccxxxiv).

Chapter 4

1. *Select Committee on the Royal Dublin Society*, 1836, p. 42.

2. *Ninth Report of the Science and Art Department*, pp. 160–1.

3. Samuel J.M.M. Alberti, 'Objects and the Museum', *ISIS*, vol. 96, no. 4, 2005, p. 564.

4. Sandford Palmer to A. Carte, 3 April 1866, MS letter box 30, National Museum of Ireland Archives, Natural History.

5. Lightman, *Victorian Popularizers of Science*, p. 4.

6. Gates, 'Ordering Nature', p. 179.

7. Andrew Pickering (ed.), *Science as Practice and Culture* (Chicago: University of Chicago Press, 1992), p. 1.

8. Bruno Latour, *Reassembling the Social: An introduction to actor-network-theory* (Oxford: Oxford University Press, 2005), p. 128.

9. James Bennett, 'Why the History of Science Matters in Ireland', in David Attis and Charles Mollan (eds), *Science and Irish Culture: Why the history of science matters in Ireland*, vol. I (Dublin: Royal Dublin Society, 2004), pp. 5–6.

10. J. Leslie Foster, 'Biographical Sketch of Sir Charles Lewis Metzler von Giesecke', *The Dublin University Magazine*, vol iii, 1834, p. 161; E. Charles Nelson, 'William Henry Harvey', in *Oxford Dictionary of National Biography*.

11. Patrick N. Wyse-Jackson, 'Haughton, Samuel', in *Dictionary of Irish Biography*.

12. Petra Coffey, 'George Victor du Noyer: Artist, geologist and antiquary', *The Journal of the Royal Society of Antiquaries of Ireland*, vol. 123, 1993, pp. 102–19.

13. Both are represented in the correspondence and donations to the museum, as well as in the *Journal of the Royal Dublin Society* and the *Proceedings of the Natural History Society of Dublin*.

14. Robert K. Nutall, San Francisco, to A. Carte, 1858, MS letter box 30, National Museum of Ireland (hereafter NMI) Archives.

15. All references to donations here were taken from these sources; the National Library of Ireland holds a full set of this journal, volumes I to VII. The open-source internet archive Archive.org also holds a number of them, which are searchable and may be downloaded. The author has compiled an extensive database list of donations, which she is happy to share with researchers.

16. Barton, 'Men of Science', pp. 81–7.

17. Ibid., p. 95.

18. Nutall to Carte, 1858, MS letter box 30, NMI Archives.

19. James Bennett, 'Science and Social Policy in Mid-Nineteenth-Century Ireland', in Peter J. Bowler and Nicholas White (eds), *Science and Society in Ireland: The social context of science and technology in Ireland, 1800–1950* (Belfast: Queen's University Belfast, 1997), p. 39.

20. Ibid.

21. *JRDS*, vol. I, pp. 285, 431.

22. Ibid., p. 285.

23. Ibid., p. 432; vol. II, pp. 360, 157.

24. *JRDS*, vol. I, p. 286.

25. Ibid., p. 432; vol. V, pp. 61, 239.

26. *JRDS*, vol. I, p. 46; vol. II, p. 193.

27. Sherrard to Carte, 9 July 1868, MS letter box 30, NMI Archives. There is also a letter in the files from Edward Evans of Gortmerron House, donating specimens from his greenhouses, suggesting that Sherrard developed her interest in natural history within her family context.

28. Dictionary of Irish Architects, http://www.dia.ie/architects/view/4941/sherrard-davidhenry; Sarah Bendell (ed.), *Dictionary of Land Surveyors and Local Map-makers of Great Britain and Ireland, 1530–1850*, 2nd edn (London: The British Library Publishing Division, 1997), vol II, p. 462.

29. Rebekah Higgit and Charles W.J. Withers, 'Science and Sociability: Women as audience at the British Association for the Advancement of Science, 1831–1901', *Isis*, vol. 99, 2008, pp. 1–27.

30. O'Riordan, *The Natural History Museum, Dublin*; Clara Cullen, 'Starry Eyed: Women in science in nineteenth-century Ireland', in Brendan Walsh, *Knowing Their Place: The intellectual life of women in the nineteenth century* (Dublin: The History Press, 2014, e-book edition). In the early to mid-century there are notable anomalies such as naturalist Mary Ward and entomologist Mary Ball, but they are the exceptions that confirm the rule.

31. RDS Natural History Committee, 1831–54, 14 September 1853.

32. *RDS Proceedings*, 6 November 1861 to 24 June 1862 (Dublin, 1862), pp. cixi–cixii.

33. Clibborn to A. Carte, 2 October 1865, MS letter box 30, NMI Archives.

34. Natural History Museum Register, 1851–72 (compiled by Alexander Carte; held in the National Museum Archives, Natural History).

35. *Eighteenth Report of the Board of Public Works, Ireland* (London, 1850), p. 198.

36. Dr William Frazer, 'On the Distribution of *Isocordia cor* along the Irish Coast, with Record of its Discovery in Dungarvan Bay by John Good, Esq', in *Proceedings of the Natural History Society of Dublin*, vol. V (Dublin, 1871), pp. 189–90.

37. *JRDS*, vol. IV, pp. 137, 284; vol. V, pp. 240, 403; NUI Galway Landed Estates Database: Families A–Z, Riall, www.landedestates.ie

38. NUI Galway Landed Estates Database: Families A–Z, Palmer, www.landedestates.ie

39. Palmer to Carte, 28 May 1864, MS letter box 30, NMI Archives.

40. *JRDS*, vol. V, p. 521.

41. *JRDS*, vol. I, p. 285; a Miss Nangle is listed at this address in the 1849 *Dublin Almanac and General Register of Ireland*, but again with no additional information.

42. Patricia M. Byrne, 'Townsend, Richard', in *Dictionary of Irish Biography*. Richard was the son of Helena and Thomas; Thomas Townsend died in 1848.

43. *JRDS*, vol. II, p. 246.

44. Townsend to A. Carte, no date, MS letter box 30, NMI Archives. This letter must date prior to 1863, the year of Helena Townsend's death.

45. David Murphy, 'Talbot, James', in *Dictionary of Irish Biography*.

46. *Proceedings of the Royal Irish Academy*, vol. IX, 1864–6 (Dublin, 1866), pp. 390–95.

47. Powerscourt to Carte, 25 December 1865, MS letter box 30, NMI Archives.

48. See Lightman, *Victorian Science in Context*; Jardine et al. (eds), *Cultures of Natural History*; David E. Allen, *The Naturalist in Britain: A social history* (Princeton: Princeton University Press, 1995); John M. Mackenzie, *Museums and Empire: Natural history, human cultures and colonial identities* (Manchester: Manchester University Press, 2009); David N. Livingstone, *Putting Science in its Place: Geographies of scientific knowledge* (Chicago: University of Chicago Press, 2003); Sarah Longair and John McAleer, *Curating Empire: Museums and the British imperial experience* (Manchester: Manchester University Press, 2012).

49. See the introduction to Longair and McAleer, *Curating Empire.*

50. Mackenzie. *Museums and Empire,* p. 8.

51. Robert A. Stafford, 'Scientific Exploration and Empire', in Andrew Porter and William Roger Louis (eds), *The Oxford History of the British Empire. Volume V: The Nineteenth Century* (Oxford: Oxford University Press, 1999), p. 310. This chapter gives an overview of the relationship between collecting and colonialism.

52. Kevin Kenny, *Ireland and the British Empire* (Oxford: Oxford University Press, 2004), p. 2.

53. Joe Cleary, *Literature, Partition and the Nation State: Culture and conflict in Ireland, Israel and Palestine* (Cambridge: Cambridge University Press, 2002), p. 253.

54. Fitzpatrick, 'Ireland and the Empire', pp. 509–10.

55. Comerford, 'Ireland, 1850–70', p. 372; Barry Crosbie's *Irish Imperial Networks: Migration, social communication and exchange in nineteenth-century India* offers an examination of Irish participation in a specific colonial context (Cambridge: Cambridge University Press, 2012).

56. See Johnathan Jeffrey Wright, 'A Depot for the Productions of the Four Quarters of the Globe: Empire, collecting, and the Belfast Museum', in Diarmid A. Finnegan and Johnathan Jeffrey Wright, *Spaces of Global Knowledge: Exhibition, encounter and exchange in an age of empire* (New York: Routledge, 2016).

57. *JRDS,* vol. I, p. 157.

58. *Supplement to the London Gazette,* 5 March 1858. The actions of British and French forces in the city were reported in newspapers from November 1857 through to the spring of 1858.

59. *Freeman's Journal,* 26 November 1858.

60. *Freeman's Journal,* 14 February 1858.

61. *JRDS,* vol. V, p. 60. A lachrymatory is a ceremonial vessel for containing or collecting tears.

62. Henry Manner Chichester, 'Cunynghame, Sir Arthur Augustus Thurlow', *Oxford Dictionary of National Biography.*

63. *JRDS,* vol. I, p. 432. The *Herald* was a diplomatic frigate that travelled extensively across the globe, and Maguire had been attached to one of the many missions sent in search of Sir John Franklin.

64. *JRDS,* vol. III, p. 173.

65. Laura Franey, 'Ethnographic Collecting and Travel: Blurring boundaries, forming a discipline', *Victorian Literature and Culture,* vol. 29, no. 1, 2001, pp. 219–39.

66. Benedict Anderson, *Imagined Communities,* 2nd edn (London: Verso Books, 1991), p. 184.

67. *JRDS,* vol. I, p. 358.

68. Robert McDonnell, 'Observations on the Habits and Anatomy of the Lepidosiren Annectens', *JRDS,* vol. II, pp. 398–407.

69. Ibid. McDonnell cites Carte as a co-author of the study. Carte also exhibited the animal to the Dublin University Botanical and Zoological Society in 1859 (see *Journal of the Dublin University Botanical and Zoological Society,* vol I, 1860, p. 153).

70. Randolph Cock, 'Scientific Servicemen in the Royal Navy and the Professionalization of Science', in David M. Knight and Matthew Eddy (eds), *Science and Beliefs: From natural philosophy to natural science, 1700–1900* (Aldershot: Ashgate, 2005), pp. 95–112.

71. Bruno Latour, 'Visualization and Cognition: Thinking with eyes and hands', in *Knowledge and Society: Studies in the sociology of culture past and present,* vol. 6 (Stamford: JAI Press, 1986), p. 21.

72. Ibid., p. 7. Emphasis in the original.

73. Ibid., pp. 7–11.

74. See Richard Drayton, *Nature's Government: Science, imperial Britain and the 'improvement' of the world* (New Haven and London: Yale University Press, 2000); Janet Browne, 'Biogeography and Empire', in Jardine et al. (eds), *Cultures of Natural History*, pp. 305–21; Roy MacLeod (ed.), *Government and Expertise: Specialists, administrators and professionals, 1860–1919* (Cambridge: Cambridge University Press, 1998); Lucile H. Brockway, *Science and Colonial Expansion: The role of the British Royal Botanic Garden* (New Haven: Yale University Press, 1979).

75. *JRDS*, vol. III, p. 93.

76. J.D. Hooker, 'David Lyall', *Journal of Botany, British and Foreign*, vol. 33, 1895, pp. 209–11.

77. 'Obituary; William Carte, FRCSI', *The British Medical Journal*, 29 April 1899, p. 1067. An 1859 letter to Alexander Carte from celebrated ornithologist and artist John Gould regarding the 'birds brought back from the Crimea by your cousin' suggests that William and Alexander Carte were related, strengthened by the fact that William's obituary noted he was also from Newcastle West, County Limerick.

78. *JRDS*, vol. I, p. 42.

79. Ibid., pp. 250–80.

80. William Carte, 'Observations during the Campaign of 1854, 1855 and 1856 on the Crimea, its Climate and Zoology', *JRDS*, vol. I, 1856–7, p. 252.

81. Ibid., pp. 253–4.

82. *JRDS*, vol. I, pp. 250–80.

83. *JRDS*, vol. I, p. 277. Made at the site of some of the most difficult battles in the war, this place name was still fresh in the public consciousness through press accounts.

84. *JRDS*, vol. I, pp. 277–8.

85. David Murphy, 'McClintock, Sir Francis Leopold', in *Dictionary of National Biography*. The Scott Polar institute at Cambridge University holds a collection of McClintock's correspondences and papers.

86. David Murphy's book *The Arctic Fox: Francis Leopold McClintock, discoverer of the fate of Franklin* (Cork: The Collins Press, 2004) is a concise account of McClintock's career and its relationship to the Franklin saga; pages 129–36 describe the events of this discovery.

87. Murphy, *The Arctic Fox*, p. 179.

88. The letters on file from McClintock derive primarily from his post-Arctic postings, ranging from Barbados, Jamaica, London and Dublin: MS letter box 30, NMI Archives.

89. McClintock to Carte, 23 April 1866, MS letter box 30, NMI Archives.

90. Mackenzie, *Museums and Empire*, pp. 8–9.

91. *JRDS*, vol. I, p. 286; vol. V, p. 238.

92. Robert Patterson, 'Memoir of the Late Robert Ball', in *Proceedings of the Dublin University Zoological and Botanical Association*, vol. I (Dublin, 1858), p. 7.

93. V. Ball to Carte, 12 November 1867, MS letter box 30, NMI Archives.

94. Ibid.

95. Mackenzie, *Museums and Empire*, pp. 9–10.

96. Patrick N. Wyse-Jackson. 'Ball, Valentine', in *Dictionary of Irish Biography*.

97. R.M. Hague, 'Jeffcott, Sir William (1850–1855)', *Dictionary of Australian Biography*; Obituary, *The Argus* (Melbourne), 22 January 1856.

98. Hague, 'Jeffcott, Sir William'.

99. Obituary, *The Straits Times*, 30 October 1855.

100. Ibid.

101. *JRDS*, vol. I, pp. 41–6.

102. Ibid., p. 46.

103. Catherine Levy, *William Thomas March, 1804–1872*, unpublished research, June 2013, accessed via academia.edu, and correspondence with Levy, a Jamaican ornithologist.

104. Alexander Carte, 'On an Undescribed Species of Petrel from the Blue Mountains of Jamaica', *Proceedings of the Zoological Society of London* (London: Longman Greene, 1866), pp. 93–5.

105. Jean-Marc Drouin and Bernadette Bensaude-Vincent, 'Nature for the People', in Jardine et al. (eds), *Cultures of Natural History*, p. 417.

106. Wyse-Jackson, 'Haughton, Samuel'.

107. *Eighth Report of the Science and Art Department of the Committee of Council on Education* (London, 1861), pp. 155–65; *Eleventh Report of the Science and Art Department of the Committee of Council on Education* (London, 1864), pp. 207–19.

108. An author search on the National Library of Ireland's Sources database, sources.nli.ie, yields over thirty-five papers by Kinahan, most for *the Journal of the Natural History Society of Dublin*, but also for the Geological Society of Dublin, the Royal Dublin Society, and the Royal Irish Academy.

109. William Andrews, 'Obituary of Professor John Robert Kinahan', in *Proceedings of the Natural History Society of Dublin, for the sessions 1862–63, 1863–64, 1861–65*, vol. IV (Dublin, 1865), pp. 33–7.

110. For instance, see Kinahan, 'Remarks on the habits and distribution of marine crustacea', pp. 112–49.

111. Bryan P. Beirne, 'Irish Entomology: The first hundred years', *The Irish Naturalists' Journal*, vol. 21, Special Entomological Supplement, 1985, pp. 17–18.

112. Edwin Birchall, 'Catalogue of the Lepidoptera of Ireland', in *Proceedings of the Natural History Society of Dublin for the Session 1865–66* (Dublin, 1866), pp. 57–87.

113. Beirne, 'Irish Entomology', p. 17.

114. Edwin Birchall, 'Notes on the Lepidoptera of Ireland', *The Entomologist's Monthly Magazine*, vol. I, 1865, pp. 270–2.

115. J.M. Chalmers-Hunt, 'On Some Interesting Irish Lepidoptera in the National Museum of Ireland', *The Irish Naturalists' Journal*, vol. 20, no. 12, 1982, pp. 531–7.

116. NUI Galway Landed Estates Database: Families A–Z, Warren, www.landedestates.ie

117. C.B. Moffat, 'Robert Warren', *The Irish Naturalist*, vol. 25, no. 3, 1916, pp. 33–44.

118. MacDonagh, 'Ireland and the Union', p. lix.

119. As quoted in Siegel, *Emergence of the Modern Museum*, p. 259.

120. *Report upon the Royal Dublin Society, the Museum of Irish Industry and on the System of Scientific Instruction in Ireland*, HCPP 1863 (3180), p. 48.

Chapter 5

1. Bourke, *The Story of Irish Museums*, pp. 159–62.

2. Ibid., pp. 144–5. The *Journal of the Geological Society* itself lists donations within the minutes of meetings, from which a sense of its collections may be gleaned.

3. Wyse-Jackson, 'Geological Collections of Trinity College', pp. 263–74.

4. The fourth chapter in Adelman's *Communities of Science*, 'Museums and Exhibitions', focuses on the museums of the Queen's Colleges.

5. *First Annual Report of the Dublin Natural History Society* (Dublin, 1839), and Minute Book: Dublin Natural History Society, 1838 (Royal Irish Academy, MS 12 P 2). The Natural History Society drew members from a wide range of other learned societies.

6. The letters for Carte's curatorship are primarily held in MS letter box 30 in the National Museum of Ireland: Natural History archives.

7. Andrews was examined extensively by the Select Committee for the Scientific Institutions of Dublin in 1864.

8. Linda Lunney, 'Andrews, William', in *Dictionary of Irish Biography*.

9. A search for Andrews in the National Library of Ireland's Sources database yields over forty results for papers on diverse topics, but most focusing on aspects of the fisheries.

10. *Irish Times*, 23 January 1863.

11. For example, William Andrews, 'On the Sea Fisheries of Ireland, and with Reference to Trawling', *JRDS*, vol. IV; 'Notes on the Salmon Fisheries of Ireland', *JRDS*, vol. IV; 'On Certain Branches of Industry in Ireland, with Special Reference to the Steps Taken by the Royal Dublin Society for their Promotion', *JRDS*, vol. V.

12. J.A.N. Parnell, 'Harvey, William Henry', in *Dictionary of Irish Biography*.

13. *Eighth Report of the Science and Art Department of the Committee of Council on Education* (London, 1861), pp. 155–65; *Eleventh Report of the Science and Art Department of the Committee of Council on Education* (London, 1864), pp. 207–19. See also William Henry Harvey, *A Manual of the British Algae: Containing generic and specific descriptions of all the known British species of sea-weeds, and of conferae, both marine and fresh-water* (London, 1841); and *The Sea-side Book* (London, 1849).

14. Parnell, 'Harvey, William Henry', in *Dictionary of Irish Biography*.

15. E. Charles Nelson, 'Harvey, William Henry', in *Oxford Dictionary of National Biography*.

16. Helen Andrews, 'Wright, Edward Perceval', in *Dictionary of Irish Biography*.

17. Ibid.; also *Proceedings of the Natural History Society of Dublin*, vol I, 1849–1855 (Dublin, 1855), p. 4.

18. Wyse-Jackson, 'Haughton, Samuel'. See also Wyse-Jackson, 'Geological Collections of Trinity College', pp. 263–6.

19. Sir C.A. Cameron, *History of the Royal College of Surgeons in Ireland* (Dublin: Fannon and Co., 1916), pp. 330–3; Barker is included in Table 5.1.

20. Livingstone and Withers, *Geographies of Nineteenth-Century Science*, pp. 21–2.

21. Alberti, 'The Status of Museums', pp. 51–72.

22. Ibid., p. 52.

23. Ibid.

24. See Alexander Carte, 'On an Undescribed Species of Petrel from the Blue Mountains of Jamaica', in *Proceedings of the Zoological Society of London*, 1866, pp. 93–5; 'On Some Indented Bones of the *Cervus megaceros*, Found near Lough Gur, County of Limerick', *Journal of the Royal Geological Society of Ireland*, vol. I, 1866, pp. 151–4; Alexander Carte and W.H. Baily, 'Description of a New Species of Plesiosaurus from the Lias, near Whitby, Yorkshire', *JRDS*, vol. IV, 1863–5 (Dublin, 1866), pp. 160–70.

25. Comerford, 'Ireland, 1850–70', p. 373.

26. Morgan to Carte, September 18 1865, MS letter box 30, NMI Archives.

27. J. Reed to Carte, 25 May 1864, MS letter box 30, NMI Archives.

28. Freeman to Carte, 1871, MS letter box 30, NMI Archives.

29. Mayne to Carte, 9 October 1862, MS letter box 30, NMI Archives. There is a small note from Carte at the top indicating that he replied, though there is no indication of whether or not he complied.

30. Anne Secord, 'Corresponding Interests: Artisans and gentlemen in nineteenth-century natural history', *The British Journal for the History of Science*, vol. XXVII, no. 4, 1994, p. 384.

31. White to Carte, 14 January 1859, MS letter box 30, NMI Archives.

32. King to Carte, 29 September 1871, MS letter box 30, NMI Archives.

33. Saunders to Carte, 16 April 1866, MS letter box 30, NMI Archives. Emphasis in the original.

34. Foot to Carte, 3 November 1864, MS letter box 30, NMI Archives. Emphasis in the original.

35. Warren to Carte, 11 May 1866, MS letter box 30, NMI Archives.

36. *Proceedings of the Natural History Society of Dublin*, vol. V (Dublin, 1866), p. 31.

37. Hutton to Carte, 1 Mar 1869, MS letter box 30, NMI Archives.

38. *Proceedings of the Natural History Society of Dublin*, vol. V, part I (Dublin, 1866), p. 5; *Proceedings of the Natural History Society of Dublin*, vol. V, part II (Dublin, 1866), p. 165.

39. Peter Bowler, 'Charles Darwin and his Dublin critics; Samuel Haughton and William Henry Harvey', in *Proceedings of the Royal Irish Academy*, section C, vol. 109 (Dublin, 2009), pp. 409–20.

40. McDonnell, 'Habits and Anatomy of the Lepidosiren Annectens', p. 406.

41. Reynolds to Carte, in a letter dated 19 March, but with no year. However, it appears to be part of a small series of letters dated 1868. MS letter box 30, NMI Archives.

42. H.N. Parton, 'Hutton, Frederick Wollaston', in *Dictionary of New Zealand Biography*.

43. Jim Burton, 'Robert FitzRoy and the Early History of the Meteorological Office', *British Journal for the History of Science*, vol. 19, no. 2, July 1986, p. 173.

44. Scott to Carte, 20 June, no year recorded, MS letter box 30, NMI Archives. It is part of a sequence that appears to have been written in 1868.

45. B.B. Woodward, 'Busk, George', in *Oxford Dictionary of National Biography*; the Darwin correspondence project notes that Darwin consulted with him on both bryozoans and medical matters.

46. Alexander Carte, 'On the Former Existence of the Polar Bear in Ireland, as is probably shown to be the fact by some remains recently discovered at Lough Gur, Co. of Limerick', *Journal of the Geological Society of Dublin*, vol. X, 1864, pp. 114–19.

47. Comerford, 'Ireland, 1850–70', p. 375.

48. Anthony J. Gaston, 'Leith-Adams, Andrew', in *Oxford Dictionary of National Biography*.

49. Fifteen letters from Leith-Adams can be found in MS letter box 30, NMI Archives.

50. Adams to Carte, 8 October 1862, MS letter box 30, NMI Archives.

51. Adams to Carte, nd, MS letter box 30, NMI Archives. Emphasis in the original.

52. MS letter box 30, NMI Archives contains one letter from Owen and eleven from Sclater.

53. Alexander Carte and Alexander Macalister, 'On the Anatomy of Balaenoptera Rostrata', in *Philosophical Proceedings of the Royal Society of London, 1868* (London, 1868), pp. 201–61. There are seven letters from Flower in the archives.

54. For example, the museum's archives hold manuscript lists of purchases from fossil dealer James Marder of Lyme Regis, 1870–4, and a series of lists and invoices from Edouard Verreaux, a Parisian dealer in natural history specimens. Information is also provided in Natural History Museum Register of Purchases, 1866–1872.

55. Purchases from Maison Verreaux are recorded on 9 March and 20 September 1867. Natural History Museum Register (purchases) 1866–72, NMI Archives.

56. Natural History Society of Dublin, minute book (Royal Irish Academy MS 12 P 2), 19 March 1838.

57. Warren to Carte, 6 May 1867.

58. Scott to Carte, 20 June, no year recorded, MS letter box 30, NMI Archives. It is part of a sequence that appears to have been written in 1868.

59. Williams to Carte, 26 August 1868, MS letter box 30, NMI Archives. Also see Natural History Museum Register (purchases), 1866–1872, in NMI Archives.

60. Wright to Carte, 30 October 1867, MS letter box 30, NMI Archives. Also Natural History Museum Register (purchases), 1866–1872, in NMI Archives.

61. Marder to Carte, letters from 1868–71, MS letter box 30, NMI Archives. Also see Natural History Museum Register (purchases), 1866–1872, in NMI Archives, and folder labelled Purchases: James W. Marder, Lyme Regis.

62. Natural History Museum Register (purchases), 1866–1872, in NMI Archives.

63. Enniskillen to Carte, 30 April, no year, MS letter box 30, NMI Archives. The *Journal of the Natural History Society* recorded an obituary notice for Admiral Jones in March 1868.

64. Enniskillen to Carte, 30 April, no year, MS letter box 30, NMI Archives.

65. Enniskillen to Carte, 9 September 1869 and 14 September 1869, MS letter box 30, NMI Archives.

66. Juliana Adelman also notes the lack of biographical information about Hinchy; see Adelman, 'An Insight into Commercial Natural History: Richard Glennon, William Hinchy and the nineteenth-century trade in giant Irish deer remains', *Archives of Natural History*, vol. 39, no. 1, 2012, p. 21.

67. Powerscourt to Carte, 30 November 1864, MS letter box 30, NMI Archives.

68. Hinchy to Carte, 8 March 1864, MS letter box 30, NMI Archives.

69. Nigel Monaghan, 'The Giant Irish Deer or "Irish elk"', *Geological Curator*, vol. 6, no. 4, 1995, pp. 171–3. This drawing is now in the collection of the National Museum of Ireland; Terry Clavin, 'Loftus, Adam', in *Dictionary of Irish Biography*.

70. Thomas Molyneaux, 'A Discourse Concerning the Large Horns Frequently Found Under Ground in Ireland, concluding from them that the great American deer, call'd a moose, was formerly common in that island', in *The Philosophical Transactions of the Royal Society. Vol. 19: 1695–1697* (London, 1697), pp. 498–512.

71. Hinchy to Carte, 8 March 1864, MS letter box 30, NMI Archives.

72. Ibid.

73. Carte, 'On the Former Existence of the Polar Bear in Ireland', p. 115.

74. Carte, 'On Some Indented Bones of the *Cervus megaceros*', pp. 151–4.

75. Carte to Waterhouse, 22 March 1864; Baily to Waterhouse, 9 May 1986, in British Museum, Natural History archives, Department of Paleontology, ref. no. DF100/11/12.

76. See Alexander Carte and J. Emerson Reynolds, 'Abstract of a Report on Continental Museums', *JRDS*, vol. V, 1866, p. 260.

77. *JRDS*, vol. I, pp. 41–2.

78. Montgomery to Carte, 25 April 1866; draft reply from Carte attached, MS letter box 30, NMI Archives.

79. Simpson's career has largely been erased with the passage of time. The Whitby Museum website has a short biography in its Personalities section: https://whitbymuseum.org.uk/whitby-history/whitby-personalities/martin-simpson/

80. Moore to Carte, 5 December 1868, MS letter box 30, NMI Archives.

81. RDS Natural History Committee, 1854–1877, 11 November 1856.

82. Carte to Waterhouse, 2 April 1864, British Museum, Natural History archives, Department of Paleontology, ref. no. DF100/11/12.

83. Waterhouse to Carte, 25 June 1870, MS letter box 30, NMI Archives.

84. Scott to Carte, 17 July 1869, MS letter box 30, NMI Archives.

85. Kaup to Carte, 25 August 1869, MS letter box 30, NMI Archives.

86. Natural History Museum Register (purchases), 1866–1872, 17 December 1869.

87. Kaup to Carte, 1869–70, MS letter box 30, NMI Archives.

88. Latour, *Reassembling the Social*, p. 17.

89. For instance, there are only seven letters from Carte listed in the archives at the Natural History Museum in London, and enquiries to places corresponding to Carte's letter files, such as the Whitby Museum and Henry Ward's archives at the University of Rochester, New York, yielded no results.

90. Locke to Carte, 22 May, no year, MS letter box 30, NMI Archives.

91. Byrne, 'Alexander Carte', in *Dictionary of Irish Biography*.

92. Latour, *Reassembling the Social*, pp. 66–7.

Chapter 6

1. Latour, *Reassembling the Social*, p. 71. Emphasis in the original

2. Ibid., pp. 70–5.

3. Secord, 'How Scientific Conversation Became Shop Talk', p. 26.

4. Richard Griffith, 'The Localities of the Irish Carboniferous Fossils, arranged according to the stratigraphical subdivisions of the carboniferous system adopted in the geological map of Ireland, with the Irish mining localities as appended to the synoptical table of fossils, engraved on the margin of that map, and as originally compiled for the use of the general valuation of Ireland', *Journal of the Geological Society of Dublin*, vol. IX, 1860–2 (Dublin, 1862), pp. 21–155.

5. Griffith, 'Irish Carboniferous Fossils', pp. 21–2. The carboniferous period occurred during the late Paleozoic era, about 350–300 million years ago, and was named in England after the coal deposits that correspond with it.

6. Minutes of the Royal Dublin Society, MS vol. 18, 1844–6, 24 March 1844 (Archives of the Royal Dublin Society); G.L. Herries-Davies, *Sheets of Many Colours: The mapping of Ireland's rocks, 1750–1890* (Dublin: Royal Dublin Society, 1983), p. 6.

7. Minutes of the RDS, MS vol. 18, 24 March 1844.

8. Ibid.

9. Ibid.

10. G.L. Herries-Davies, 'Richard Griffith: His life and character', in G.L. Herries-Davies and R.C. Mollan (eds), *Richard Griffith, 1784–1878* (Dublin: Royal Dublin Society, 1980), p. 5.

11. Patrick N. Wyse-Jackson, 'Griffith, Sir Richard John', *Dictionary of Irish Biography*; Peter J. O'Keefe, 'Richard Griffith: Planner and builder of roads', in Herries-Davies and Mollan, *Richard Griffith, 1784–1878*, pp. 57–75.

12. Herries-Davies, *Sheets of Many Colours*, p. 47.

13. William E. Vaughan, 'Richard Griffith and the Tenement Valuation', in Herries-Davies and Mollan, *Richard Griffith, 1784–1878*, pp. 103–4.

14. Wyse-Jackson, 'Griffith, Sir Richard John', *Dictionary of Irish Biography*; Ronald C. Cox, 'The Engineering Career of Richard Griffith', in Herries-Davies and Mollan, *Richard Griffith, 1784–1878*, p. 49.

15. Herries-Davies, 'Richard Griffith: His life and character', p. 21.

16. Richard Griffith, *Geological and Mining Report on the Leinster Coal District* (Dublin, 1814), p. xvi.

17. Berry, *A History of the Royal Dublin Society*, p. 168.

18. Matt T. Greene, 'Geology', in Bowler and Pickstone, *Cambridge History of Science*, pp. 167–75; Anthony Hallam, *Great Geological Controversies* (Oxford: Oxford University Press, 1989).

19. David R. Oldroyd, *Thinking about the Earth: A history of ideas in geology* (Cambridge: Cambridge University Press, 1996), p. 131.

20. T.R. Marchant and G.D. Sevastopulo, 'Richard Griffith and the Development of Stratigraphy in Ireland', in Herries-Davies and Mollan, *Richard Griffith, 1784–1878*, p. 181.

21. Jean B. Archer, 'Richard Griffith and the First Published Geological Maps of Ireland' and Vaughan, 'Richard Griffith and the Tenement Valuation', in Herries-Davies and Mollan, *Richard Griffith, 1784–1878*.

22. Griffith, as quoted in Archer, 'Richard Griffith and the First Published Geological Maps', p. 158.

23. Marchant and Sevastopulo, 'Richard Griffith and the Development of Stratigraphy', p. 190.

24. Frederick McCoy, *A Synopsis of the Characters of the Carboniferous Limestone Fossils in Ireland* (Dublin, 1844), p. iii.

25. Gareth Knapman, 'Curiosities of Science in the National Museum of Victoria: Procurement networks and the purpose of a museum', in Longair and McAleer, *Curating Empire*, pp. 82–103.

26. Wyse-Jackson, 'Fluctuations in Fortune', p. 103.

27. This map, still in pristine condition, is held in the National Museum of Ireland, Natural History archives.

28. Archer, 'Richard Griffith and the First Published Geological Maps', pp. 158–61.

29. *Freeman's Journal*, 28 August 1857.

30. Lunney, 'Andrews, William'. For example, 'On the Sea Fisheries of Ireland, and with Reference to Trawling', *JRDS*, vol. IV, 1863–5 (Dublin, 1866), pp. 295–324; 'On the Ichthyology of the South-West Coast of Ireland and a Collection of Zoological Specimens Obtained for the Society during the Summer and Autumn of 1868', *JRDS*, vol. V, 1866–70 (Dublin, 1870), pp. 379–89; 'Observations on the Salmon, Parr, and Gravelling', in *Proceedings of the Natural History Society of Dublin*, vol. I (Dublin, 1856), pp. 111–17.

31. Andrews, 'On Certain Branches of Industry in Ireland', p. 204.

32. Kane, *The Industrial Resources of Ireland*, p. 427.

33. Berry, *A History of the Royal Dublin Society*, pp. 62–70.

34. RDS Natural History Committee, 1831–54, 26 October 1853; Carte to Lamprey, draft reply, 10 November 1865, MS letter box 30, NMI Archives.

35. Alexander Carte, 'Report on the Progress and State of the Museum of Natural History of the Royal Dublin Society', *JRDS*, vol. I, pp. 43–5.

36. *JRDS*, vol. I, pp. 284–5, 430–2.

37. William Andrews, *On the Fisheries of the Coasts of Ireland, Addressed to Rear-Admiral Sir Thomas Ussher* (Dublin, 1847); National Library of Ireland, P1053(6), p. 14.

38. Andrews, 'On Certain Branches of Industry in Ireland', pp. 201–2. Trevelyan was instrumental in establishing the Royal Irish Fisheries Company by royal charter in 1848.

39. Patent of the Royal Irish Fisheries Company, 8 June 1848, Public Record Office, Dublin, M. 1369. As manager at the Royal Irish Fisheries Company, Andrews responded to a paper by fellow RDS member William Barker on the manufacture of fertiliser from fish, *Reports of the Proceedings, 1848–1855*, pp. 217–21.

40. Andrews, 'Notes on the Salmon Fisheries of Ireland', p. 86.

41. Ibid.

42. For instance, a paper delivered to the Natural History Society in 1855 detailed field research, collections and observations of the breeding and young of the salmon, describing early experiments in identification and tagging of fish. See Andrews, 'Observations on the Salmon, Parr, and Gravelling'.

43. *Report of the Fishery Commissioners, Ireland, for the Year 1862*, 1863 (3225); Salmon fisheries (Ireland), A bill to assimilate the law of Ireland as to salmon fisheries to that of England, HCPP 1862 (47); Salmon fisheries (Ireland), A bill to assimilate the law of Ireland as to salmon fisheries to that of England, HCPP 1863 (1).

44. Andrews, 'Notes on the Salmon Fisheries of Ireland', pp. 81–5.

45. Ibid., pp. 81–9.

46. Ibid., p. 82.

47. *Irish Times*, 23 January 1863.

48. Ibid.

49. Andrews, 'Notes on Salmon Fisheries of Ireland', pp. 97–100; *Irish Times*, 23 January 1863.

50. Andrews, 'Notes on the Salmon Fisheries of Ireland', p. 84.

51. *JRDS*, vol. IV, p. 137; Andrews to Carte, 27 August 1864, MS letter box 30, NMI Archives.

52. Alexander Carte, 'On an Undescribed Species of Petrel from the Blue Mountains of Jamaica', in *Proceedings of the Zoological Society of London* (London, 1866); Entry for 26 June 1855, Natural History Museum Register, 1851–72 (compiled by Alexander Carte), NMI Archives. March sent a pair, a male and female. Why March chose to donate to the RDS, or how he was connected to Carte, is unclear.

53. Catherine Levy, 'William Thomas March, 1804–1872', unpublished research, June 2013, accessed via academia.edu

54. Gould to Carte, 2 March 1859, MS letter box 30, NMI Archives.

55. John Gould, *The Birds of Europe*, vols I–V (London, 1837); *The Birds of Australia*, vols I–VII (London, 1848); *An Introduction to the Birds of Great Britain* (London, 1873).

56. March to Carte, 6 July 1865, MS letter box 30, NMI Archives.

57. March to Carte, 6 July 1865, MS letter box 30, NMI Archives; Carte, 'On an Undescribed Species of Petrel', pp. 93–5.

58. Obituary of Charles H. Gatty, *Quarterly Journal of the Geological Society of London*, vol. 60, 1903, p. lxxvii.

59. Gatty to Carte, 15 December 1865, MS letter box 30, NMI Archives.

60. Sclater to Carte, 27 June 1865, MS letter box 30, NMI Archives.

61. MS copy of a letter from Gray to Sclater, 18 December 1865, sent from Sclater to Carte, 28 December 1865, MS letter box 30, NMI Archives.

62. Sclater to Carte, 28 December 1865, MS letter box 30, NMI Archives.

63. Carte, 'On an Undescribed Species of Petrel', pp. 93–5.

64. Gatty to Carte, 19 February 1866, MS letter box 30, NMI Archives.

65. BirdLife International, factsheet on the Jamaican petrel, *Pterodroma caribbaea*, at http://www.birdlife.org/datazone/species/factsheet/22698097

66. Ibid.

67. Alexander Carte and W.H. Baily, 'Description of a New Species of *Plesiosaurus* from the Lias, near Whitby, Yorkshire', *JRDS*, vol. IV, 1863–5, pp. 160–2; Taylor to Carte, 20 December 1862, MS letter box 30, NMI Archives; Normanby to Carte, 23 November 1862, MS letter box 30, NMI Archives.

68. Carte and Baily, 'Description of a New Species of *Plesiosaurus*'; *Freeman's Journal*, 4 May 1853.

69. O'Riordan, *The Natural History Museum, Dublin*, p. 53; Adam Stuart Smith, 'Anatomy and Systematics of the Rhomaleosauridae (Sauropterygia: Plesiosauria)', PhD thesis, University College Dublin, 2007, p. 30.

70. Carte and Baily, 'Description of a New Species of *Plesiosaurus*'.

71. Though the letters are from various people, they are filed under N for Normanby in MS letter box 30, NMI Archives.

72. Taylor to Carte, 26 December 1862, MS letter box 30, NMI Archives.

73. Carte and Baily, 'Description of a New Species of *Plesiosaurus*'.

74. Simpson to Carte, 6 January 1863, in MS letter box 30, NMI Archives. This is one of the only references to photography in the correspondence, but J. Emerson Reynolds had been an amateur photographer from the early days of photography in Dublin, and perhaps took this image.

75. Carte and Baily, 'Description of a New Species of *Plesiosaurus*'; Smith, 'Anatomy and Systematics of the Rhomaleosauridae (Sauropterygia: Plesiosauria)', p. 30.

76. Baily to Carte, 7 October 1862, MS letter box 30, NMI Archives; *Report of the Thirty-Second Meeting of the British Association for the Advancement of Science, Held at Cambridge in October 1862* (London, 1863), p. 68 (Abstracts section).

77. Smith, 'Anatomy and Systematics of the Rhomaleosauridae (Sauropterygia: Plesiosauria)', pp. 27–37.

78. T. Moore to Carte, 5 December 1863, MS letter box 30, NMI Archives.

79. Draft reply, Carte to Moore, 8 December 1863, MS letter box 30, NMI Archives.

80. C. Moore to Carte, 24 March 1866; Bennett to Carte, 16 January 1866; Guillou to Carte, 18 September 1869, MS letter box 30, NMI Archives.

81. Carte to C. Moore, in the margins of C. Moore to Carte, 24 March 1866, MS letter box 30, NMI Archives.

82. Mary P. Winsor, 'Museums', in Bowler and Pickstone, *Cambridge History of Science*, p. 71.

83. Henry Ward, *Catalogue of Casts of Fossils from the Principal Museums of Europe and America* (Rochester, 1866); and *Ward Series of Casts of Fossils: Academy series* (Rochester, 1870).

84. Ward, *Ward Series of Casts of Fossils: Academy series*, front matter. Emphasis in the original.

85. Ward, *Catalogue of Casts of Fossils*, p. 19. Ward used Richard Owen's designation of the species rather than Cuvier's *Cervus megaceros*, used by Carte.

86. Ward to Carte, 11 November 1863, MS letter box 30, NMI Archives.

87. Ward to Carte, 21 November 1864, MS letter box 30, NMI Archives.

88. Ward to Carte, 26 September 1865, MS letter box 30, NMI Archives. Emphasis in the original.

Conclusion

1. Nicholas Whyte, *Science and Colonialism in Ireland* (Cork: Cork University Press, 1999), pp. 147–8; Bourke, *The Story of Irish Museums*, pp. 330–3.

2. Bourke, *The Story of Irish Museums*, pp. 330–3.

3. Whyte, *Science and Colonialism*, p. 148.

4. For a discussion of the focus on antiquities in the formation of identity in the early Free State, see Elizabeth Crooke, *Politics, Archaeology and the Creation of a National Museum in Ireland: An expression of national life* (Dublin: Irish Academic Press, 2000), pp. 139–47.

5. Dáil Éireann, vol. 29, 17 April 1929, Committee on Finance, vote 49, science and art. Alton was a professor of classics at Trinity College, and an independent unionist. Tierney, Law, Briscoe and Esmonde voiced their support in debates.

6. Seanad Éireann, vol. 48, 11 December 1957, Tourist Traffic Bill 1957.

7. Ibid.

8. For examples of the shifts which took place, consult Eilean Hooper Greenhill, *Museums, Media, Message* (New York: Routledge, 1995) and Pearce, *Museums, Objects and Collections*.

9. The closure was announced in the *Irish Independent*, 12 July 1988; the dates for reopening were debated in the Dáil throughout 1989, finally reopening in November. Funding was provided by the newly inaugurated National Lottery Fund, established in 1987.

10. Stephen Jay Gould, 'Cabinet Museums Revisited', *Natural History*, vol. 103, no. 1, 1994, pp. 12–20. Later re-published as 'Alive, Alive-O', in *Dinosaur in a Haystack* (New York: Three Rivers Press, 1996).

11. Gould, 'Alive, Alive-O', p. 240.

12. Ibid., p. 241.

13. Roland Barthes, *Mythologies* (New York: Noonday Press, 1972), p. 109.

14. On 5 July 2007, a cantilevered stone staircase collapsed in a restricted area of the building, injuring several teachers who were visiting the museum. In the aftermath, a safety audit deemed that the museum should be closed so that necessary repairs could be undertaken. Press accounts on 6 July 2007 and 22 April 2010 covered the events, and an excellent summary, titled 'Natural History Museum: A history of neglect?', may be found on Eoin Lettice's blog Communicate Science: http://www.communicatescience.eu/2010/04/natural-history-museum-history-of.html

15. *Irish Times*, 22 April 2010.

16. MacDonagh, 'Ireland and the Union', p. lix.

17. Murphy, *Abject Loyalty*, p. 110.

18. Comerford, 'Ireland, 1850–70', p. 372.

19. McDonnell was a comparative anatomist and a member of four of the learned societies covered in Chapter 4. His lecture on mesmerism was reported in the *Freeman's Journal*, 4 April 1862. The exhibition of wax models included lectures demonstrating human anatomy with the models. It was advertised in the *Freeman's Journal*, 14 February 1863.

20. John Pickstone, 'Science in Nineteenth-Century England: Plural configurations and singular politics', in Martin Daunton (ed.), *The Organisation of Knowledge in Victorian Britain* (Oxford: Oxford University Press, 2005), p. 30.

21. *Freeman's Journal*, 28 August 1857.

BIBLIOGRAPHY

Unpublished and manuscript material

Natural History Division Correspondence, 1854–86, A–Z, archive box 30, National Museum of Ireland Archives

Natural History Museum Register, 1834–51 (compiled by John Scouler), National Museum of Ireland Archives

Natural History Museum Register, 1851–72 (compiled by Alexander Carte), National Museum of Ireland Archives

Natural History Museum Register of Purchases, 1866–72, National Museum of Ireland Archives

Richard John Griffith Collection; manuscript lists of Carboniferous and Silurian fossil collections, in taxonomic order within stratigraphic units, National Museum of Ireland Archives

Minutes of the Royal Dublin Society, MS volume 18, 1844–6, RDS Library and Archives

Minutes of the Natural History Committee, Royal Dublin Society, 1831–54, RDS Library and Archives

Minutes of the Natural History Committee, Royal Dublin Society, 1854–77, RDS Library and Archives

Natural History Society of Dublin, minute book, Royal Irish Academy, MS 12 P 2

Larcom Papers, National Library of Ireland (letters and documents pertaining to the Royal Dublin Society, the Museum of Irish Industry and the development of science and art in Ireland. There are also papers treating the development of the fisheries.)

Catalogues of collections and exhibitions (in chronological order)

Dublin Society, *Catalogue of the Subjects of Natural History in the Museum of the Right & Hon. Dublin Society* (Dublin, 1818)

Giesecke, Charles, *A Descriptive Catalogue of a New Collection of Minerals in the Museum of the Royal Dublin Society* (Dublin, 1835)

Catalogue of the Library of the Royal Dublin Society (Dublin, 1839)

McCoy, Frederick, *A Synopsis of the Characters of the Carboniferous Limestone Fossils in Ireland* (Dublin, 1844)

—— *A Synopsis of the Characters of the Silurian Fossils of Ireland* (Dublin, 1846)

Catalogue of Articles of Manufactures, Produce and Invention Exhibited at the Royal Dublin Society's House, July 8, 1850 and Following Days (Dublin, 1850)

The Official Catalogue of the Great Exhibition of the Works of Industry of All Nations, 1851 (London, 1851)

A Catalogue of the Mammals in the Museum of the Hon. East-India Company (London, 1851)

The Irish Industrial Exhibition of 1853: A detailed catalogue of its contents (Dublin, 1854)

Wilde, William, *A Descriptive Catalogue of the Antiquities of Stone, Earthen and Vegetable Matter in the Museum of the Royal Irish Academy* (Dublin, 1857)

Ward, Henry, *Catalogue of Casts of Fossils from the Principal Museums of Europe and America* (Rochester, 1866)

More, A.G., *Guide to the Natural History Department, Series I, Vertebrate Animals (Recent), Part I, Mammals and Birds* (Dublin, 1887)

Ball, Valentine, *General Guide to the Science and Art Museum, Dublin*, 2nd edn (Dublin, 1890)

Lydekker, R., *Catalogue of Fossil Mammals, Birds, Reptiles, and Amphibians in the Science and Art Museum* (Dublin, 1891)

Journals and proceedings

Royal Dublin Society, *Reports of the Proceedings of Meeting for the Discussion of Subjects Connected with Practical Science and Art, 1848–1855* (Dublin, 1855)

Proceedings of the Royal Dublin Society

Journal of the Royal Dublin Society

Proceedings of the Royal Irish Academy

Journal of the Geological Society of Dublin

Proceedings of the Natural History Society of Dublin

Proceedings of the Dublin Statistical Society

Proceedings of the Dublin University Zoological and Botanical Association

Transactions of the Kilkenny Archaeological Society

Memoirs of the Natural History Society of Edinburgh

Parliamentary papers and reports (in chronological order)

Report from the Select Committee on the Royal Dublin Society, 1836, HCPP 1836 (445)

Report from the Select Committee on the British Museum, 1836, HCPP 1836 (440)

Report of the Commissioners Appointed to Inquire into the Constitution and Government of the British Museum: with Minutes of Evidence, HCPP 1850 (1170)

Public Libraries and Museums (Ireland), A Bill for Further Promoting the Establishment of Free Public Libraries and Museums in Ireland, 1854–5 (63)

Public Works, Ireland, Twenty-third Report from the Board of Public Works, Ireland, with Appendices, 1854, 1854–5 (1929)

Copy of Minute of the Lords' Committee of Privy Council for Trade, dated 11 April, in Reference to the Estimates for the Royal Dublin Society, and Report of the Council of the Society in Reference Thereto, HCPP 1854 (330)

Museum of Industry (Dublin), Statements of the Amount Voted by Parliament, or Expended from other Sources, for the Museum of Industry, Dublin, Stephen's Green, Dublin, since the Formation of that Institution, HCPP 1854 (331)

Royal Dublin Society, Copies of Memorials or other Correspondence which has Taken Place, since 1859, between the Various Departments of the English and Irish Governments and the Royal Dublin Society, Respecting any Increase of Public Grants to the Royal Dublin Society, 1862 (264)

Report of the Fishery Commissioners, Ireland, for the Year 1862, 1863 (3225)

Report upon the Royal Dublin Society, the Museum of Irish Industry and the System of Scientific Instruction in Ireland, HCPP 1863 (3180)

Scientific Institutions (Dublin), Copy of Correspondence between the Lord Lieutenant of Ireland or any other Member of the Irish Executive and the Treasury, or the Department of Science and Art, on the report of the commissioners appointed to inquire into the scientific institutions of Dublin in connexion with the Department of Science and Art, and on the proposed amalgamation of the Museum of Irish Industry with the Royal Dublin Society, 1863 (401)

Salmon Fisheries (Ireland), A Bill to Assimilate the Law of Ireland as to Salmon Fisheries to that of England, 1862 (47)

Salmon Fisheries (Ireland), A Bill to Assimilate the Law of Ireland as to Salmon Fisheries to that of England, 1863 (1)

Salmon Exportation, A Bill for Prohibiting the Exportation of Salmon at Certain Times, 1863 (42)

Report from the Select Committee on Scientific Institutions (Dublin), HCPP 1864 (495)

Scientific Institutions and Instruction in Dublin, Copy of Minute of Committee of Council on Education Relative to Scientific Institutions and Instruction in Dublin, HCPP 1866 (42)

Reports from the Commission on the Science and Art Department in Ireland together with the Minutes of Evidence, Appendix and Index, 1868–9, HCPP (4103)

The Dublin Science and Art Museum Act, 1877 (40 & 41 Vict. c. ccxxxiv)

Reports (in chronological order)

Griffith, Richard, *Geological and Mining Report on the Leinster Coal District* (Dublin, 1814)

'Proposed plan for rendering the nomenclature of zoology uniform and permanent, being the report of a committee for the consideration of the subject appointed by the British Association for the Advancement of Science', in *The Annals and Magazine of Natural History, including Zoology, Botany and Geology,* vol. XI (London, 1843)

Eighteenth Report of the Board of Public Works, Ireland (London, 1850)

Report of the Twenty-Seventh Meeting of the British Association for the Advancement of Science, Held at Dublin in August and September, 1857 (London, 1858)

Seventh Report of the Science and Art Department of the Committee of Council on Education (London, 1860)

Eighth Report of the Science and Art Department of the Committee of Council on Education (London, 1861)

Ninth Report of the Science and Art Department of the Committee of Council on Education (London, 1862)

Report of the Thirty-Second Meeting of the British Association for the Advancement of Science, Held at Cambridge in October, 1862 (London, 1863)

Report of the Thirty-Third Meeting of the British Association for the Advancement of Science, Held at Newcastle-on-Tyne in August and September, 1863 (London, 1864)

Eleventh Report of the Science and Art Department of the Committee of Council on Education (London, 1864)

Sixteenth Report of the Science and Art Department of the Committee of Council on Education (London, 1869)

Lithberg, Nils, *Report of the Committee of Enquiry into the National Museum of Ireland and Report on the Same,* 1927, Irish Free State Parliamentary Papers

Selected papers from the *Journal of the Royal Dublin Society (JRDS)*, vols I–V

Andrews, William, 'On the Cod and Ling Fisheries of Ireland', *JRDS,* vol. III, 1860–1 (Dublin, 1862), pp. 224–39

—— 'On the Sea Fisheries of Ireland, and with Reference to Trawling', *JRDS,* vol. IV, 1863–5 (Dublin, 1866), pp. 295–324

—— 'Notes on the Salmon Fisheries of Ireland', *JRDS,* vol. IV, 1863–5 (Dublin, 1866), pp. 81–100

—— 'On the Herring Fisheries of Ireland', *JRDS,* vol. V, 1866–70 (Dublin, 1870), pp. 12–26

—— 'On Certain Branches of Industry in Ireland: With special reference to the steps taken by the Royal Dublin Society for their promotion', *JRDS,* vol. V, 1866–70 (Dublin, 1870), pp. 192–205

—— 'On the Ichthyology of the South-West Coast of Ireland and a Collection of Zoological Specimens Obtained for the Society during the Summer and Autumn of 1868', *JRDS*, vol. V, 1866–70 (Dublin, 1870), pp. 379–89

Anonymous, 'Museum of Natural History: Ceremony of laying the foundation stone', *JRDS*, vol. I, 1856–7 (Dublin, 1858), pp. 50–6

—— Meeting of the British Association for the Advancement of Science', *JRDS*, vol. I, 1856–7 (Dublin, 1858), pp. 431–40

Baily, William H., 'On Fossils from the Crimea, with Descriptions of Some New Species Principally in the Collections of the Royal Dublin Society', *JRDS*, vol. II, 1858–9 (Dublin, 1860), pp. 233–40

Carte, Alexander, 'Report on the State and Progress of the Museum of Natural History of the Royal Dublin Society for the Year 1855', *JRDS*, vol. I, 1856–7 (Dublin, 1858), pp. 40–6

—— 'Nidification of the Ivory Gull', *JRDS*, vol. I, 1856–7 (Dublin, 1858), pp. 57–60

—— 'Description of the Fossil Bones Discovered by Mr Brennan at Shandon, Near Dungarvan', *JRDS*, vol. II, 1858–9 (Dublin, 1860), pp. 351–6

Carte, Alexander and W.H. Baily, 'Description of a New Species of *Plesiosaurus* from the Lias, Near Whitby, Yorkshire', *JRDS*, vol. IV, 1863–5 (Dublin, 1866), pp. 160–70

Carte, Alexander and J. Emerson Reynolds, 'Abstract of a Report on Continental Museums', *JRDS*, vol. V, 1866–70 (Dublin, 1870), p. 260

Carte, William, 'Observations during the Campaigns of 1854, 1855 and 1856, on the Crimea, its Climate and Zoology', *JRDS*, vol. I, 1856–7 (Dublin, 1858), pp. 250–80

Foot, Frederick J., 'Notes on a Tour in Norway', *JRDS*, vol. V, 1866–70 (Dublin, 1870), pp. 96–114

Giesecke, Charles, 'Catalogue of Geological and Geographical Collections of Minerals from the Arctic Regions, from Cape Farewell to Baffin's Bay', *JRDS*, vol. III, 1860–1 (Dublin, 1862), pp. 198–215

Griffith, Richard, 'On the Remains of Fossil Plants Discovered in the Yellow Sandstone Strata, situated at the base of the Carboniferous Limestone Series of Ireland, in connection with a communication on that subject received from M. Adolphe Brongniart', *JRDS*, vol. I, 1856–7 (Dublin, 1858), pp. 313–25

Haughton, Samuel, 'On the Fossils Brought Home from the Arctic Regions in 1859 by Captain Sir F.L. McClintock', *JRDS*, vol. III, 1860–1 (Dublin, 1862), pp. 53–83

Hoare, John, 'The Resources of the Sea Fisheries of Ireland', *JRDS*, vol. V, 1866–70 (Dublin, 1870), pp. 2–12

Kinahan, John Robert, 'Remarks on the Habits and Distribution of Marine Crustacea on the Eastern Shores of Port Phillip, Victoria, Australia; with descriptions of unidentified species and genera', *JRDS*, vol. I, 1856–7 (Dublin, 1858), pp. 111–34

—— 'Remarks on Crustacea Collected in Peru, on the High Seas and in South Australia, with Descriptions of Undescribed Species', *JRDS*, vol. I, 1856–7 (Dublin, 1858), pp. 328–52

Kirby, W.F., 'Account of a Natural History Excursion to the Continent in the Spring of 1869', *JRDS*, vol. V, 1866–70 (Dublin, 1870), pp. 436–44

McClintock, Captain F.L., 'Reminiscences of Arctic Ice-Travel in Search of Sir John Franklin and His Companions, with Geological Notes and Illustration by Samuel Haughton, M.A., Fellow of Trinity College, and Professor of Geology in the University of Dublin', *JRDS*, vol. I, 1856–7 (Dublin, 1858), pp. 183–250

McDonnell, Robert, 'Observations on the Habits and Anatomy of the *Lepidosiren Annectens*', *JRDS*, vol. II, 1858–9 (Dublin, 1860), pp. 388–404

Reeves, Robert William Cary, 'On the Irish Salmon Fisheries', *JRDS*, vol. IV, 1863–5 (Dublin, 1866), pp. 101–13

Scott, Robert H., Remarks on a Collection of Fossils from the Neighbourhood of Dresden', *JRDS*, vol. III, 1860–1 (Dublin, 1862), pp. 269–71

—— 'On the Mineral Localities of Donegal, as Ascertained by Sir Charles Giesecke, and by the British Association Committee', *JRDS*, vol. IV, 1863–5 (Dublin, 1866), pp. 114–25

Walker, David, 'Ice Observations', *JRDS*, vol. II, 1858–9 (Dublin, 1860), pp. 373–80

—— 'Notes on the Zoology of the Last Arctic Expedition under Sir F.L. McClintock, R.N.', *JRDS*, vol. III, 1860–1 (Dublin, 1862), pp. 61–77

Relevant scientific papers from learned societies

Andrews, William, 'Remarks on Harbour Fish and Formation of Piscinae', in *Proceedings of the Natural History Society of Dublin*, vol. I (Dublin, 1856), pp. 122–5

—— 'Observations on the Salmon, Parr, and Gravelling', in *Proceedings of the Natural History Society of Dublin*, vol. I (Dublin, 1856), pp. 111–17

—— 'Notes on the Fishes of the Western Coasts, and Record of the Occurrence of the Boar-Fish (*Capros Aper*) in the Irish Seas', in *Proceedings of the Natural History Society of Dublin*, vol. II (Dublin, 1860), pp. 104–7

—— 'Remarks on the Salmonidae', in *Proceedings of the Natural History Society of Dublin*, vol. IV (Dublin, 1865), pp. 53–7

Baily, William Hellier, 'On the Occurrences of Some Characteristic Graptolites and other Fossils, Indicating Certain Divisions of the Lower Silurian Rocks in the Counties of Meath, Tipperary and Clare', *Journal of the Geological Society of Dublin*, vol. IX, 1860–2 (Dublin, 1862), pp. 800–5

Birchall, Edwin, 'Notes on the Lepidoptera of Ireland', *The Entomologist's Monthly Magazine. Vol. I: 1864–5* (London, 1865)

—— 'Catalogue of the Lepidoptera of Ireland', in *Proceedings of the Natural History Society of Dublin*, vol. V (Dublin, 1866), pp. 57–85

Carte, Alexander, 'On an Undescribed Species of Petrel from the Blue Mountains of Jamaica', in *Proceedings of the Zoological Society of London for the Year 1866* (London, 1866), pp. 93–5

—— 'On Some Indented Bones of the *Cervus megaceros*, Found Near Lough Gur, County of Limerick', *Journal of the Royal Geological Society of Ireland*, vol. I, 1866, pp. 151–4

—— 'On the Anatomy of *Balaenoptera rostrata*, by Alexander Carte, and Alexander Macalister', in *Philosophical Proceedings of the Royal Society of London, 1868* (London, 1868), pp. 201–61

Griffith, Richard, 'The Localities of the Irish Carboniferous Fossils, arranged according to the stratigraphical subdivisions of the carboniferous system adopted in the geological map of Ireland, with the Irish mining localities as appended to the synoptical table of fossils, engraved on the margin of that map, and as originally compiled for the use of the general valuation of Ireland', *Journal of the Geological Society of Dublin*, vol. IX, 1860–2 (Dublin, 1862), pp. 21–155

Molyneaux, Thomas, 'A Discourse Concerning the Large Horns Frequently Found Under Ground in Ireland, concluding from them that the great American deer, call'd a moose, was formerly common in that island', in *The Philosophical Transactions of the Royal Society. Vol. 19: 1695–7* (London, 1697)

'Obituary of Sir Charles Lewis von Giesecke', *The Dublin University Magazine*, vol. III, 1834, p. 161

'Obituary; William Carte, FRCSI', *The British Medical Journal*, 29 April 1899, p. 1067

Wilde, William, 'Upon the Unmanufactured Animal Remains Belonging to the Academy', in *Proceedings of the Royal Irish Academy*, ser. I, vol. VII: 1857–61 (Dublin, 1861), pp. 181–212

Pamphlets

Andrews, William, *On the Fisheries of the Coasts of Ireland: Addressed to Rear-Admiral Sir Thomas Ussher*, National Library of Ireland, P 1053(6)

Allman, George J., *The Importance of Natural History Studies to the Artist: A lecture delivered at the seventh public distribution of prizes to the pupils of the Royal Dublin Society Drawing School* (Dublin, 1849), National Library of Ireland, P 1177(9)

Hart, John, *A Description of the Skeleton of the Fossil Deer of Ireland,* Cervus megaceros, *drawn up at the instance of the Committee of Natural Philosophy of the Royal Dublin Society* (Dublin, 1825), National Library of Ireland, P 1811(3)

Harvey, William, *Botany Considered in Reference to the Arts of Design: An introductory address delivered in the theatre of the Royal Dublin Society* (Dublin, 1849), National Library of Ireland, P 1177(10)

Periodicals and newspapers

The British Medical Journal

Dublin Evening Post

Dublin Evening Mail

Dublin Penny Journal

The Dublin Quarterly Journal of Science

Dublin University Magazine

The Entomologist's Monthly Magazine

The Evening Freeman

The Freeman's Journal

The Gentleman's Magazine

The Irish Naturalist

The Illustrated London News

The Irish Times

Journal of Botany, British and Foreign

The Morning Register

The Nation

The Natural History Review and Quarterly Journal of Biological Science

Saunder's News-Letter

The Weekly Times

Period scientific publications with relevance to Dublin and/or the Natural History Museum

Adams, Andrew Leith, *Wanderings of a Naturalist in India* (Edinburgh, 1867)

Baily, William Hellier, *Rambles on the Irish Coast, Especially Relating to Its Geology, Natural History and Antiquities* (Dublin, 1886)

Cole, Henry, *The Functions of the Science and Art Department* (London, 1857)

Cuvierian Society of Cork, *Contributions toward a Flora and Fauna of Cork* (London, 1845)

Kane, Robert, *The Industrial Resources of Ireland* (Dublin, 1844)

Kirwan, Richard, *Elements of Mineralogy* (London, 1810)

Harvey, William Henry, *The Genera of South African Plants: Arranged according to the natural system* (Cape Town, 1838)

—— *A Manual of the British Algae: Containing generic and specific descriptions of all the known British species of sea-weeds, and of conferae, both marine and fresh-water* (London, 1841)

—— *The Sea-side Book* (London, 1849)

Owen, Richard, *On the Extent and Aims of a National Museum of Natural History* (London, 1862)

Playfair, Leon, *On Scientific Institutions in Connexion with the Department of Science and Art* (London, 1857)

Thompson, William, *The Natural History of Ireland, in Four Volumes* (London, 1856)

Ussher, Richard J. and Robert Warren, *The Birds of Ireland* (London, 1900)

Watters, John J., *The Natural History of the Birds of Ireland, Indigenous and Migratory* (Dublin, 1853)

Relevant period volumes

Address of the President of the Belfast Natural History Society on the Opening of the Belfast Museum (Belfast: John Hodgson, 1831)

Brewer, J.N., *The Beauties of Ireland* (London, 1825)

Davis, Thomas Osborne, 'Institutions of Dublin', in D.J. O'Donoghue (ed.), *Essays, Literary and Historical. By Thomas Davis. Centenary edition, including several pieces never before collected* (Dundalk, 1914), pp. 329–39

McClintock, F. Leopold, *The Voyage of the 'Fox' in the Arctic Seas: A narrative of the discovery of the fate of Sir John Franklin and his companions* (London, 1859)

McGregor, John James, *New Picture of Dublin: Comprehending a history of the city, an accurate account of its various establishments and institutions, and a correct description of all the public edifices connected with them* (Dublin, 1821)

McLeod, John, *Voyage of His Majesty's Ship* Alceste *along the Coast of Corea to the Island of Lewchew* (London, 1818)

Ruskin, John, *Modern Painters. Vol. 1: Of general principles, and of truth*, 2nd edn (London: George Allen, 1898)

Shaw, Henry, *The Dublin Pictorial Guide and Directory* (Dublin, 1850)

Thackeray, William Makepeace, *The Irish Sketchbook* (London, 1842)

Trevelyan, Charles, *The Irish Crisis* (London, 1848)

Dictionaries of Biography

The Oxford Dictionary of National Biography

The Dictionary of Irish Biography

The Australian Dictionary of National Biography

Dictionary of New Zealand Biography

Books

Adelman, Juliana, *Communities of Science in Nineteenth-Century Ireland* (London: Routledge, 2009)

Adelman, Juliana and Éadaoin Agnew (eds), *Science and Technology in Nineteenth-Century Ireland* (Dublin: Four Courts Press, 2011)

Alberti, Samuel J.M.M., Alexander, Edward Porter and Mary Alexander, *Museums in Motion: An introduction to the history and functions of museums*, 2nd edn (New York: Altamira Press, 2008)

Allen, David E., *The Naturalist in Britain: A social history* (Princeton: Princeton University Press, 1995)

—— 'Tastes and Crazes', in N. Jardine, J.A. Secord and E.C. Spary (eds), *Cultures of Natural History* (Cambridge: Cambridge University Press, 1996)

—— 'Amateurs and Professionals', in Peter Bowler and John V. Pickstone (eds), *Cambridge History of Science. Vol. 6: Modern biological and earth sciences* (Cambridge: Cambridge University Press, 2009)

Anderson, Benedict, *Imagined Communities*, 2nd edn (London: Verso Books, 1991)

Archer, Jean B., 'Richard Griffith and the First Published Geological Maps of Ireland', in G.L. Herries-Davies and R.C. Mollan (eds), *Richard Griffith, 1784–1878* (Dublin: Royal Dublin Society, 1980)

Attis, David and Charles Mollan (eds), *Science and Irish Culture*, vol. I (Dublin: Royal Dublin Society, 2004)

Auerbach, Jeffrey A., *The Great Exhibition of 1851: A nation on display* (New Haven: Yale University Press, 1999)

Auerbach, Jeffrey A. and Peter H. Hoffenberg (eds), *Britain, the Empire and the World at the Great Exhibition of 1851* (London: Routledge, 2008)

Barber, Lynn, *The Heyday of Natural History, 1820–1870* (London: Johnathan Cape, 1980)

Barthes, Roland, *Mythologies* (New York: Farrar, Strauss & Giroux, 1972)

Bellon, Richard, 'Science at the Crystal Heart of the World', in Aileen Fyfe and Bernard Lightman (eds), *Science in the Marketplace* (Chicago: University Press of Chicago, 2007)

Bendell, Sarah (ed.), *Dictionary of Land Surveyors and Local Map-Makers of Great Britain and Ireland, 1530–1850*, 2nd edn (London: The British Library Publishing Division, 1997)

Bennett, James, 'Why the History of Science Matters in Ireland', in David Attis and Charles Mollan (eds), *Science and Irish Culture: Why the history of science matters in Ireland*, vol. I (Dublin: Royal Dublin Society, 2004)

—— 'Science and Social Policy in Mid-Nineteenth-Century Ireland', in Peter J. Bowler and Nicholas Whyte (eds), *Science and Society in Ireland: The social context of science and technology in Ireland, 1800–1950* (Belfast: Queen's University Belfast, 1997)

Bernstein, Susan David, 'Supposed Differences: Lydia Becker and Victorian women's participation in the BAAS', in David Clifford, Elisabeth Wadge, Alex Warwick and Martin Willis (eds), *Repositioning Victorian Sciences: Shifting centres in nineteenth-century thinking* (London: Anthem Press, 2006)

Berry, Henry F., *A History of the Royal Dublin Society* (London: Longmans, Green & Co., 1915)

Bourke, Marie, *The Story of Irish Museums, 1790–2000: Culture, identity and education* (Cork: Cork University Press, 2011)

Bowler, Peter and John V. Pickstone (eds), *Cambridge History of Science. Volume 6: Modern biological and earth sciences* (Cambridge: Cambridge University Press, 2009)

Bowler, Peter and Nicholas Whyte (eds), *Science and Society in Ireland: The social context of science and technology in Ireland, 1800–1950* (Belfast: Queen's University Belfast, 1997)

Bowler, Peter J., *Evolution: The history of an idea* (Berkeley: University of California Press, 1983)

Bright, Kevin, *The Royal Dublin Society, 1815–45* (Dublin: Four Courts Press, 2004)

Brockway, Lucile H., *Science and Colonial Expansion: The role of the British Royal Botanic Garden* (New Haven: Yale University Press, 1979)

Browne, Janet, 'Biogeography and Empire', in N. Jardine, J.A. Secord and E.C. Spary (eds), *Cultures of Natural History* (Cambridge: Cambridge University Press, 1996)

Burnett, James E. and A.D. Morrison-Low, *Vulgar and Mechanick: The scientific instrument trade in Ireland, 1650–1921* (National Museums of Scotland, 1989)

Cameron, C.A., *History of the Royal College of Surgeons in Ireland* (Dublin: Fannon & Co., 1916)

Carroll, Patrick, *Science, Culture and Modern State Formation* (Berkeley: University of California Press, 2006)

Cleary, Joe, *Literature, Partition and the Nation State: Culture and conflict in Ireland, Israel and Palestine* (Cambridge: Cambridge University Press, 2002)

—— *Outrageous Fortune: Capital and culture in modern Ireland* (Dublin: Field Day Publications, 2007)

Clifford, David, Elisabeth Wadge, Alex Warwick and Martin Willis (eds), *Repositioning Victorian Sciences: Shifting centres in nineteenth-century thinking* (London: Anthem Press, 2006)

Comerford, R.V., 'Ireland, 1850–70: Post-Famine and mid-Victorian', in W.E. Vaughan (ed.), *A New History of Ireland. Vol. V: Ireland under the union, 1801–70* (Oxford: Oxford University Press, 1989)

Cox, Ronald C., 'The Engineering Career of Richard Griffith', in G.L. Herries-Davies and R.C. Mollan (eds), *Richard Griffith, 1784–1878* (Dublin: Royal Dublin Society, 1980)

Cock, Randolph, 'Scientific Servicemen in the Royal Navy and the Professionalization of Science', in David M. Knight and Matthew Eddy (eds), *Science and Beliefs: From natural philosophy to natural science, 1700–1900* (Aldershot: Ashgate, 2005)

Coolahan, John, *Irish Education: History and structure* (Dublin: Institute of Public Administration, 1981)

Crooke, Elizabeth, *Politics, Archaeology and the Creation of a National Museum in Ireland: An expression of national life* (Dublin: Irish Academic Press, 2000)

Crosbie, Barry, *Irish Imperial Networks: Migration, social communication and exchange in nineteenth-century India* (Cambridge: Cambridge University Press, 2012)

Cullen, Clara, 'Starry Eyed: Women in science in nineteenth-century Ireland', in Brendan Walsh (ed.), *Knowing Their Place: The intellectual life of women in the nineteenth century*, e-book edn (Dublin: The History Press, 2014)

Daly, Mary E., *The Spirit of Earnest Inquiry: The Statistical and Social Inquiry Society of Ireland, 1847–1997* (Dublin: Institute of Public Administration, 1997)

Daunton, Martin, *The Organisation of Knowledge in Victorian Britain* (Oxford: Oxford University Press, 2005)

Drayton, Richard, *Nature's Government: Science, imperial Britain and the 'improvement' of the world* (New Haven: Yale University Press, 2000)

Drouhin, Jean-Marc and Bernadette Bensaude Vincent, 'Nature for the People', in N. Jardine, J.A. Secord and E.C. Spary (eds), *Cultures of Natural History* (Cambridge: Cambridge University Press, 1996)

Finnegan, Diarmid A. and Johnathan Jeffrey Wright (eds), *Spaces of Global Knowledge: Exhibition, encounter and exchange in an age of empire* (New York: Routledge, 2016)

Fitzpatrick, David, 'Ireland and the Empire', in Andrew Porter (ed.), *The Oxford History of the British Empire. Vol III: The nineteenth century* (Oxford: Oxford University Press, 1999)

Foster, John Wilson, *Recoveries: Neglected episodes in Irish cultural history, 1860–1912* (Dublin: UCD Press, 2002)

Foster, John Wilson and Helena C.G. Chesney (eds), *Nature in Ireland: A scientific and cultural history* (Dublin: The Lilliput Press, 1997)

Fyfe, Aileen and Bernard Lightman (eds), *Science in the Marketplace: Nineteenth-century sites and experiences* (Chicago: University Press of Chicago, 2007)

Gates, Barbara T., 'Ordering Nature: Revisioning Victorian science culture', in Bernard Lightman (ed.), *Victorian Science in Context* (Chicago: University Press of Chicago, 1997)

Golinski, Jan, *Making Natural Knowledge: Constructivism and the history of science* (Cambridge: Cambridge University Press, 1998)

Gould, Stephen Jay, *Dinosaur in a Haystack* (Cambridge: Harvard University Press, 1996)

Gray, Peter (ed.), *Victoria's Ireland? Irishness and Britishness, 1837–1901* (Dublin: Four Courts Press, 2004)

Greene, Matt T., 'Geology', in Peter Bowler and John V. Pickstone, *Cambridge History of Science. Vol. 6: Modern biological and earth sciences* (Cambridge: Cambridge University Press, 2009)

Gribbin, John, *Science: A history, 1543—2001* (London: Penguin Books, 2003)

Hallam, Anthony, *Great Geological Controversies* (Oxford: Oxford University Press, 1989)

Hayley, Barbara and Enda McKay (eds), *Three Hundred Years of Irish Periodicals* (Dublin: The Lilliput Press, 1987)

Herries-Davies, G.L. and R. Charles Mollan (eds), *Richard Griffith, 1784–1878* (Dublin: Royal Dublin Society, 1980)

Herries-Davies, G.L., *Sheets of Many Colours: The mapping of Ireland's rocks, 1750–1890* (Dublin: Royal Dublin Society, 1983)

Hewison, Robert, *John Ruskin* (Oxford: Open University Press, 2007)

Heyck, T.W., *The Transformation of Intellectual Life in the Victorian Period* (New York: St Martin's Press, 1982)

Hooper-Greenhill, Eilean, *Museums and Education: Purpose, pedagogy, performance* (New York: Routledge, 2007)

Hoppen. K.T., *Ireland since 1800: Conflict and conformity* (London: Longman, 1989)

Houghton, Walter E., *The Victorian Frame of Mind* (New Haven: Yale University Press, 1957)

Howarth, O.J.R., *The British Association for the Advancement of Science: A retrospect* (London: The Association, 1922)

Inkster, Ian and Jack Morrell, *Metropolis and Province: Science in British culture* (London: Routledge, 2007)

Jardine, N., J.A. Secord and E.C. Spary (eds), *Cultures of Natural History* (Cambridge: Cambridge University Press, 1996)

Kelham, Brian B. and Douglas McMillan, 'Experimental Science in Ireland and the Scientific Societies', in Norman McMillan (ed.), *Prometheus's Fire: A history of scientific and technical education in Ireland* (Kilkenny: Tyndall Books, 2000)

Gareth Knapman, 'Curiosities of Science in the National Museum of Victoria: Procurement networks and the purpose of a museum', in Sarah Longair and John McAleer (eds), *Curating Empire: Museums and the British imperial experience* (Manchester: Manchester University Press, 2012), pp. 82–103

Latour, Bruno, *Science in Action: How to follow scientists and engineers through society* (Cambridge: Harvard University Press, 1987)

—— 'Visualization and Cognition: Thinking with eyes and hands', *Knowledge and Society: Studies in the sociology of culture past and present*, vol. 6, 1986, pp. 1–40

—— *Reassembling the Social: An introduction to actor-network-theory* (Oxford: Oxford University Press, 2005)

Laudan, Rachel, *From Mineralogy to Geology: The foundations of a science 1650–1830* (Chicago: University of Chicago Press, 1987)

Leapman, Michael, *The World for a Shilling; How the Great Exhibition of 1851 shaped a nation* (London: Faber & Faber, 2001)

Lightman, Bernard, *Victorian Popularizers of Science: Designing nature for new audiences* (Chicago: University Press of Chicago, 2007)

Lightman, Bernard, (ed.), *Victorian Science in Context* (Chicago: University Press of Chicago, 1997)

Linnie, Martyn J., *The Zoological Museum, School of Natural Science, Trinity College Dublin: History, current status and developments* (Dublin: Trinity College, 2008)

Livingstone, David N., *Putting Science in its Place: Geographies of scientific knowledge* (Chicago: University of Chicago Press, 2003)

Longair, Sarah and John McAleer (eds), *Curating Empire: Museums and the British imperial experience* (Manchester: Manchester University Press, 2012)

Kenny, Kevin, *Ireland and the British Empire* (Oxford: Oxford University Press, 2004)

MacDonald, Sharon (ed.), *A Companion to Museum Studies* (Sussex: Wiley Blackwell, 2011)

MacGregor, Arthur, *Curiosity and Enlightenment: Collections from the sixteenth to the nineteenth century* (New Haven: Yale University Press, 2007)

MacLeod, Roy (ed.), *Government and Expertise: Specialists, administrators and professionals, 1860–1919* (Cambridge: Cambridge University Press, 1998)

Mackenzie, John M., *Museums and Empire: Natural history, human cultures and colonial identities* (Manchester: Manchester University Press, 2009)

Mayr, Ernst, *The Growth of Biological Thought: Diversity, evolution and inheritance* (Cambridge: Belknap Press, 1982)

MacDonagh, Oliver, 'Ireland and the Union, 1801–70', in W.E. Vaughan (ed.), *A New History of Ireland. Vol. V: Ireland under the union, 1801–70* (Oxford: Oxford University Press, 1989)

McDonough, Terence (ed.), *Was Ireland a Colony? Economics, politics and culture in nineteenth-century Ireland* (Dublin: Irish Academic Press, 2005)

McDowell, R.B., 'The Main Narrative', in T. Ó Raifeartaigh (ed.), *The Royal Irish Academy: A bicentennial history, 1785–1985* (Dublin: RIA, 1985)

MacLeod, Roy (ed.), *Government and Expertise: Specialists, administrators and professionals, 1860–1919* (Cambridge: Cambridge University Press, 1998)

Marchant, T.R. and G.D. Sevastopulo, 'Richard Griffith and the Development of Stratigraphy in Ireland', in G.L. Herries-Davies and R.C. Mollan (eds), *Richard Griffith, 1784–1878* (Dublin: Royal Dublin Society, 1980)

Meadows, Jack, *The Victorian Scientist: The growth of a profession* (London: The British Library, 2004)

Meenan, James and Desmond Clarke (eds), *The Royal Dublin Society, 1731–1981* (Dublin: The Royal Dublin Society, 1981)

Miller, Edward, *That Noble Cabinet: A history of the British museum* (London: Andre Deutsch, 1973)

Mollan, Charles, William Davis and Brendan Finucane (eds), *Some People and Places in Irish Science and Technology* (Dublin: Royal Irish Academy, 1985)

—— *More People and Places in Irish Science and Technology* (Dublin: Royal Irish Academy, 1990)

—— *Irish Innovators in Science and Technology* (Dublin: Royal Irish Academy, 2002)

Mollan, Charles, *It's Part of What We Are: Who was who in Irish science, 1566–1990*, vols 1 & 2 (Dublin: Royal Dublin Society, 2007)

Morrell, Jack and Arnold Thackray (eds), *Gentlemen of Science: Early correspondence of the British Association for the Advancement of Science* (London: Royal Historical Society, 1984)

Morrell, Jack, 'Professionalization', in G.N. Cantor, J.R.R. Christie, M.J.S. Hodge and R.C. Olby (eds), *Companion to the History of Modern Science* (London: Routledge, 1996)

Murphy, David, *The Arctic Fox: Francis Leopold McClintock* (Cork: The Collins Press, 2004)

Murphy, James H., *Abject Loyalty: Nationalism and monarchy in Ireland during the reign of Queen Victoria* (Cork: Cork University Press, 2001)

Murphy, Sherra, 'The Learned Gentlemen are in Town: The British Association meeting of 1857 in Dublin's popular press', in Juliana Adelman and Éadaoin Agnew (eds), *Science and Technology in Nineteenth-Century Ireland* (Dublin: Four Courts Press, 2011)

Nelson, E. Charles, *John Scouler (c. 1804–1871), Scottish Naturalist: A life, with two voyages* (Glasgow: Glasgow Natural History Society, 2014)

O'Keefe, Peter J., 'Richard Griffith: Planner and builder of roads', in G.L. Herries-Davies and R.C. Mollan (eds), *Richard Griffith, 1784–1878* (Dublin: Royal Dublin Society, 1980)

Oldroyd, David R., *Thinking about the Earth: A history of ideas in geology* (Cambridge: Harvard University Press, 1996)

Ó Raifeartaigh, T. (ed.), *The Royal Irish Academy: A bicentennial history, 1785–1985* (Dublin: Royal Irish Academy, 1985)

O'Riordan, C.E., *The Natural History Museum, Dublin* (Dublin: National Museum of Ireland, 1983)

Pearce, Susan M., *Museums, Objects and Collections: A cultural study* (Leicester: Leicester University Press, 1992)

—— *Interpreting Objects and Collections* (Leicester: Leicester University Press,1994)

Pickering, Andrew (ed.), *Science as Practice and Culture* (Chicago: University Press of Chicago, 1992)

—— *The Mangle of Practice: Time, agency and science* (Chicago: University Press of Chicago, 1995)

Pickstone, John, 'Science in Nineteenth-Century England: Plural configurations and singular politics', in Martin Daunton (ed.), *The Organisation of Knowledge in Victorian Britain* (Oxford: Oxford University Press, 2005)

Plunkett, John, *Victorian Print Media: A reader* (Oxford: Oxford University Press, 2005)

Porter, Andrew (ed.), *The Oxford History of the British Empire. Vol III: The nineteenth century* (Oxford: Oxford University Press, 1999)

Praeger, Robert Lloyd, *Some Irish Naturalists: A biographical note-book* (Dundalk: W. Tempest, 1949)

Pyenson, Lewis and Susan Sheets-Pyenson, *Servants of Nature: A history of scientific institutions, enterprises and sensibilities* (New York: WW Norton & Co., 2000)

Ritvo, Harriet, 'Zoological Nomenclature and the Empire of Victorian Science', in Bernard Lightman (ed.), *Victorian Science in Context* (Chicago: University of Chicago Press, 1997), p. 336

Roche, Daniel, 'Natural History in the Academies', in N. Jardine, J.A. Secord and E.C. Spary (eds), *Cultures of Natural History* (Cambridge: Cambridge University Press, 1996)

Rudwick, Martin J.S., *Bursting the Limits of Time: The reconstruction of geohistory in an age of revolution* (Chicago: University Press of Chicago, 2005)

Secord, James, 'How Scientific Talk Became Shop Talk', in Aileen Fyfe and Bernard Lightman (eds), *Science in the Marketplace* (Chicago: University Press of Chicago, 2007)

Siegel, Jonah (ed.), *The Emergence of the Modern Museum: An anthology of nineteenth-century sources* (Oxford: Oxford University Press, 2008)

Spary, E.C., *Utopia's Garden: French natural history from old regime to revolution* (Chicago: University of Chicago Press, 2000)

Robert A. Stafford, 'Scientific Exploration and Empire', in Andrew Porter and William Roger Louis (eds), *The Oxford History of the British Empire. Vol. V: The nineteenth century* (Oxford: Oxford University Press, 1999)

Vaughan, W.E. (ed.), *A New History of Ireland. Vol. V: Ireland under the union, 1801–70* (Oxford: Oxford University Press, 1989)

—— 'Richard Griffith and the Tenement Valuation', in G.L. Herries-Davies and R.C. Mollan (eds), *Richard Griffith, 1784–1878* (Dublin: Royal Dublin Society, 1980)

Walsh, Brendan, *Knowing Their Place: The intellectual life of women in the nineteenth century*, e-book edn (Dublin: The History Press, 2014)

Whyte, Nicholas, *Science, Colonialism and Ireland* (Cork: Cork University Press, 1999)

Winsor, Mary P., 'Museums', in Peter Bowler and John V. Pickstone (eds), *Cambridge History of Science. Vol. 6: Modern biological and earth sciences* (Cambridge: Cambridge University Press, 2009)

Wright, Johnathan Jeffrey, 'A Depot for the Productions of the Four Quarters of the Globe: Empire, collecting and the Belfast Museum', in Diarmid A. Finnegan and Johnathan Jeffrey Wright (eds), *Spaces of Global Knowledge: Exhibition, encounter and exchange in an age of empire* (New York: Routledge, 2016)

Wyse-Jackson, Patrick N., 'Fluctuations in Fortune: Three hundred years of Irish geology', in John Wilson Foster and Helena C.G. Chesney (eds), *Nature in Ireland: A scientific and cultural history* (Dublin: The Lilliput Press, 1997)

Yanni, Carla, *Nature's Museums: Victorian science and the architecture of display* (London: The Athlone Press, 1999)

Journal Articles

Adelman, Juliana, 'Evolution on Display: Promoting Irish natural history and Darwinism at the Dublin Science and Art Museum', *The British Journal of the History of Science*, vol. 38, no. 4, 2005, pp. 411–36

—— 'An Insight into Commercial Natural History: Richard Glennon, William Hinchy and the nineteenth-century trade in giant Irish deer remains', *Archives of Natural History*, vol. 39, no. 1, 2012

Alberti, Samuel J.M.M., 'Conversaziones and the Experience of Science in Victorian England', *Journal of Victorian Culture*, vol. 8, no. 2, 2003, pp. 208–30

—— 'Placing Nature: Natural history collections and their owners in nineteenth-century England', *The British Journal for the History Of Science*, vol. 35, no. 3, 2002, pp. 291–311

—— 'Objects and the Museum', *Isis*, vol. 96, no. 4, 2005, pp. 559–71

—— 'Constructing Nature Behind Glass', *Museum and Society*, vol. 6, no. 2, 2008, pp. 73–97

Barton, Ruth, 'Men of Science: Language, identity and professionalization in the mid-Victorian scientific community', *History of Science*, vol. 43, 2003, pp. 73–119

Beirne, Bryan P., 'Irish Entomology: The first hundred years', *The Irish Naturalists' Journal*, vol. 21, Special Entomological Supplement, 1985

Bennett, Jim, 'Museums and the History of Science: Practitioner's postscript', *Isis*, vol. 96, no. 4, 2005, pp. 602–8

Bowler, Peter, 'Charles Darwin and His Dublin Critics: Samuel Haughton and William Henry Harvey', in *Proceedings of the Royal Irish Academy*, section C, vol. 109 (Dublin, 2009)

Burton, Jim, 'Robert FitzRoy and the Early History of the Meteorological Office', *British Journal for the History of Science*, vol. 19, no. 2, 1986

Classen, Constance, 'Museum Manners: The sensory life of the early museum', *Journal of Social History*, vol. XL, no. 4, Summer 2007

Clarke, Desmond, 'An Outline of the History of Science in Ireland', *Studies: An Irish quarterly review*, vol. 62, nos. 247/8, 1973, pp. 287–302

Cleary, Joe, 'Amongst Empires: A short history of Ireland and empire studies in international context', *Éire/Ireland*, vol. 42, nos 1 & 2, 2007, pp. 11–57

Chalmers-Hunt, J.M., 'On Some Interesting Irish Lepidoptera in the National Museum of Ireland', *The Irish Naturalists' Journal*, vol. 20, no. 12, 1982

Cook, Jim, 'The Dublin Mechanics' Institute, 1824–1919', *Dublin Historical Record*, vol. 52, no. 1, Spring 1999

Cullen, Clara, 'The Museum of Irish Industry, Robert Kane and Education for All in the Dublin of the 1850s and 1860s', *History of Education*, vol. 38, no. 1, 2009, pp. 99–113

DeArce, Miguel, 'Darwin's Irish Correspondence', *Biology and Environment: Proceedings of the Royal Irish Academy*, vol. 108B, no. 1, 2008, pp. 43–56

Forgan, Sophie, 'Building the Museum: Knowledge, conflict, and the power of place', *Isis*, vol. 96, no. 4, 2005, pp. 572–85

—— 'The Architecture of Display: Museums, universities and objects in nineteenth-century Britain', *Journal of the History of Science*, vol. 32, 1994, pp. 139–62

Franey, Laura, 'Ethnographic Collecting and Travel: Blurring boundaries, forming a discipline', *Victorian Literature and Culture*, vol. 29, no. 1, 2001, pp. 219–39

Herries-Davies, Gordon L., 'Notes on the Various Issues of Sir Richard Griffith's Quarter-Inch Geological Map of Ireland', *Imago Mundi,* vol. 29, 1977, pp. 35–44

Higgit, Rebekah and Charles W.J. Withers, 'Science and Sociability: Women as audience at the British Association for the Advancement of Science, 1831–1901', *Isis,* vol. 9, no. 1, March 2008, pp. 1–27

Jarrell, Richard A., 'The Department of Science and Art and the Control of Irish Science, 1853–1905', *Irish Historical Studies,* vol. 23, no. 92, 1983, pp. 330–47

Leaney, Enda, 'Missionaries of Science: Provincial lectures in nineteenth-century Ireland', *Irish Historical Studies,* vol. 34, no. 135, May 2005, pp. 266–88

—— 'Vested Interests: Science and medicine in nineteenth-century Ireland', *Field Day Review,* vol. II, 2006, pp. 284–93

—— 'Evanescent Impressions: Public lectures and the popularization of science in Ireland', *Éire/Ireland,* vol. 43, nos. 3 & 4, 2008, pp. 157–82

Levy, Catherine, 'William Thomas March, 1804–1872', unpublished research, June 2013, accessed via academia.edu and personal correspondence

Lysaght, Sean, 'Themes in the History of Irish Science', *The Irish Review,* no. 19, 1996, pp. 87–97

McLeod, Roy, 'Nature and Empire: Science and the colonial enterprise', *Osiris,* 2nd series, vol. 15, 2000, pp. 1–13

Moffat, C.B., 'Robert Warren', *The Irish Naturalist,* vol. 25, no. 3, 1916

Monaghan, Nigel, 'The Giant Irish Deer or "Irish Elk"', *Geological Curator,* vol. 6, no. 4, 1995, pp. 171–3

Pickstone, John, 'Museological Science? The place of the analytical/comparative in nineteenth-century science, technology and medicine', *History of Science,* vol. 32, 1994, pp. 111–38

Secord, Anne, 'Corresponding Interests: Artisans and gentlemen in nineteenth-century natural history', *The British Journal for the History of Science,* vol. 27, no. 4, 1994, pp. 383–408

Shapin, Steven, 'Here and Everywhere: Sociology of scientific knowledge', *Annual Review of Sociology,* vol. 21, 1995, pp. 289–321

Turpin, John, 'Exhibitions of Art and Industries in Victorian Ireland, Part I', *Dublin Historical Record,* vol. 35, no. 1, 1981, pp. 2–13

—— 'The School of Design in Victorian Ireland', *Journal of Design History,* vol. 2, no. 4, 1989, pp. 243–56

White, H.B., 'The History of the Science and Art Institutions of Dublin', *Museum Bulletin* (National Museum of Science and Art), vol. 1, 1911

Withers, Charles, Rebekah Higgit and Diarmid Finnegan, 'Historical Geographies of Provincial Science: Themes in the setting and reception of the British Association for the Advancement of Science in Britain and Ireland, 1831–*c.* 1939', *British Journal for the History of Science,* vol. 41, no. 3, 2008, pp. 385–415

Wyse-Jackson, Patrick, 'Sir Charles Lewis Giesecke (1761–1833) and Greenland: A recently discovered mineral collection in Trinity College Dublin', *Irish Journal of Earth Sciences,* vol. 15, 1996

—— 'The Geological Collections of Trinity College Dublin', *The Geological Curator,* vol. 5, no. 7, 1992

Theses

Adelman, Juliana, 'Communities of Science: The Queen's Colleges and scientific culture in provincial Ireland, 1845–1875', PhD thesis, National University of Ireland, Galway, 2006

Cullen, Clara, 'The Museum of Irish Industry (1845–1867): Research environment, popular museum and community of learning in mid-Victorian Ireland', PhD thesis, University College Dublin, 2008

Smith, Adam Stuart, 'Anatomy and Systematics of the Rhomaleosauridae (Sauropterygia: Plesiosauria)', PhD thesis, University College Dublin, 2007

Whyte, Nicholas, 'The Social Context of Science in Ireland, 1890–1930', PhD thesis, Queen's University Belfast, 1996

Web Sources

National University of Ireland, Galway: Landed Estates Database, www.landedestates.ie

National Museum of Ireland, Natural History, https://www.museum.ie/en-IE/Museums/Natural-History

The Scott Polar Research Institute, https://www.spri.cam.ac.uk/

The Whitby Museum, www.whitbymuseum.org.uk

INDEX

Page locators in italics refer to illustrations